Between Reform & Revolution

POLITICAL STRUGGLES IN THE
PERUVIAN ANDES,
1969-1991

Program in Agrarian Studies,
Yale University

Between
Reform & Revolution

POLITICAL STRUGGLES
IN THE PERUVIAN ANDES,
1969-1991

Linda J. Seligmann

Stanford University Press

Stanford, California 1995

Stanford University Press
Stanford, California
©1995 by the Board of Trustees of the
Leland Stanford Junior University
Printed in the United States of America

CIP data appear at the end of the book

Stanford University Press publications are distributed
exclusively by Stanford University Press within the United
States, Canada, Mexico, and Central America; they are distributed exclusively
by Cambridge University Press throughout the rest of the world.

To the memory of Cecilia Irqo Paqo and José de la Vega
To the future of Erlán Pantoja Zanabria

Preface

I am not sure whose ethnography this is, because so many voices have spoken, listened, retorted, and responded to me over the years. There is definitely a point of view to the book, though. That is what intrigues me. More and more, it seems that my concerns and those of people I met dwelling in the cities and countryside of the Andean highlands of Peru intersect and coincide in ways that surprise and provoke me to wonder about how ethnographies are born and take on lives of their own.

I have spent most of my life engaged in straddling worlds. Whatever worlds I bridge, sometimes looking into a chasm below, sometimes unaware that I'm standing on a bridge at all, sometimes knowing that I'll never be back, and sometimes longing to stay in one place forever, I've found myself grateful for community. As a busy, (almost) obsessed bricoleur, I have constructed community again and again, as have the people I've come to know in the Andes, fashioning it out of some of the same materials I've used before, but always mixing in new, unexpected ingredients. My community resembles not so much a nucleus as a staggering number of crisscrossing pathways.

My passion for community (and the idea of community) leads me to acknowledge, in however attenuated and impoverished a fashion, the many people who have participated in the process of creating this book with me, guiding and sometimes admonishing me. Certainly they have challenged me to look at the world in new ways. Their loyalty and trust, beyond their knowledge, wit, and fine critical sense, have mattered most. In the end, although the point of view of this book is my own, and in that sense I am responsible for it as a product, I have been influenced greatly by the conversations, readings, words, and deeds of specific individuals whom I've encountered and enjoyed, and from whom I've learned an extraordinary amount that I now hope to pass on to others.

I worked in four different regions of the southern Andean highlands: Santa Barbara, Combapata, Ayapata, and, finally, Huanoquite, the subject of this book. The comparative perspective I obtained from people in each of these places has been invaluable. I mourn the deaths of some of the friends I made there over the years. This book is dedicated to two of them, Cecilia Irqo Paqo and José de la Vega. I also dedicate this book to Erlán Pantoja Zanabria, my godson, who recovered from tuberculosis. I am especially grateful to Erlán's parents, Demetrio Pantoja Bejar and Victoria Zanabria Rado of Huanoquite, who welcomed me into their home and made me a part of their daily lives with patience, good humor, and occasional irritation at my clumsy understanding of what was going on.

Two research centers were crucial in helping me to become oriented when I began work in Peru, and they were generous in permitting access to their resources: the Centro de Estudios Regionales Andinos "Bartolomé de Las Casas" in Cusco, and the Instituto de Estudios Peruanos in Lima. They prodded me to reflect upon my own biases and assumptions as I continued to do research in the highlands. In particular, I would like to thank Heraclio Bonilla, Leonidas Casas, Carlos Iván Degregori, Juan Carlos Godenzzi, Gabriela Ramos, Marisa Remy, and Henrique Urbano. Juan Ossio Acuña of the Social Science Division of the Pontificia Universidad Católica del Perú, offered me an affiliation when I first came to do my doctoral field research in Huanoquite under the auspices of a Fulbright grant. Miguél Ayala and Silvia León became my very good friends in Cusco. Their long experience working with microdevelopment projects and peasant organizing gave them unique perspectives, which, in turn, helped me to revise my thinking. I especially recall that sense of community as we sat around a table, talking, and drinking hot soup with their family.

It is always risky to allow someone you do not know to interview you and pry into your life. I was particularly interested in talking with attorneys, judges, and bureaucrats who, in one way or another, had participated in the reform process. Special thanks to Victor Angles, Prudencio Carcausto, Nerio Gonzales, and Noé Hanco in Cusco, and Guillermo Figallo in Lima, for allowing me to interview them and sharing their writings with me, as well as for their genuine interest in what I was trying to do at a time when talking politics meant taking a risk.

Buzz Alexander, Kathy Fine, Christine Harris, Lucy Mathiak, and Debbie Poole have been great friends who have shared many ups and downs with me over the years. Marisol de la Cadena and Chuck

Walker were stalwart companions with a great sense of humor during those days in Cusco when few other anthropologists were doing any work at all in the highlands. Stephen G. Bunker accompanied me for part of the time I was in Huanoquite, and I benefited from our very different perspectives as we did field work, as well as from his smooth skill in achieving dialogue with just about anyone.

The academy can be a lonely and nasty world sometimes, especially since recognition rather than monetary remuneration is generally the reward one receives for achievement. Under these conditions, community can be a hard thing to forge. The late Joe Casagrande, Enrique Mayer, Sabine MacCormack, Frank Salomon, Irene Silverblatt, Steve Stern, Norman E. Whitten, Jr., and Tom Zuidema challenged me to find my own intellectual path and gave me sustained support as I sought to do so. I am grateful for a Fulbright-Hayes award, and research grants from the Wenner-Gren Foundation and from the Nave Foundation at the University of Wisconsin-Madison's Latin American and Iberian Studies Program, which made it possible for me to do the research upon which this book is based. I was also fortunate to receive a fellowship in the Program in Agrarian Studies at Yale University. Most of this book was written there. Jim Scott's energy, wonderful sense of humor, remarkable intellect, and great joy in bringing together people allowed me to make important personal and professional transitions in my life. Louise Scott opened her home to all of us and we had a grand old time at dinners that lasted well into the night. Kay Mansfield watched over us, facilitating our work, and making connections between us. Jane Gray and Kamal Sheel, two fellows in the program, carefully read some of the chapters that went into the making of this book and offered excellent suggestions. Helen Siu gathered us together for a memorable Sunday Dim Sum and ice cream and cookies in her backyard. That was as important as the experiences she shared with me from her work in China. William P. Mitchell invited me to present a paper at the New York Academy of Science. He, along with Marc Edelman, Angelique Haugerud, Mimi Keck, and William Roseberry made instructive comments on that paper, thus helping me to work out further my ideas for the book.

In a move from New Haven to the Shenandoah Valley, I once again set about creating community. My colleague Ric Thompson encouraged me as I was completing the final revisions of the book and helped me to feel welcome in my new home. He has an acute understanding of the healing and defiant powers of irony. The Department of Sociology and Anthropology of James Madison University and the Department of Sociology and Anthropology and the

College of Arts and Sciences of George Mason University generously helped defray some of the costs of the book.

Muriel Bell, John Feneron, and Peter Dreyer at Stanford University Press took a genuine and attentive interest in the form and content of the book, assisting and guiding me in ways that went beyond the usual functions of editorship. Joanne Rappaport gave this manuscript a judicious and careful reading. Her suggestions made this a far better piece of work than it was initially. I have learned from her example as a clear writer and original thinker.

My parents, Albert L. and Barbara B. Seligmann, and my sisters, . Susan Seligmann-Moreno, Ann Lyons, and Wendy Seligmann have always had faith in me. At least now they will see the fruits of some of my labor. They have also provided a haven to me and given me the courage to question. Special thanks to John Cooper, Andrew Levine, and Gus. They have repeatedly helped me not to exaggerate things or lose perspective.

L.J.S.
McGaheysville, Virginia

Contents

Maps and Figure

Maps

Figure

Between Reform & Revolution

POLITICAL STRUGGLES IN THE
PERUVIAN ANDES,
1969-1991

Introduction

Five hundred kinds of flowers of as many kinds of potatoes grow
        on the edges of the chasms unreached by your eyes;
            they grow in the earth; mixed with night and gold,
            silver and day. Those five
        hundred flowers are my brains, my flesh.
           . . .
Did I work for centuries of months and years in order that someone
                I do not know and who does not know me,
        should cut off my head with a small steel blade?
           . . .
We know that they want to misshape our faces with clay;
        exhibit us, deformed, before our children
        so that they will kill us.
We don't know what will happen. Let death walk toward us,
        let these unknown people come.
We will await them; we are the sons of the father
        of all the rivers; sons of the
        father of all the mountains.

                    José María Arguedas, "Huk docturkunaman
                    qayay" ("A Call to Some Doctors")

Peasants, the landlords will no longer eat your poverty!" General Juan Velasco Alvarado, who had seized the presidency of Peru from Fernando Belaúnde Terry in a military coup the year before, proclaimed on June 24, 1969.[1] This announcement ushered in one of the most ambitious agrarian reforms in Latin America, and possibly the most radical shift ever in Peru's agrarian policies. In attempting to transform Velasco's rhetoric into reality, it wrought significant changes in the nature of state intervention in the lives of rural inhabitants, most of whom were Quechua peasants. In both word and deed, the state sought to reshape land tenure and rural labor regimes, as well as the attitudes of the dominant mestizo classes toward Quechua peasants.

Distribution of land was so skewed in Peru prior to the 1969 reform that approximately 96 percent of the agricultural population controlled 44 percent of the cultivable land, divided into innumerable tiny plots, while 3.9 percent of the population controlled the remaining 56 percent, most of it in the form of large holdings (Matos Mar and Mejía 1980a). Transforming a countryside that for several centuries had been controlled by the landed elite, usually with the support of the state, shook the very foundations of Peruvian society. Despite their numbers, Quechua-speaking peasants had been marginalized socially, politically, and economically. Their buying and selling power had been debilitated by unequal terms of exchange on the market. They had been subjected to an extraordinary degree of exploitation by a handful of dominant landowners.

The most striking result of the passage of the reform law was that the balance of power between the landed elite, Quechua peasants, and the state shifted. Peasants gained access to state political-legal institutions from which they had been excluded in the past; estate owners were constricted in their abuses of power and their manipulation of the bureaucracy; and many young men and women, the children of peasants and landlords alike, began to occupy the broadening economic and political interstices between rural communities and urban centers.

The reform law targeted the large estates on which peasants toiled as permanent workers for expropriation. The peasants were then organized into cooperatives managed by state administrators. They were expected to farm most of the land collectively and to become the future owners and managers of the property. The government took into account other kinds of land and labor relationships among peasants but concentrated on establishing economies of scale. It established bureaucratic procedures whereby native communities could attempt to be formally recognized and to have their titles to communal land legitimized, but it more or less ignored landless laborers, sharecroppers, and the demands of many communities for lands that they considered their own, but that had been encroached upon by haciendas over the years.

In spite of these serious shortcomings, the reform gave peasants unprecedented legal means to reclaim lands they had lost. Remunerated with limited cash and bonds to be invested in urban industrial enterprises, most expropriated landowners left the countryside to reestablish themselves in the cities. While some remained, their relationships with peasants necessarily changed, and they were forced to be far more accommodating than they had been in the past. Having lost much of their land, estate owners were less able to terrorize or protect the local population.

Rather than depending upon the existing civil court system,

which was corrupt, ineffectual, and often controlled by the landed elite, the Velasco regime took the innovative step of establishing a separate system of land courts and a Superior Agrarian Tribunal to resolve disputes during the reform. Peasants could present their own cases or be represented by public defenders sympathetic to them. Judges and attorneys actually traveled to the rural areas where lands were being considered for expropriation or disputes were taking place. Peru's agrarian reform differed most notably from those in other parts of the world in terms of the legal process established to settle land disputes. Rather than remaining neutral, the judiciary, and the land judges in particular, were expected to be explicitly biased in favor of peasants.

The Velasco regime also tried to restructure ethnic relations. It assumed that once peasants had control over their land and labor, they would regain their dignity and, in a general sense, cease to be "Indians." The loyalty of Quechua peasants to the Peruvian nation would take precedence over their loyalties to small kin groups or their interest in reconstituting the territorial integrity of ethnic polities that had once existed. They would stop exhibiting cultural traits that the Hispanicized population found offensive and instead become integrated into the nation. The reform measures thus spelled out the path that Quechua peasants should follow if they wanted to receive the benefits of the reform *and* recognition as national citizens. Participation in government-sponsored political organizations and electoral politics, adherence to the principle of a free market, following proper legal procedures rather than resorting to uprisings or land invasions, demonstrating civic responsibility, and literacy in Spanish were among the values and proper behavior that the Velasco regime sought to instill in peasants. The government's goals were the continuation of a 150-year effort on the part of the Peruvian state since independence to integrate Indians into the nation.

Nevertheless, twenty-three years later, little evidence existed in Peru's countryside or cities to suggest that the Velasco regime's bold measures had succeeded in alleviating the poverty of peasants, increasing agricultural production, stimulating industrialization in the cities, or integrating peasants into the nation. Instead, Peru's economy was in shambles. Close to 30,000 people had died in a brutal civil war between the military and police forces and the Communist Party of Peru–Sendero Luminoso ("Shining Path").[2] Thousands, many of them peasants, had disappeared and were sometimes subsequently discovered in a tortured and mutilated state in mass graves. Over 56 percent of the population and 42.3 percent of the national territory were under a state of emergency in June 1991 (Youngers 1992:2).

Poverty, fanaticism, lack of institutional representation, or frustrated expectations among peasants are some of the principal explanations scholars have offered for the civil war.[3] After a close examination of the events that unfolded in highland regions of Peru after the reform, I have come to think that these explanations are too simple. This book argues instead that the mechanisms that combined to usher in one of the most violent periods of Peru's history are inextricably bound up with the 1969 reform and the peculiar ways in which it restructured political space. The reform afforded some peasants the opportunity to seize greater local power, while opening the doors for a number of other contenders to vie for control of that same space. The following pages seek to explain how political life in the countryside changed during and after the reform and why these changes contributed to the ability of Sendero Luminoso to establish a foothold, specifically in rural areas. Rather than reducing these changes and their consequences to a matter of failed modernization policies, I trace the often-contradictory ways in which the state's policies led to its own growing fragility and fragmentation.

I have chosen to portray political life in the Andean highlands from the vantage point of the people of Huanoquite, a Quechua- and Spanish-speaking district in the southern highlands of the department of Cusco (province of Paruro), where I spent a year in 1984 and several months in 1989 and 1991. Originally, I went to Huanoquite to study the roles that knowledge brokers played in introducing agricultural innovations to the region. I had chosen it as a research site on the recommendation of two colleagues who had worked in the same province. Huanoquite had a long history of interaction with market forces and national politics. Hugo Blanco Galdos, an important leader of peasant and worker uprisings that had spurred the state to craft a more substantial agrarian reform, was from Huanoquite; and the district itself was characterized by a remarkable diversity of ecological zones and high agricultural productivity. It therefore seemed like an optimal location in which to see how people selected and used new ideas about agriculture, and the kinds of decision-making processes and conflicts that accompanied the incorporation of novel information and practices into their daily lives.

Once I got to Huanoquite, I gradually discovered that the struggles Huanoquiteños were encountering in their land and labor regimes and political organizing as a consequence of the agrarian reform were

of uppermost importance in their minds. I therefore shifted my research orientation and instead concentrated on how Huanoquiteños
participated in and were affected by the reform over the 23-year
period from 1968 to 1991.

I did not create the "context" of this book by simply situating
Huanoquiteños within their agrarian history in some objective fashion. The processes and mechanisms woven into the text are the
result of my own selective rendering of that history. I was struck
repeatedly by one particular aspect of daily life in Huanoquite: the
constant talk about community and the high degree of conflict,
fission, and fusion that characterized the district. In attempting to
understand these juxtaposed processes, I found myself looking more
closely at why community was so important to Huanoquiteños and
the kinds of ideas they held about what community should be. I also
found Huanoquiteños drawing my attention to the agrarian reform as
a key moment in their history. Last, but not least, the violence and
chaos ushered in by the civil war in Peru caught many anthropologists, including me, more or less by surprise. We were not unaware of
class inequalities or ethnic discrimination in Peru. Nevertheless,
most of us had not foreseen the coming of a movement like Sendero.

Renato Rosaldo observes that a powerful tendency exists within
the social sciences, perhaps most clearly explicated by Durkheim,
that equates (and conflates) society with law and order. Thus, social
scientists often assume that social violence is the *natural* order of
things, whereas social harmony and peace is the *cultural* order of
things. Rarely have they questioned whether or not there might be an
interrelationship between these two states, or what the social causes
or place of violence might be. Rosaldo argues that the general reaction among social scientists to "impending chaos" is thus "a feeling
of panic," partly because the "nightmare qualities" of chaos "have
been left so vague," and, one might add, so poorly understood.

In social thought this dreamlike vision of chaos appears more in oblique
allusions than in the explicit conceptual treatments granted to such terms as
the cultural order and normative regulation. One rarely finds any serious
effort to specify conditions under which . . . sociocultural collapse could
occur. Nor do many analysts, in this theoretical context, inquire into the
causes of such actual human catastrophes as those in Indonesia, Bangladesh,
Uganda, Cambodia, and El Salvador. [Rosaldo 1989:99, 100]

I therefore turned to the more difficult task, especially given the
precarious conditions of doing research then in the countryside and
the clandestine nature of Sendero, of trying to anchor this "vision of

chaos" in the lives and histories of Huanoquiteños and their relationships to one another and to the state. I did not feel panic so much as confusion that the knowledge I had acquired from working in the Andes since 1974 had not prepared me to understand what I was witnessing.

The District of Huanoquite

Located 65 kilometers southwest of Cusco by truck road, Huanoquite is a fertile agricultural region with diverse microecological zones, terraces, and archaeological sites. It was of importance to the Incas, and members of the Inca nobility had lived there. Long dominated by hacendados, Huanoquite had also contributed significant economic revenues to the Spanish colonial and national regimes. Since an Inca road to the coast passes through Huanoquite, connecting the southern and central highlands, the region has also been of strategic military importance.

My first impression of Huanoquite was of a dynamic, agriculturally productive district, a community that had participated in the market economy since the Spanish conquest, and that therefore had long experience of being open to the outside world. That impression was borne out by the Huanoquiteños' social networks, which extended far beyond their territory of residential settlement. Huanoquiteños had also engaged in economic exchanges with distant regions since well before the colonial regime. Huanoquite's valuable salt mines encouraged these relationships, and its physical location permitted exploitation of a wide range of resources. It had access to plentiful water sources, sheltered valleys, and numerous ecological zones for raising livestock, growing crops at different altitudes, and tending herbs and vegetables in kitchen gardens.

Huanoquite also turned out to be an exceedingly divided community. Being close to Cusco was not synonymous with modernization or development, but the Huanoquiteños were not traditionalists. They had not elaborated an inward-looking, defensive worldview, and many of them were open to innovative technology. To bring into focus why Huanoquite was so conflict-ridden, this book discriminates carefully between the kinds of relations of production Huanoquiteños were engaged in before and after Velasco's reform, their diverse ways of remembering things, their uses of history as a resource, and the institutions (and their experiences of these institutions) that structured the options available to them.

Huanoquite's hacendados had dominated the existing economic, political, and social institutions of the district as owners of land, purveyors of merchant capital, holders of most high-level political offices, and sponsors of fiestas. Most inhabitants thus initially welcomed the reform policies, which they saw as capable of transforming the servile labor relations that characterized the area and enabling them to reclaim land they had lost.

At the same time, they were neither acquiescent nor confrontational in their attitudes toward the state after the passage of the reform. The cultural practices and mobilization strategies of peasants shaped the state's attempts to maintain social control (see Migdal 1988). Inadvertently, the changing economic and political character of rural society as a result of the reform measures, combined with the inability of the state to maintain control over the political life of civil society, led to the development of new power centers in the countryside that competed with and weakened the state (see Grindle 1977, 1986).

The Argument

The debates and struggles that characterized political life in Huanoquite during and after the 1969 agrarian reform were arguably typical of those taking place throughout the Andean highlands. The reform brought about a qualitative shift in peasant-state relations that had ramifications throughout the entire fabric of Peruvian society, which was already characterized by dramatic ecological and economic fissures. In spite of the Velasco regime's promotion of an ideology of national integration and development, it found it impossible to arrive at a comprehensive reform law that could be applied throughout the nation. Given the uniform nature of the reform law and the way relations of production and exchange had historically evolved in the countryside, conflicts arose among peasants. Few of them had access to much land before the reform, and they had therefore worked on haciendas. Nevertheless, they had entered into markedly differing kinds of labor relations with one another and with the hacendados. Similarly, different hacendados had cultivated different relations with their labor forces and with one another. Some hacendados refined their positions tactically in the face of pressure, not from the Velasco regime, but from Huanoquiteños themselves.

The heterogeneous composition of the state itself created fissures and contradictions within the bureaucracy. The state's offer to peasants of real citizenship and peasant demands for recognition of cultural differences and equality coexisted in an uneasy tension as peasants, responding to the rhetoric of the Velasco regime and the tenets of the new agrarian reform law, embarked upon defining and defending their rights to land, their visions of just labor relations, and their notions of legitimate political authority. The state believed it could uproot racial discrimination by destroying the power of the landed oligarchy, but it proved unable to achieve both economic equality and a respect for ethnic differences. Although a strong correlation existed between poverty and degree of racial discrimination, the two were not synonymous. Understanding of these dynamics helps clarify the unstable relationship between the state and civil society after the reform, which, in turn, created the conditions for civil war.

In Huanoquite, as in many other highland districts, the disappearance of the formal stratum of the landed elite after the reform created a political space that inhabitants sought to control and use for a variety of purposes. As they sought to take advantage of the expansion of political space available to them, they drew upon organizational principles and forms that were familiar to them. They also experimented with a variety of new organizations, particularly ones that they thought could be effective at the regional and national levels. They took advantage of courts of law. They became far more active in political parties and peasant federations. They turned to new religious affiliations, especially Evangelical Protestantism. Perhaps most important, they attributed great value to the benefits that rural teachers and educational institutions could bring them.

Their interest in using new kinds of organizations on a wider scale led them to rely heavily upon alternative interlocutors who were skilled at mediating between the rural and urban environments, particularly between local communities and the regional bureaucracy in Cusco. These brokers, a heterogeneous group in themselves, crucially affected political organization in the district. Bitter disputes took place among the inhabitants over how far to trust them. These men and women, especially rural teachers, introduced new ideas and values and challenged peasants to revise their assumptions about the nature of community and traditional paths to status and prestige. They took advantage of existing fault lines in communities and often created new cleavages.

The dynamics of the reform process help explain why a number of these brokers in Huanoquite became sympathizers with, or even activists in, Sendero Luminoso. Those who belonged to families of the landed elite no longer had the security of land for their livelihoods, and land and wealth in the countryside had for centuries gone together in the rural highlands. Many attempted to represent themselves as defenders of peasants, but their images of peasants did not correspond to the reality of peasant culture or economy. As Peru's economic crisis deepened, they also became unable to establish an economic or social foothold within urban society. They therefore identified with Sendero's vision of Peru's future society, which required the destruction both of a differentiated peasantry and of the corporatist state. Some of these brokers became significant mouthpieces for Sendero and proceeded to attempt to educate the rural peasant population to join the movement.

Ironically, even though they were archenemies, their comparable images of "Quechua-speaking peasants" brought the state and Sendero up against similar obstacles to the realization of their political visions. The multiple images of "Quechua-speaking peasants" within Peruvian society in part have been the product of the state's agenda as it has sought to retain control over national political and economic institutions. Yet peasants' images of themselves and those held by other sectors of Peruvian society only partially resemble one another. Differentiation within the peasantry, founded in class and ethnicity, created considerable resistance among them to the state's desire to transform all Quechua peasants into ideal Peruvian citizens. Likewise, peasants refused to conform to Sendero's vision of the ideal revolutionary proletariat. Just as many of Huanoquite's peasants rejected the single path to national integration proposed by the Velasco regime, they also rejected the unidimensional image of peasants that Sendero had imposed upon them.

Sendero had begun organizing in the late 1950's in the central highlands of Ayacucho. Although its members did not begin to wage their armed struggle until 1980, in the interim they began a long process of recruiting people into the movement through a strenuous series of military and intellectual exercises. Sendero's brand of revolution was inspired by the teachings and writings of Marx, Lenin, and Mao Tse-tung; by an early twentieth century Peruvian philosopher named José Carlos Mariátegui; and by the ideas of its own supreme leader, Abimael Guzmán Reynoso, a late twentieth century student of Kant, known by the nom de guerre Presidente Gonzalo. The intellectual vanguard of Sendero believed that if the Peruvian masses followed the proper path to scientific truth, the revolution would be successful. While they maintained some ties with peasants, many of Sendero's leaders were high school teachers and university students who rejected their own roots or disdained rural life. The discrepancy between the ideological stances that members of Sendero took and the reality that confronted them was astonishing. Nonetheless, a number of events at the local level, especially the deteriorating relationships between peasants and the state, and the growing fractiousness among multiple peasant groups, led some peasants to support Sendero initially. The dynamics of these intertwined processes and their consequences are the subject of this book.

Peasants have often been unsuccessful in attaining their political goals because of the structural limitations to which they must accommodate on a daily basis—the overwhelming power of the state and the dominant classes and the historical legacy of conquest and colonialism. Centralizing states have nonetheless also been unable to consolidate their rule, despite access to a wide array of coercive mechanisms and instruments of control, including ever-expanding bureaucracies (see Migdal 1988).

The story of the efforts of Huanoquite's peasants to make the state meet their demands is not primarily one of primitive rebels or violent adherents of armed struggle. Few peasants in Huanoquite have chosen the option of armed struggle so far as I know.[4] Instead, they have relied upon everyday forms of resistance, tactical defenses, the use of law and the courts, and participation in local and supralocal organizations in order to create sufficient political leverage to shift their relationships with the state in their favor.

Theories, Methods, and Sources

Many studies have been done of the 1969 reform.[5] Most of them have examined its effects upon highland agrarian societies in terms of broad macrolevel criteria—productivity, development, income redistribution, and the strengthening of industrial-agricultural and rural-urban ties. The general consensus is that the reform did not lead to increased agricultural productivity or economic growth. Yet few studies have assessed how the inhabitants themselves viewed the reform or what its impact was upon the direction that relationships took between rural communities and the state in the decades that followed.

Although broad economic and political indicators give us some notion of the effects of state policies upon agrarian communities, we can only draw distilled and incomplete conclusions from these indicators. To understand the complex political dynamics that evolved between highland Andean communities and the state better, I have paid far greater attention in this book to the details of local participation in the reform. At the same time, I have tried not to lose sight of events unfolding in a wider arena or the myriad relationships and ideas that went beyond highland communities.

The appropriate unit of analysis for conducting this research was always problematic. Although to some extent useful analytical tools, the terms *urban* and *rural* are misnomers. It is the constant movement between these two spheres, neither of which is homogeneous in terms of ethnicity or class, that really captures the well-trained eye and ear. Furthermore, the notion of local, regional, national, and global systems dissolves in the face of the power of mass media, the proliferation of international organizations working at the grassroots level, and the trajectories of commodities and transport routes that traverse immense spaces, contracting natural time and distances. Communities imbue music, things, words, dances, and ideas from afar with their own creative interpretations and fantasies and use them in innovative ways, transforming them into expressions of their own identity. I shall thus speak of local systems even as I seek to describe and explain how they are conjoined to other worlds that are distinguished partially by the definitions that people hold of their own identities, their values, their means of livelihood, and the differences in concentrations of economic and political power.

Throughout this book, I use the term *peasant* similarly to the way Allen Isaacman (1993:206–7) employs it. Isaacman concentrates upon relationships between peasants and colonial states in Africa, but his remarks apply equally well to relationships between peasants and postcolonial states. Although observing that "peasants are an inherently tricky concept," he argues that it is possible to examine the heterogeneity of peasant production and social reproduction, and the mechanisms that give rise to that heterogeneity, by focusing on "the defining features of the peasant labor process."[6] Control over land and labor, in turn, are crucial factors in peasant struggles over political and cultural autonomy:

The uniqueness of peasants is the degree of autonomy they had in relation to the colonial state and the appropriating classes. This autonomy was inextricably linked to their ability to mobilize their own labor power through the household and their access to land, which, together gave them command over subsistence. That state power was mediated through local political institutions and that peasants generally retained their own language, historical memories, and forms of expressive culture reinforced the autonomy derived from the labor process by limiting the degree to which an authoritative colonial discourse could penetrate rural societies. [Isaacman 1993:207, 209]

In determining the framework for this book, I found both structuralist and voluntarist explanations to be unsatisfactory. They told only parts of the story of social change (see Abu-Lughod 1991; Kriger 1992; Rosaldo 1989; Roseberry 1991; Sider 1986). A structuralist orientation tends to obliterate entirely a view of peasants as agents who have the capacity to sustain long and varied struggles against existing sociopolitical conditions and whose actions, in turn, may have an impact upon the behavior of the state, the formulation of policy, and the effects of capitalism writ large. A voluntarist orientation fails to consider that individual peasant responses to similar historical and institutional conditions may vary according to the effects of preexisting political hierarchies, material relations of production, and generational and gender relations. There is no question that the contingencies of events and personality affect responses to similar structural conditions, but individuals rarely act unimpeded by historical legacies or structural constraints and opportunities that shape their interpretations and choices. "Structuralists cannot ignore individual ideas and actions even if they wish to understand structures only; voluntarists cannot ignore how structures influence individual choices and behavior," Norma Kriger cautions (1992:32).

In analogous fashion, general theoretical approaches to state-local relationships such as dependency theory or world-systems theory (Cardoso and Faletto 1969; Frank 1967, 1978; Wallerstein 1974; Amin 1974) have tended to classify peasant communities as entities created by colonial and postcolonial policies and as victims of state policies because of their structural position. They (Tilly 1975; Migdal 1988) have also underestimated the different manners in which peasants seek to accommodate to, rather than oppose, state policies, and the creative, possibly systematic, ways in which they do resist state policies or the forces of capitalism.

Forms of resistance to the state among peasants cannot be reduced to a persistent desire to return to a traditional ideal of peasant morality (see Roseberry 1991:56–57). The capacity of the state to use coercion in order to impose its policies and its image of the nation, and to mediate among different sectors of civil society, must be recognized as an important dimension of peasant-state relationships. Nevertheless, in overemphasizing the power and autonomy of the state, scholars (Evans, Rueschemeyer, and Skocpol 1985; Stepan 1978) may pass too lightly over internal class and ethnic differences and fractions within civil society, and their role in structuring relationships between agrarian societies and states. Works that succeed in portraying the differentiated nature of peasant participation in, and responses to, state-building and expansion include Bunker 1986; Cooper, Isaacman, Mallon et al. 1993; Edelman 1993; Isaacman 1991;

Lonsdale 1981; Mallon 1983; Moore 1986; Roseberry 1991; Vincent 1982; Shue 1988; Siu 1989; Smith 1990a; Stern 1987; Urban and Sherzer 1991; and Wolf 1982.

In trying to construct an ethnography that takes account of social change but also heeds the variegated cultural dimensions that inform social change, I have encountered a major problematic: how to describe and determine the weight of the effects of both material relations and culture in the process of social change. To be sure, it would be satisfying to be able to present an argument that had no hint of a Delphic oracular pronouncement. Although I am not a historian, I am reminded of Stephen Jay Gould's references to

the historian's challenge of contingency—the "pageant" of evolution as a staggeringly improbable series of events, sensible enough in retrospect and subject to rigorous explanation, but utterly unpredictable . . . the diversity of possible itineraries does demonstrate that eventual results cannot be predicted at the outset. Each step proceeds for a cause, but no finale can be specified at the start, and none would ever occur a second time in the same way. . . . Science has been slow to admit the different explanatory world of history into its domain . . . [and] has also tended to denigrate history, when forced to a confrontation by regarding any invocation of contingency as less elegant or less meaningful than explanations based directly on timeless "laws of nature." [Gould 1989:14, 51]

I find myself thus agreeing with William Roseberry's description of the complex relationship between "material circumstances" and "cultural understandings":

The "autonomy" of culture . . . comes not from its removal from the material circumstances of life but from its connection. As one of many products of prior activity and thought, it is among the material circumstances that confront real individuals who are born in a concrete set of circumstances. As some of these circumstances change, and as people attempt to conduct the same sorts of activities under new circumstances, their cultural understandings will affect the way they view both their circumstances and their activities. . . . People's activities are conditioned by their cultural understandings, just as their activities under new circumstances may stretch or change these understandings . . . although meanings are socially produced, they may be extended to situations where a functionalist might say they do not fit, or may be applied even after the circumstances and activities that have produced them have changed. [Roseberry 1991:42]

In the pages below, although I do not ignore the weight of existing economic and political structures in setting the initial direction of and limiting social change, I shall heed the words and acts of multiple individuals who may modify (and be affected by) those directions and limitations. It is in these words and acts that class itself receives its cultural content to a large extent (see also Sider 1986:8).

In unraveling the relationships between Huanoquiteños and the state, I also offer a view of the legal nexus where the reform process unfolded. This nexus is important to comprehending how peasants interact with the state. Studies of agrarian societies often confine themselves to local-level practices or to the determinant effects upon the local system of capitalist relations. They either place great emphasis upon tactics of resistance that communities develop to confront dominant regimes or they assume that dominant economic and political regimes may simply determine the kinds of transformations that take place locally.

In reviewing earlier ethnographies of the Andes, one notes that many of them either highlight the determinant and generally positive impact upon Quechua and Aymara peasant communities of development and modernization (Adams 1959; Bourque and Warren 1981; Dobyns 1964; Doughty 1968; Escobar 1973; Stein 1961) or use structuralist models to unbury precolonial categories and principles of Andean organization rather than systematically analyzing the transformations these categories have undergone over time (Allen 1989; Bastien 1978; Earls 1971; Isbell 1978; Urton 1981). A major impetus for employing the second approach was a desire among scholars at the time to demonstrate the richness of Andean culture. In doing so, however, scholars often lost sight of the dynamic and heterogeneous nature of peasant-state relationships and resorted, usually unwittingly, to nostalgia for a fabricated tradition that had vanished because of their own imperialist history (see also Rosaldo 1989).

I also situate this book within the general approach to scale taken by more recent ethnographies of Andean society (Rappaport 1990; Rasnake 1988; Smith 1989; Weismantel 1988). These texts have striven to keep multiple sociocultural levels in touch with one another, addressing the part that peasants play in shaping their destiny while examining the historical impact of state institutions and their economic and political policies upon peasant communities.

My focus in this book is primarily ethnographic, but the voices and actions of Huanoquiteños tell only part of the story of the effects of the reform upon the district. I have drawn upon a number of sources and methodological approaches, many of which presented themselves fortuitously in my field research.

Archival sources adumbrate the historical nuances that proved to be central to people's experiences of the reform and the character of state intervention in their lives. Especially interesting are the details of political struggle that unfold in the documents—the splintering factions and coalescence of alliances; the incoherence in the policies of bureaucrats and legal personnel at different levels of government that structured the capacity of Huanoquiteños to defend their rights to land and labor and secure for themselves a greater measure of political power.

Documents pertaining to expropriation and adjudication proceedings, community recognitions, and land disputes in Huanoquite are housed in the departmental capital of Cusco in the General Archives of the Agrarian Reform Office; the Second Land Court; the private property registers in the Ministry of Justice; the Office of Peasant Communities, a division of the Ministry of Agriculture; and various lawyers' offices. Other such documents are held by the communities, cooperatives, and district council of Huanoquite.

These documents are valuable because they simultaneously center upon local political processes and are interwoven with considerations emanating from the regional and national bureaucracies. They also record land disputes among Huanoquiteños. Indigenous authorities of different *ayllus*, fractions of the hacendados' labor forces, and hacendados themselves often passionately stated their positions, which were recorded verbatim. The texts of these documents not only reveal an awareness among peasants of the economic and political institutions that have dominated them, but also demonstrate the ability of peasants to pierce through a supposed "hegemony of knowledge" and make use of it for themselves.

The process of gaining access to these documents was a saga in itself, and the difficulty of access made me share many feelings with peasants. I came to treasure and privilege these yellowing pieces of paper—hoarded behind locked doors and often mislaid—that carried such weight in legal rulings. When Huanoquite's authorities finally trusted me enough to lend me locally housed documents, they did so with great hesitance and usually demanded that I return tomes of 100 pages or more of scrawled script to them within 24 hours.

Since the time of the Spanish conquest, legal documents have been respected and recognized as valid claims in Latin America, since colonists needed them to defend their rights to land and Indian labor. Native inhabitants rapidly seized upon this common ground, using the same form, the same procedures, and often even the same content, to defend *their* claims. Important differences existed, however, in the capacities of Indians and colonists to take advantage of these documents. The former encountered great difficulty in trying to search out documents they did not have under lock and key in their communities. They were also rarely able to gain a hearing in courts of law because of the expense, and because legal personnel placed numerous obstacles in the path of an Indian seeking justice. The vagaries of access are condensed in my most recent experience of attempting to peruse again documents housed in the General Archives of the Agrarian Reform Office in Cusco in 1991. I sought to do so just as President Alberto Fujimori announced "the reform of the Agrarian Reform" and ordered massive "voluntary resignations" by public servants. Only one woman, the director of the archives, held the key to the room that housed the documents, and she resigned from her position the day after I began working there. The remaining employees went on strike. Lines of peasants who had traveled great distances to Cusco found themselves in the same predicament I did. The only difference was that for them, this was the continuation of a long, costly, and frustrating tradition.

I also interviewed teachers, politicians, lower-level bureaucrats and technocrats, private attorneys, public defenders, and judges in Cusco, and the first president of the Agrarian Tribunal in Lima, about their opinions of the reform, how it had been implemented, the judicial system in general, their lives, and their views of peasant communities and the contemporary political situation in Peru. Whether or not they lived in Huanoquite, these individuals played crucial roles in rural political life. Most important, some of them had the power to make policy; some had been directly involved in designing, implementing, and modifying the agrarian reform law. They could facilitate or place obstacles in the way of peasant demands for land, education, or state resources. Some of them became godparents to the children of peasants; others desperately believed that a hard hand à la Pinochet was needed to restore order in Peru; many thought the institutions in which they worked were corrupt; still others nostalgically remembered peace that had prevailed under the landed elite. Among national- or regional-level bureaucrats, coherent policy did not exist.

I also attended numerous gatherings of peasants in the district of Huanoquite and demonstrations in Cusco. These meetings helped me understand the more subtle issues at stake for peasants, as well as the hidden historical background and agendas that people often either assumed knowledge of or obscured in their public demeanor and discourse.

The art of conversation came to be central to my fieldwork. I recognized that it was far more difficult for me to talk with people who identified little with peasants and characterized them as lazy, unthinking barbarians, lacking in spiritual and moral fiber and drunk on the power and alcohol the reforms had made available to them. Many of these same individuals were also highly critical of the state. Some of the most outspoken critics of peasant ways of life were politicians who had spent little time in the countryside; others were landowners who had been forced to devise a new means of livelihood in the cities. The great majority hailed from the countryside. They were teachers, small-scale merchants and truck drivers, law enforcement agents, and wealthier landowners who made their living from peasants but rejected their way of life (and often their own roots) vehemently. At the same time, they often behaved brutally toward peasants, drank excessively, and failed to comply with their duties as truck drivers or schoolteachers.

These individuals were central to what was happening on the political and cultural horizon, and I needed most to develop my skills in dialogue and diplomacy in order that my conversations with them continue to flow. Their perceptions of peasants and the state were a key to understanding the exacerbation of social conflict in rural areas. I recall one incident in which the art of conversation failed me when a teacher sympathetic to Sendero challenged me about my research. He ended his diatribe about the imperialist nature of my work with a question: "Yes or yes?"

What troubled me most in my field research was the current political climate in the district. From my work in other highland communities, I had gradually learned that even though it was possible to become adept at mastering the wide spectrum of etiquette that could engender trust, much depended upon how people assessed the value of my research and my personal character. That members of Sendero and a special police force were active in Huanoquite weighed heavily in people's decisions about whether or not they could risk trusting me. At the beginning of my research, I had a terrifying and angry encounter with the chief of police in Huanoquite. As I had always done before, I visited the local civil guard post to present my identification documents. In the past, I had done so because it was expected of me. This time, in addition, I really did want evidence of my identification to be recorded. The chief of police angrily confronted me and refused to accept my documents: "I don't know why you insist on presenting your documents," he said. "If you are pure, if you are doing 'sanitary' research, why are you worried about showing me your documents?" He finally did accept my documents, but such moments made the world seem topsy-turvy.

Toward the end of my field research, it became clear to me just how fragile a trust I had been able to establish. Although my residence in the district had been formally approved in a general assembly attended by representatives of all of the district's communities and cooperatives, it had nevertheless been the subject of much informal discussion and debate. One morning, when I was walking toward the cooperative of Inkaq Tiyanan de Tihuicte with Leonardo Herrera, one of its former leaders, he expressed cheerful satisfaction that I had been able to do the interviews I wanted. Leonardo and a few others had spent many hours talking with cooperative members, persuading them to "judge my sincerity" before deciding whether I was dangerous. In retrospect, I realized that their fears had been well founded. I had been dangerous because I might inadvertently have created further conflicts between political forces at work in the district that were largely outside the control of any one single individual. (A year and a half before my arrival, Sendero had dynamited the cooperative's tractor.)

The district of Huanoquite serves as one example of the kinds and outcomes of political struggles in which Quechua peasants participated during this period of time. The archival and field materials I was able to obtain for the region offer a window onto the details of daily life in the Peruvian countryside, capturing the immediate concerns and interests of villagers. These materials have encouraged me to consider more cautiously the kinds of generalizations one might draw from structural explanations alone.

The design of the agrarian reform law, its implementation, and the uses and interpretations that peasants, landlords, state officials, and legal personnel made of it illuminate the social order that the state was attempting to promote and sometimes uphold, as well as the clashes within the ranks of bureaucrats, the landed elite, and peasants over the interpretation of the law. The disputes that resulted from the passage of the law tell us a great deal about the history of ethnic and class relations in the highlands. The ways in which Huanoquiteños sought to interpret the reform law and the actions they took represented tactics they had arrived at after long experience of generating their own communities, cultural worlds, and economic livelihoods within the streams of political forces that had already been in motion before the arrival even of the Incas. To be sure, some of these forces had hardened into institutional and ideological systems, but others had not yet crystallized or been captured by dominant regimes. It is precisely the articulation of peasants to the state that helps to make sense of the heterogeneity that characterizes Peru's Andean agrarian society.

There is no single causal explanation that accounts for the course of political events in Peru since the reform. Nevertheless, a study of the history of the agrarian reform process brings to light significant mechanisms that explain the growing weakness of the state and of Andean highland communities.

The Structure of the Book

This book is about political life in Andean highland communities: what it means to those who live at 11,000 to 13,000 feet above sea level. What can their political lives tell us about the ways people in communities interact with one another? What resources do they draw upon as they engage in politics? How do the actions and ideas of people outside these communities affect those of people who live in rural villages and vice versa? And how do they represent themselves to one another?

In Chapter 1, I describe Huanoquite's economic, political, and agrarian history in the local, regional, and national contexts. As I grew familiar with the landmarks and terrain of Huanoquite, I was struck by the staggering number of roads and footpaths that led in multiple directions, some to a destination, others fading out in the middle of nowhere. The physical web of roads and the social and economic patterns of exchange networks were a central cultural representation for Huanoquiteños of the battles they had waged over the centuries to enhance their local economic and political power, and the effects of those efforts. The chaotic physical infrastructure had its own history and was an indelible reminder for Huanoquiteños of the lack of state assistance for numerous locally initiated projects of development, as well as of the extent to which local political authorities were corrupt. I therefore offer readers a sense of the history of these battles and what they have meant to people.

In Chapter 2, I review the history of agrarian reform in Peru, the principal tenets of the 1969 Agrarian Reform Law, and the manner in which the law was designed and implemented. The law itself was the product of a curious blend of models from other socialist societies, including those of Eastern Europe and Algeria, modified to take into account Peru's particular needs. It embodied values derived from French socialist humanism and liberalism and from the ideology of modernization promoted by the U.S.-created Alliance for Progress.

The officials who participated in implementing the reform at the regional level were important to the direction that the reform took. They directly interceded on behalf of peasants; they interpreted the tenets promulgated by the state; and they faced the difficulties of resisting corruption in confronting the machinations and vengeance of many landlords. They also frequently disagreed with the design and objectives of the national policies that they were responsible for implementing.

In Chapters 3 and 4, I examine the testimony rural inhabitants constructed to defend their rights to land and labor during the agrarian reform. In particular I discuss the strategic responses to state initiatives and policies that peasants and landlords elaborated in their defenses and the consequences of the positions they took. A crucial concern for peasants in crafting their claims was the position of the state. In particular, they were faced with figuring out how to respond to the discrepancies between the state's ulterior and immediate motives.

A close examination of the content and form of peasant claims, which were often mediated or transcribed by either private lawyers or public defenders, helps to make sense of the apparent chaos that superficially characterized much of the testimony. Even more significant, the differences in the testimonies of peasants as they responded to the reform law played a crucial role in creating dissent among them. These conflicts diminished the capacity of all peasants to form a united political front.

In Chapter 5, I review the history of one prolonged land dispute, tracing the stances that participants took in order to demonstrate how they sought to transform the political fields in which they were situated. Of particular interest to me as I reconstructed the course of this dispute through a combination of oral histories, documents, and interviews was how, and on what grounds, new kinds of authority figures came to play important roles in the district. Although a formal resolution to the dispute was eventually reached, I suspect that it is only a temporary one. The dispute itself had become yet another principal vehicle Huanoquiteños used to define themselves culturally, politically and economically. It brought together their ideas about the interrelationships between territorial control, political authority and leadership, and corporate identity.

Between 1975 and 1980, when the reform gradually came to a halt, a new economic and political geography had taken root in rural society, reflected in growing economic differentiation between households and corporate units, particularly state-managed cooperatives and recognized communities. New kinds of linkages also characterized relationships between the city and countryside. In Chapter 6, I discuss the mechanisms that generated inequality in the district and the impact they had upon the ability of Huanoquiteños to make demands upon the state and to organize collectively.

Even as Huanoquiteños diverged in their economic practices and political activities after the reform, some individuals were able to temper the vicious backbiting among inhabitants and enhance the probability that they would be able to organize around particular issues in a unified manner. Chapter 7 provides the life histories, briefly narrated, of two peasants of equal economic and political standing who had become well-respected leaders in Huanoquite despite the multiple factions that existed. Their biographies demonstrate the kinds of resources, knowledge, and personality traits rural inhabitants came to consider as leadership qualities that could unite rather than divide them.

Chapter 8 reviews the kinds of organizations that peasants sought to use for political purposes, and the backgrounds of individuals who became intermediaries between the state and the district. The reform law delegitimized the authority of large landowners. At the same time, though, the state attempted to control all peasant political participation at the local and regional levels by establishing governmental agrarian leagues and associations. While peasants took advantage of these organizations in order to press their demands upon the state, the state had narrowly defined the degree of political mobilization that could take place within these bodies. Intense differences grew among peasants concerning the goals they ought to pursue. Peasants began to organize politically outside the law in order to resist landowners' abuses and the state's failure to meet their demands. They also created alternative forums that better reflected their own needs and objectives. They continued to use these organizations to counteract subsequent reversals in agrarian policy following the overthrow of the Velasco regime.

The unmet promises of the state and the often paradoxical efforts of rural inhabitants to combine their moral principles, their conceptualizations of their ethnic and class identities, and their interpretations of the legal tenets of the reform law directly and indirectly contributed to the emergence of Sendero in the district.

Chapter 9 briefly discusses the philosophy and history of Sendero Luminoso as a political movement and then turns to relationships between members of Sendero and peasants in the district. Despite their very different political orientations, Sendero members and state officials alike have tended to misunderstand or deliberately view peasants as potentially undifferentiated, homogeneous, and as having little capacity to take independent action as agents of their own history. This tendency, in turn, has played a significant role in encouraging peasants not to sacrifice their partial autonomy from both Sendero and the state. It has also contributed to the degree of violence used by both Sendero and the state in order to force peasants to conform to their respective models of them.

The following pages seek to delineate some of the deeper historical processes underlying the violence and instability that characterize Peru today. They are also intended to serve as a testimony to the concerted efforts of Quechua peasants of the Peruvian highlands to clarify and fortify their own positions vis-à-vis the state through local action, discussion, and contention. The political struggles described in this book depict the culture of Peru's highland peasants as neither pure nor wholly autonomous. Rather, a large part of political life in the highlands has to do with the laborious efforts of people to nurture the seeds that have provided them with spiritual and physical nourishment for centuries. These are the seeds of power and knowledge as well as those that grow from the land. Members of Andean agrarian societies, as is true of so many other peoples who live with the legacy of invasion, conquest, and colonialism, have forged their identities out of a recognition simultaneously of a sense of loss and of awakening. Their awareness of loss, their capacity to imagine alternatives, and their struggles to transform into reality the possibilities that present themselves provide the space and time for political life in the Andean highlands.

— 1 —

Structuring Huanoquite's Regional Space

Huanoquite is the westernmost district of the province of Paruro. It borders the province of Anta to the north and west. To the east, it is separated from the district of Paruro by the river that descends from the heights of Vilcacunca or Limatambo and falls to the Apurimac above the Huacachaca Bridge. The district is completely mountainous. Many brooks and streams break it up. Its northwest section is very flat. There is the best and most abundant livestock. Huanoquite is a much-traveled district. It is a boon to the travelers who make the journey from Abancay to Cusco. The district was created by Bolívar and has more than 4,000 inhabitants. It is of such ancient antiquity that its age dates from a prehistoric epoch. Its inhabitants are descendants of the ancient families of Paccarectambo who dominated the heights between Paruro and Cusco.

La Crónica (1918)

My first journey to Huanoquite began at 3 A.M. in the chilly dawn at Belén Pampa in Cusco, the departmental capital. All the trucks headed for the province of Paruro depart from there. I arrived early, being unsure of the customary pattern of travel. A truck was already there, warming up its engine, and I boarded it. We huddled in the cold. The truck was overcrowded with people sandwiched among baskets, sacks, and bundles of noodles, fruit, oil, sugar, flour, and clothes, plastic containers of kerosene, home-brewed beer, and alcohol. Nobody looked too happy. They had a better idea than I of the onerousness of the journey that was to follow.

Soon after I had settled myself, Aristedes García, a young man, leaped astride the high wooden racks enclosing the flat bed of the truck, as so many other men had done. He greeted us, announcing, "Here we are, f—d over as usual!" A few of us laughed. The sullen silence of the rest was more telling.

The rainy season had begun with a vengeance. Slowly, the truck departed, leaving behind the city. The potholed pavement ended abruptly at the edge of the city, and the truck skidded wildly, unable to find traction in the deep mud as it climbed out of Cusco's steep valley. It continued to strain, ascending the even-steeper grade of the road to Oqhupata. In Oqhupata, it stopped briefly to discharge passengers. A vast, undulating *puna* (high altitude pasture and potato lands) of little vegetation, broken up by a dizzying number of furrowed fields, surrounded us. Bright green potato plants had pushed their way up from the rust-colored earth, creating a contrast to the barren landscape. Spindly legged llamas grazed on the puna. They stared quizzically at us from afar and then darted away, frightened by the sound of the truck. The truck took off again, down a steeply winding road in even worse condition than that we had already covered.

By the time we reached Yaurisque, midway between Cusco and Huanoquite, the remaining passengers were anxious to get home. Emilio Mora, the owner of the truck and a powerful cattle dealer, had other plans, however. A sallow, lanky man with bloodshot eyes, he strode resolutely into the local restaurant and ordered a beer. After one beer, he ordered another, then another. He was careful to invite the most powerful passengers on the truck—the mayor, the president of the community, and the president of the cooperative—to imbibe with him. Meanwhile, the driver tried to fend off the impatient, irritated passengers huddled in the rain. Several hours later, Emilio staggered out to the truck. No one said a word.

The truck moved slowly through the mud, then stopped abruptly. A bridge was missing several timbers, and there was a good chance that the truck might go over the side if the driver attempted to cross. Aristedes nimbly jumped off the truck. He had assessed the situation and recognized danger. Emilio climbed out of the cab and confronted him aggressively. By taking matters into his own hands, Aristedes had become a challenge to Emilio's authority, and the two men exchanged verbal insults. The passengers maintained a grim silence at first but began to protest when the heated argument turned to blows. Aristedes persisted in refusing to board the truck until it had crossed the bridge. No one else, myself included, bothered to get out. The truck heaved and groaned but succeeded in crossing the bridge without a mishap.

It continued through the narrow, fertile Yaurisque Valley, carved out by the Corcca River. We passed two estates, elegant haciendas in times gone by, now in disrepair. Nevertheless, all the fields surrounding these crumbling structures were intensively planted with maize. A little further to the west, across the river, a cluster of houses that constituted the community of Molle Molle appeared. Shortly afterward, we came to the edge of the river. The water raged turbulently over the rough, rocky riverbed. I could see the concrete foundations of a bridge that had washed away. The truck lurched across the river, guided by the driver's assistants, who tested the riverbed, walking thigh-deep in the freezing water.

After crossing the river, the truck toiled up the last, long hill, carefully executing the many hairpin curves on the narrow road. Finally, ten hours after leaving Cusco, we arrived at the entrance to the village. The rains had made the road to the plaza impassable, so we paid our fares and trudged into Huanoquite with our bundles. During my year's stay in Huanoquite, truck rides fraught with danger, discomfort, and frustration were the norm.

Huanoquite's social geography has changed over time. Situating Huanoquite historically sheds light upon the paradox of it being a highly productive agricultural region whose multiple exchange networks have contracted as it has been incorporated into the market economy. Its marginality to the national economy is a cause of great concern to the village authorities, who address this problem almost every time they meet. Huanoquiteños have striven to fortify their links to Cusco, especially by improving roads and truck service. They have also, at various times, attempted to revitalize trade networks that existed in the past.

The choices the Peruvian state has made about where roads and bridges should go, and the success or failure of villagers in pressing their demands, provide multiple images of the politics underlying relationships between the state and Huanoquite's rural inhabitants. They also tell us how, over time, Huanoquiteños have sought to remold these relationships more along the lines of their own ideas about how coherent regional space should be constructed. In a country as vast and differentiated as Peru, the inhabitants of the urban centers of power associate the lack of communication and exchange infrastructure in rural regions with isolation and abandonment. Urbanites tend to view peasants as barbaric, ignorant, and potentially uncontrollable. The prejudice against rural society began long ago when the Spanish conquerors brought their love of cities and disdain of manual labor with them from the Mediterranean. Rural inhabitants must weigh their desire to take advantage of what roads and markets can offer them against their awareness that this infrastructure will not necessarily create a more dynamic local economy for them or do away with the racist stereotypes that mestizos in particular have of them.

The significance of extractive resources such as minerals for local and national power and expansion, the imposition of national administrative boundaries upon territory that has been organized over time according to different principles, and the impact upon Huanoquiteños of international and national cycles of commerce serve as an essential backdrop to understanding better how Huanoquiteños viewed the state during and following the 1969 reform.

Social Geography, Environment, and Polity

The district of Huanoquite spreads over a vast geographic expanse. It encompasses fifteen "centers," including nine formally recognized communities and several annexes (see Map 1). It is larger than any of the other six districts that together with it make up the province of Paruro, and its population, which numbered approximately 4,082 in 1989, is greater too.

Today, the inhabitants of the community of Maska and the cooperative of Inkaq Tiyanan de Tihuicte reside in the district capital of Huanoquite. Most of the remaining landed elite, merchants, police, and teachers also live or board in the capital. Their residences surround an unkempt, grassy plaza, whose focal point is an immense colonial church and bell tower. Nearby the district capital lie the communities of Inkakuna Ayllu Chifia, Tantarcalla, and Molle Molle and the cooperatives of Chanka and Llaspay. Within each community, the houses, most of which are simple adobe huts with thatched roofs, are clustered together. These communities maintain close ties with the cooperative of Tihuicte and the community of Maska. Tihuicte and Maska show far more variation in their architectural styles, a reflection of greater economic differentiation and proximity to the Cusco market. A jumble of adobe huts and two-story whitewashed mansions with attached patios and tiled or corrugated iron roofs meet the eye. Together these communities constitute the core of Huanoquite. Various important economic and social exchanges also take place with more distant and dispersed population centers of the district.

The Huanoquite region formerly had what can best be described as a "nested" or "embedded" form of social structure. Multiple smaller units of equivalent form called *ayllus* were encapsulated within larger ones. Units of differing scale had economic and sociopolitical links among them. In keeping with the kind of flexiblity of social organization characteristic of Andean highland regions, Inkakuna Ayllu Chifia and Maska were moieties or "halves," each of

Prov: CUSCO
Distr: SANTIAGO

Prov: PARURO
Distr: YAURISQUE

Prov: PARURO
Distr: PACCARECTAMBO

Prov: CUSCO
Distr: CORCCA

Chifia

Tantarcalla

Tihuicte

Maska

HUANOQUITE

Molle
Molle

Toctohuaylla

Rocco

Vilcabamba

Llaspay

Roccoto

Prov: PARURO
Distr: CCAPI

Chanca

Qenqonay

Huanca
Huanca

Arabito

Pacco

Paccas

Prov: ANTA
Distr: CHINCHAYPUQUIO

DEPART: APURIMAC

Boundaries

—— Department
—·—·— Province
------ District

0   10 km

Map 1. The District of Huanoquite

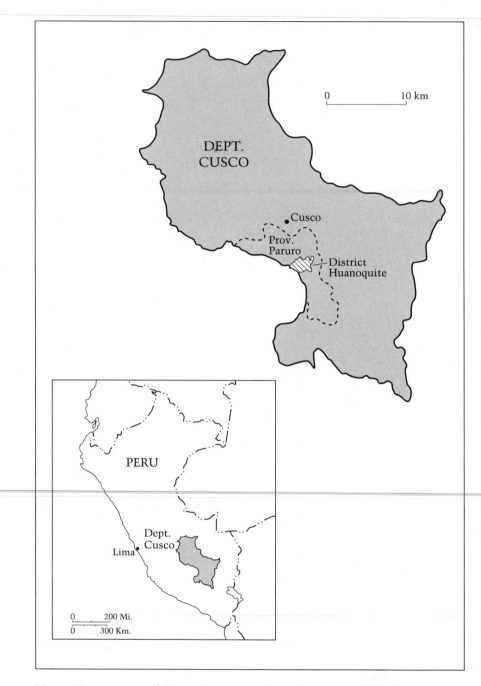

Map 2. Department of Cusco, Province of Paruro, Department of Huanoquite

which was composed of multiple ayllus. Tantarcalla and Chanka were maximal ayllus, each with its own principal political authority, or *kuraka*. In turn, these maximal ayllus were composed of minimal ayllus.

The term *ayllu*, which will appear frequently in the following pages, changes in meaning according to time and place in the Andes. It can refer precisely to a social unit composed of kin related within three generations. On the other hand, it may be a more general kind of sociopolitical unit, composed of households related to one another by ethnicity, common landholdings, rank, or class. A woman's ayllu may be her extended family, but also her lineage, probably her bilateral kin, and even the members of her community or province. Catherine Allen (1988:108–9) notes that Quechua inhabitants generally conceive of ayllus as "processes or modes of relatedness" and suggests that they can best be thought of as distinct groups of people united by a common focus, which may often include social, political, religious, and work values, beliefs, and activities. Ayllu members usually have obligations in the form of labor to the ayllu in return for the usufruct of corporate lands and other resources that may be considered to belong to the ayllu as a whole. They also claim the same local shrines and sacred places (see Fuenzalida 1976:235–40; González Holguín [1608] 1952:39).

In Huanoquite, *ayllu* corresponds best to Allen's definition. Communities, and new kinds of administrative units such as cooperatives, often also exhibit the kinds of relationships that create unifying ties and distinguish one ayllu from another. In Huanoquite, outsiders are occasionally incorporated into ayllus or ayllu-like structures. Ayllu members reside in the same territory, although migrants may be absent for long periods of time.

A dynamic tension characterizes ethnic identity and relations in the district. Many inhabitants speak both Quechua and Spanish. Although far fewer women than men speak Spanish, many of them understand Spanish. Most generally, those who labor directly upon the land, speak Quechua, reside permanently in the district, belong to a community or cooperative, and interact primarily with other peasants usually identify themselves as *campesinos* or *comuneros*. Those who rely mainly upon others' labor to work their properties, speak Spanish, orient their social lives and values toward urban centers, do not belong to a community or cooperative, and primarily interact with others in a similar position usually think of themselves as *vecinos*. However, these are not fixed categories. Education, achievement, language, skill in functioning in urban settings, and occupation provide a degree of economic upward mobility and class stratification among campesinos. Likewise, vecinos have experienced downward economic mobility as a consequence of the reform. Nevertheless, institutionalized idioms of ethnicity and relationships of power play significant roles in maintaining status categories despite class stratification.[1]

The present-day capital of Huanoquite is located at 3,383 meters above sea level (msl), midway (*chaupi*) between the lower valley (*qheshwa*), which ranges roughly from 3,100 msl to 3,600 msl, and the higher reaches of the upper valley (*puna*), which ranges from 3,800 msl to 4,200 msl. In the lower valley, peasants primarily cultivate maize, early potatoes, and wheat. In addition, during the dry season, they bring down their livestock from the upper valley to pasture in this area. In the higher puna, peasants herd and cultivate a few kinds of frost-resistant potatoes. Lower down, they grow barley, broad beans, lupines, and a wide range of potatoes and other kinds of tubers.

The inhabitants of the Andean highlands have always attempted to achieve control over a wide range of production zones, located in different ecological niches. In contrast to natural ecological zones or political administrative units, production zones are "where farmers grow their particular crops in specific ways." These zones combine natural and social processes. In Enrique Mayer's formal definition, a production zone is

a communally managed set of specific productive resources in which crops are grown in distinctive ways. It includes infrastructural features, a particular system of rationing resources (such as irrigation water and natural grasses), and the existence of rule-making mechanisms that regulate how these resources are to be used. . . . Individual production units (such as households) hold access rights to specific portions of these resources. They have full rights to all products obtained by them from their labor and they have the right to transmit them to others. [Mayer 1985:48–51]

By controlling multiple production zones, peasants can offset environmental risks, have a more diverse diet, and respond more easily to an unpredictable market.

Despite this ideal, the interspersal of large areas of private property among parcels of cooperative and community lands held according to different tenure regimes impedes access to and management of many of these zones (see Maps 3 and 4). This patchwork of privately and collectively farmed zones has resulted from complex transformations in land tenure rights, brought about by Huanoquite's incor-

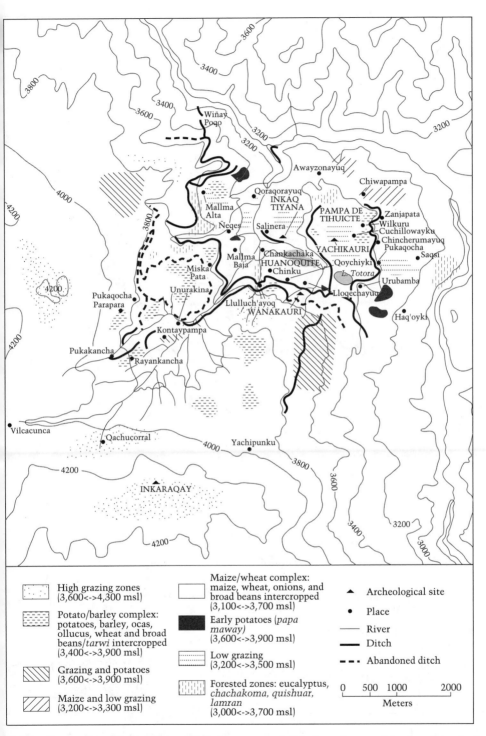

Map 3. Production Zones, Huanoquite (map prepared with the assistance of Stephen G. Bunker)

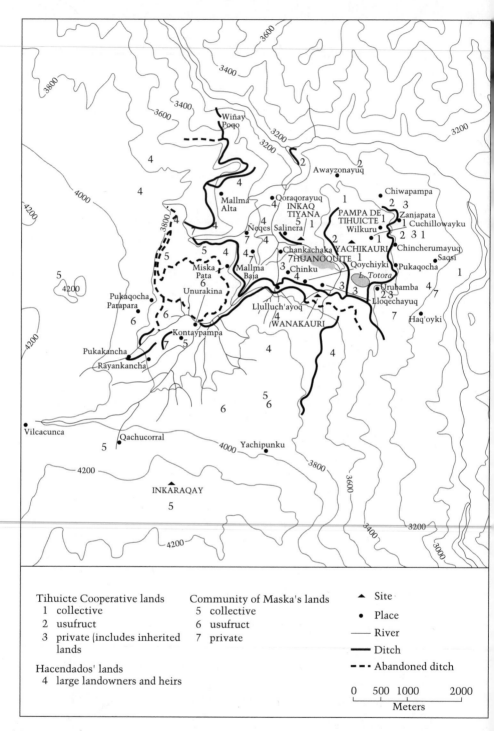

Map 4. Land Tenure Patterns, Huanoquite (map prepared with the assistance of Stephen G. Bunker

poration into the Inca, Spanish colonial, and Peruvian national regimes, and by demographic processes. For example, when ayllu lands were encroached upon and privatized by estates, the estates themselves fought over access to the best ayllu lands and divided them up even further. European-style estates frequently did not heed the indigenous logic of creating multiple production zone "strips" that went from low to high altitude but rather preferred the logic of large contiguous properties, thus cutting across numerous "strips" of communal land.

Precolonial Settlement Patterns and Exchange Networks

Huanoquite's changing economic and political status in a wider regional context has been as important as transformations in its settlement and land-tenure patterns. The tremendous difficulties of transportation epitomize the ambiguities, tensions, and challenges of Huanoquiteños' growing, but still incomplete, participation in wider regional and national systems. Their participation in these systems affects their engagement in different kinds of economic production and exchange and their efforts to secure a measure of local political power.

Huanoquite is the westernmost district of the province of Paruro, formerly known as the province of Chilques and Mascas, located in the department of Cusco (see Map 2). The turbulent Apurimac River divides the district from the department of Apurimac, which lies to its southwest. One of its tributaries, the Corcca/Molle Molle River, divides the district from the rest of the province of Paruro, which lies to its southeast.

Attempting the journey fromCusco to Huanoquite gives one a remarkable sense of the ruggedness of the terrain, the obstacles to building enduring infrastructure, and the space and time that physically separate Huanoquite from urban centers. In addition to the truck road that wends and weaves its way 65 kilometers from Cusco to Huanoquite, there is a beautifully constructed, stone-cobbled footpath and animal trail built by the Incas. The Inca road extends 22 kilometers from Cusco through Huanoquite, crossing the Apurimac River into the central highlands at the Waca Chaca Bridge and eventually reaching the coast.

Several tributaries of the Apurimac River pass through the district of Huanoquite, and the valley that the river has carved out is so rugged that only ten points of access exist along it (Escobar 1977). Five bridges cross this valley into the province of Paruro. The military importance and grandeur of this valley have been remarked upon by the explorer Victor von Hagen, who writes:

The river Apurimac emerges from the edge of the western Andes as a mere rill, fed by the runoff from the glaciers of the lofty Cerro Huachahui (17,787 feet high). Flowing in a northwesterly direction, it receives a number of tributary rivers and streams, and gouges out an impressive canyon on its way to join the Amazon. By the time it reaches the site of the [Waca Chaca] bridge, it has descended from a height of 10,000 feet to one of 5,000 feet. Heard from above the high canyon walls, its cascading waters have a dull, echoing roar, and it is this that gives it its name of Apurimac, "The Great Speaker."

It had been the Rubicon of the Incas since, for a century, it had held them in check, and prevented them from extending their empire northwards. It remained a considerable obstacle until 1350, when the engineers serving the sixth Inca, Roca, made the first attempt to bridge it. That bridge, the Huaca-Chaca or "Holy Bridge" was *huaca* to the Incas because it was thought to possess Soul. On its Cusco side, a very important oracle was erected; this spoke through the deafening roar of the river to those who implored it. Pedro Pizarro, writing in his old age, said that it was known as "The Lord that Speaks," or the Apurimac, "The Great Speaker." It was in a richly painted hut which contained an idol, a thick log spattered with blood. [Von Hagen 1976:75]

The Waca Chaca Bridge has now been reconstructed and renamed the Mariscal Gamarra Bridge, in memory of General Agustín Gamarra, a powerful prefect of Cusco. Gamarra envisioned himself as a leader of the resurrection of the Inca empire following the Wars of Independence of the early nineteenth century.[2] In addition to its religious significance, the bridge was crucial to the extension of Huanoquite's exchange networks into the Apurimac region, and to the Incas' and Spaniards' military strategies of conquest.

From these regions, especially Chumbivilcas and Cotabambas, great llama caravans loaded with wool, llama dung, and medicinal herbs once wended their way to Huanoquite, where the Chumbivilcanos and Cotabambinos traded them for salt, boiled corn, potatoes, and corn on the cob (see Map 5). The journey was arduous, and the round-trip from the most distant communities took approximately two months (De la Bandera 1965 [1557]:324–25). Magnus Mörner (1977:104–5) describes the experience of crossing these kinds of bridges with livestock: "For the livestock, it was very narrow, and because the bridge moved a lot . . . , only one [llama] at a time could pass, and until it had crossed, another did not start to cross for fear that they would fall into the river (which frequently occurred) or the bridge would break."

Huanoquite probably received its name from the presence in great

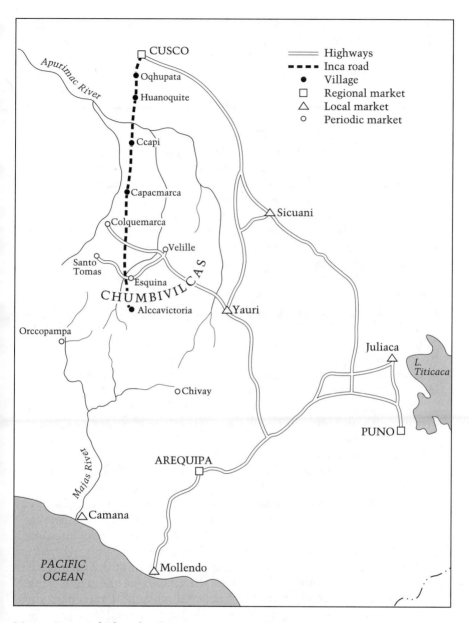

Map 5. Route of Chumbivilcas Llama Caravans (adapted from Glynn Custred, "Llame-ros y comercio interregional," in Giorgio Alberti and Enrique Mayer, eds., *Reciprocidad e inter-cambio en los andes peruanos* [Lima: IEP, 1974], 263)

numbers of these llamas, which left behind valuable fertilizer in the shape of their dung (Paz Soldán 1877:408). Jorge Lira (1982:106) translates the Quechua word *wanukiti* as *con tendencia al abono* ("a propensity toward llama dung"). It is interesting, however, that most Huanoquiteños, young and old, offer an alternative etymology of their community's name. Their explanation reflects their awareness of the former presence of Inca authority in their territory and their incorporation into the Inca radius of power, an experience they did not find entirely to their liking. They recount the story of an Inca princess (*ñusta*) who fled her comfortable and rich surroundings. Some say she escaped from Ccapi, which lies to the south of Huanoquite; others claim she traveled from Cusco, which lies to the north of Huanoquite. An Inca noble pursued her and caught her near Huanoquite, where she was weaving. The Huanoquiteños say that the noble hung her at one of two sites, Vilcaqunka (Sacred Neck) or Ñusta Warkuna (Hanging Site of the Princess). As he strangled her, he queried, "Wanaykita?"—"Have you reformed your ways? Have I punished you enough?" Thus, Huanoquite received its name. The ñusta probably originally came from the Huanoquite region and had been married off to an Inca in Cusco in order to establish a political alliance. Apocryphal or not, the story is repeated frequently enough by Huanoquiteños to suggest that, anecdotally, the death of the rebellious damsel was a lesson to them not to flee the authority of the Incas, and, by extension, that of the state.

Huanoquiteños' most important pre-Inca ties were with regions to the south and west of the district. From the province of Chumbivilcas, in exchange for Huanoquite's corn and salt, came wool, meat, and the prized green-glazed ceramics of Charamoray; from Chanka came potatoes, broad beans, and chuño (freeze-dried potatoes) for Huanoquite's excellent corn; and from Pacco came fruit and corn seed to renew Huanoquite's stock. Huanoquiteños and Vilcabambinos traveled back and forth as well, the Huanoquiteños exchanging early potatoes for delicious prickly pears, peppers, passion fruit, and avocados from the Vilcabambinos.

With the rise of the Incas and the construction of the Inca road, Huanoquite was brought closer into the circuit to the north with Cusco. As an extremely fertile agricultural zone, it attracted members of the Inca nobility, who controlled agricultural and pasture lands there. Groups resettled by the Inca state (*mitmaqkuna*) in a plan of enforced colonization also lived in Huanoquite. It was the site of three valuable salt mines, and of zinc, lead, silver and gold mines (Bueno 1951; Aparicio Vega 1967). It also served as a strategic military garrison for the Incas in their ongoing efforts to conquer the Chankas and other rebellious ethnic polities that lay to the south and west of Huanoquite in what is now the department of Apurimac.[3]

The Inca road from Cusco tilted Huanoquite's interests to the north. Huanoquite retained its vitality because it was a transit point on the Inca road, and because the Incas had considerable economic and political interests in the region. Their imposition of sumptuary laws and enforcement of Quechua as the lingua franca of the empire created a more homogeneous space than had existed previously. Inca rule, because of its policy of economic redistribution, also put a damper on the kinds of traditional exchanges that had previously flowed freely between Huanoquite and its neighboring polities.

Under Inca imperial rule, other non-Inca groups were dislocated and resettled in Huanoquite, among them Maskas, Tantars, and In-kakunas, ethnic groups also scattered in other parts of Paruro; and Wankas and Chankas, whose original home had been in the central highlands and who opposed Inca rule more than other ethnic groups.[4] Archaeological sites along the Inca road include terraces, an irriga-tion ditch, the remains of a way station (*tambo*), and several Inca "thrones" (*Inkaq tiyanan*) located near the salt mines, whence the name of the Inkaq Tiyanan de Tihuicte cooperative. (These "thrones" consist of stepped platforms carved of stone; they were intended either for high-ranked personages or for use as altars.) Although Huanoquite may not have been among the most important Inca way stations, its lookout posts, well-terraced hillsides, and the early de-velopment of its extensive irrigation system attest to its significance to both the Incas and the Spanish conquistadores.

Colonial Settlement Patterns and Exchange Networks

The present-day district capital of Huanoquite was established as a *reducción* in the late sixteenth century as a consequence of the Toledan reforms. These reforms, which took place between 1569 and 1571, forcibly centralized multiple ayllus into what were known as *reducciones* in order to secure better control over the native popula-tion for purposes of Christianization and collecting tribute from them.[5]

In addition, portions of *ayllu* populations were incorporated into labor grants known as *encomiendas*. Encomiendas of indigenous inhabitants were doled out by Francisco Pizarro to victorious con-quistadores. The encomendero was expected to serve the Crown's needs and take care of the spiritual and physical well-being of his

Indians. In turn, he had the right to collect tribute from them and use their labor as he saw fit. Eventually, many of these encomiendas became transformed into workers on haciendas.

In 1689, the cleric Miguél de Velasco, reporting to the bishop of Cusco, Manuel de Mollinedo y Angulo, described the parish of "Guanoquite and its spiritual jurisdiction" as consisting of

a small population of Spaniards living on their estates, the rest of whom live in the city. Outside of the estates surrounding the whole village and its valleys are the lands of the Indians of this village, which are divided from the community into portions by their Caciques, depending upon the quality of the persons. . . . There are two *parcialidades* [moieties], each with its principal cacique, even though only one is governor of all of them, and to that are added two others . . . one called Tantarcalla . . . the other called Chanca, whose Indians reside principally in an outlying *estancia* [hamlet] that belongs to d. Basco de Valverde, and in this village they have only their houses and patios, without lands that have been distributed to them. . . . the people do not remain in their villages or on their lands: some of them help in the village, others on the estates of the Spaniards. [Villanueva 1982:433–40]

De Velasco also mentions three "annexes," Corca, Guanca Guanca, and San Juan de Coror.

The colonial policy of resettlement instituted by the Toledan reforms was not entirely successful. Many of the original population centers of Huanoquite remained scattered throughout the district. Over the centuries, some of these centers have coalesced with others, split off, or become transformed into landed estates. Precisely this flexibility has made it difficult to ascertain the history of Huanoquite's sociopolitical organization. In addition, documentation is sparse. Colonial officials frequently failed to understand the logic of preexisting indigenous sociopolitical organization. Their data were often incomplete or incorrect. The changes in the parameters of administrative units also meant that multiple communities were incorporated into a single larger unit within the region; others came to be considered members of a different administrative unit altogether; and still others were divided into two different units. This process of coalescence and fragmentation is ongoing in the Andes and responds to changing pressures on the land base, disputes over land and labor rights within sociopolitical units, and state policies. (See Appendix A for details of Huanoquite's changing sociopolitical structure and population.)

The events of Spanish conquest and colonization caused shifts in Huanoquite's economic and political relationships to the state. During the colonial period, Huanoquiteños attempted to return to and elaborate upon some of the exchanges they had engaged in prior to Inca hegemony. The context in which they attempted to do so had changed, however, and social and economic strategies that had once worked well for them no longer achieved the same results.

Commenting on the principal economic attractions of Huano-quite and the province of Paruro in general for the Spaniards, Jeanine Brisseau Loayza remarks: "As forgotten and poor a province as Paruro is today, [it] then had a flourishing cereal and textile artisan econ-omy. . . . Significant amounts of rustic cloth were produced in the provinces of Paruro and Quispicanchis" (Brisseau 1975:220–21). Sev-eral textile sweatshops (*obrajes*) functioned near Huanoquite (Mos-coso 1965; Tamayo 1981:50; Oricain 1906 [1790]:363–64). The San Juan de Taray and Parpay obrajes, owned first by the Jesuits and then by the Augustinians, and the Molle Molle *chorrillo*, owned by the marqués de Rocafuerte, were all attached to landed estates and active near Huanoquite.[6] In almost all cases, the exploitation of wool for this primitive manufacturing industry enhanced the productivity of agricultural estates.

In seventeenth-century church tithe (*diezmo*) records, Huano-quite is also documented as having become the third highest wheat-producing district in the department of Cusco, surpassed only by Anta and Pisac. Even in the early twentieth century, although other provinces in the department of Cusco had outstripped Paruro com-mercially, Huanoquite still produced the greatest quantity of wheat, corn, and potatoes in the province of Paruro (Fuentes 1905:226).

By 1689, at least seventeen estates had been established in Hua-noquite (Villanueva 1982:433–40), and Mörner (1977:50, 141) reports fifteen substantial estates in the parish of Huanoquite, a higher num-ber than found at that time in any of the other six parishes belonging to Paruro (figures for estates in the other parishes range from three to eight). Many of these haciendas belonged to individuals, but Catholic orders also owned substantial amounts of land in Huanoquite and exerted an important economic and political influence. They exacted high tithes, amounting to a tenth of the annual output of hacen-dados, whose productivity depended upon the resident indigenous labor force. Between 1777 and 1826, Huanoquite consistently con-tributed the highest percentage of tithes of all of Paruro's parishes (Huertas and Carnero 1983). The church collected these tithes in return for the "privilege" of Christianizing the native population.

Religious sodalities (*cofradías*) were also established in the region by the end of the sixteenth century, providing important economic revenues to the church and serving as an additional weapon in Christianization. The church controlled some of the best flat, irrigated lands in the area, and Horacio Villanueva Urteaga (1982:433–40) reports that fifteen lay sodalities existed in the region by 1689. The grandeur of the church at Huanoquite and the number of valuable paintings housed in it, including some done by the finest colonial artists of the Cusco School, attest to its symbolic and economic power.

By the eighteenth century, the impact of haciendas and colonial rule on production and commerce in Huanoquite had increased. Based on Viceroy Toledo's inspection of indigenous communities between 1570 and 1575, Noble David Cook, Alejandro Malaga, and Therese Bouysse (1975:xxxvii) report a total population of 1,037 for the reducción of Huanoquite. Toledo's inspection found 250 male tribute payers (heads of household) and 564 women, a ratio that reveals the decline of the male population following the conquest and the institutionalization of harsh forced labor in locations often distant from people's homes. Devastating epidemics also produced an absolute decline, and the population rose so slowly thereafter that by 1689, Huanoquite had only 1,150 inhabitants (Mörner 1977). By 1786, the population had grown to 1,463 (Mörner 1977), and 2,566 were reported by 1877 (Paz Soldán 1877:408). It should be remembered, however, that the demographic increase was partially owing to the number of people fleeing forced labor in the mines or who had lost their lands in other places and were seeking to attach themselves to new communities.

During the early part of the colonial period, because of the demographic decline of the native population, land grabs by the Spaniards affected indigenous living conditions less than the harsh labor conditions the colonial regime instituted, including forced work in the distant mines and in textile sweatshops. Huanoquite's Spanish landed elite took advantage of already-existing trade networks, but used them to market their own products, primarily in Cusco. They relied upon the Inca road, using mules to transport agricultural products and textiles to the Cusco market and the mines of Potosí. "One could find the most archaic system, in which the peasant worked the land without ever receiving a salary, and in addition had to use his own means of transport to convey the harvest to the urban residence of the landowner in Cusco," comments José Tamayo Herrera (1981:136).

Many of Huanoquite's landed elite also became engaged in cattle dealing. Livestock began to be raised in large numbers by the eighteenth century, reflected in the tithe records and the numerous complaints of authorities and native inhabitants that hacendados were abusing *yerbaje*, the levy native inhabitants had to pay hacendados to pasture their herds on lands that no longer belonged to their ayllus. Rafael Serrano, subprefect of Paruro, criticized the practice:

> With this, they charge an annual fee for each head of cattle, sheep, or horse. Since none of the landlords have fenced in their lands, they constantly abuse the unhappy native, charging him for each head of livestock that he herds next to their estates. . . . since the exploitation of natives still persists, it is not rare that each time they charge them, they take away one of more of their cattle or horses.[7]

Firewood and wool also became important commercial products in the colonial era. The cutting of firewood for Cusco stripped and eroded many of Huanoquite's slopes. The raising of livestock and the increased reliance of landlords upon mules and horses for transport accelerated damage to footpaths and irrigation ditches.

Huanoquiteños participated in the Tupac Amaru uprisings that swept the southern Andean highlands from 1781 to 1783, although the precise details of their involvement are not known. The horrible labor conditions in the textile sweatshops and the forced redistribution of goods (*repartimiento de mercancías*) to the native population in an effort by the colonial regime to accumulate further revenues set the stage for the rebellion. The efforts of the Crown to recuperate control over the colonies in the face of the growing economic and political power of the colonial bureaucracy also played an important role in both the uprising and the subsequent Wars of Independence.[8]

Tupac Amaru, who spearheaded the rebellion, was a muleteer. Quintessentially a mediator, he was able to take advantage of the numerous networks the muleteers had established in their travels, and they helped him greatly in his "campaign to reconstitute the ancient nation" (*La Crónica* [1918]). In 1984, Huanoquiteños still recounted stories of the mistreatment muleteers had suffered at the hands of the landlords of Tihuicte, one of Huanoquite's largest properties.

Although we do not know precisely why Huanoquiteños decided to support the rebellion, we may surmise that the Inca road from Cusco to the coastal regions of Arequipa was important for exporting the textiles manufactured in Huanoquite and the province of Paruro in general, as well as for transporting the luxury goods that native inhabitants were forced to purchase. As the crucial link between the highlands and coast, the road was thus also the necessary focus of any military strategy, and the rebels devoted much thought to whether they should burn the Waca Chaca bridge to prevent troops arriving from Lima (Mörner 1977:121–22).

Although the Tupac Amaru rebellion was put down, the Bourbon reforms, passed by the Crown in 1783–84, officially abolished the forced redistribution of goods, a mainstay of the colonial economy. This was done in part because of the rebellion and in part because the Crown was seeking to wrest control of the colonial economy from bureaucrats of the colonial state apparatus who were appropriating its revenues. At the same time that the Spanish Crown tried to diminish the power of Peru's colonial bureaucrats, it also tried to restrict the relative autonomy of native polities by eliminating the official titles of native authorities (*kurakas*).

By the end of the colonial period, the Inca road had become increasingly important to Huanoquite, but it primarily served the landed elite rather than the native inhabitants. Because of the cumulative effects of the forced labor draft, the demographic decline, and the passage of various *composiciones de tierra*, the ayllus of Huanoquite had lost much of their land. Begun in 1591 and continued periodically through the eighteenth century, the policy of composiciones de tierra permitted the Spanish Crown to grab up ayllu lands beyond the minimum allotted to ayllu members and required that landholders, including the native inhabitants, purchase titles to their land from the Crown.

The most significant thing about the policy of composiciones de tierra was that it gave individuals the right to purchase titles from the Crown for what appeared to be fallow or abandoned lands. The population decline and the permanent movement of the indigenous population for purposes of forced labor had disrupted traditional control over lands in different ecological zones, leaving much land unused. The decree facilitated the ability of Spaniards, as well as wealthier ayllu members, particularly those who had been kurakas, to purchase titles for large tracts of land cheaply from Crown officials, who were authorized to throw lands defined as vacant onto the market (Mellafe 1969:40–42; Spalding 1984:181–83). This practice decreased the amount of land available to members of smaller ayllu units and increased the opportunity for the colonial landed elite and larger, more powerful ayllus to expand their holdings and gain greater access to the labor of dispossessed Indians. It also privatized lands that had frequently been used by multiple sociopolitical units.

Many households in Huanoquite thus became attached to haciendas, and their direct participation in local and long-distance commerce diminished. Those who had been kurakas or ethnic lords and had held a higher status were in a far better position than other inhabitants to take advantage of the benefits of the colonial regime, to exploit their own polities, and to engage in commerce. They were also more able to establish useful alliances with the landed elite and colonial bureaucrats than were other Huanoquiteños.[9] Despite the diminishing economic and political power of Huanoquite's indigenous population, Huanoquite itself remained a significant agricultural region, and one to which royal, colonial, and ecclesiastical administrative officials paid considerable attention. Ironically, the very prosperity of the region hastened the impoverishment of Huanoquite's indigenous population.

Exchange Networks in the Nineteenth and Twentieth Centuries

> When the Lord and St. Peter were roaming the world planting seeds wherever they wanted towns to sprout, a small seed dropped out of the sack onto the rocky summit where the village now stands. Saint Peter noticed the mistake and wanted to retrieve the seed, but the Lord, who was in a great hurry to reach more important places, told his disciple to move on and let the people fend for themselves.
>
> Roland Sarti, *Long Live the Strong:*
> *A History of Rural Society in the Apennine Mountains*

During the early nineteenth century, the orientation of Huanoquite's regional space shifted gradually but dramatically. These shifts resulted from national and international economic dynamics and ideologies as well as from changes in local administrative policies and commerce. Surprisingly few data are available on how Huanoquiteños participated in the changes of the Republican period. The Wars of Independence (1820–23) encouraged the establishment of frontiers between nations and the abolition of protectionist policies. At the local level, Simón Bolívar's decrees of 1825 ordered that private title to community lands be established (Davies 1970; De Trazegnies 1979), and abolished tribute, replacing it with a "personal contribution." These decrees protected lands held with clear title, but the majority of these were in the hands of the wealthier inhabitants and members of the landed elite. The privatization of corporate lands also fragmented existing ethnic units and ayllus.

Collusion increased among merchants, priests, and former kurakas to throw off the yoke of state control. They often supported indigenous inhabitants in their efforts to abolish "personal contributions" to the state, so that they could siphon off the surplus instead. Conflicts between traditional ethnic lords who had been heirs to their positions before the Bourbon reforms and individuals who knew Spanish and had acquired useful skills of mediation with colonial society were exacerbated. Powerful local bosses (*caudillos*) dominated the political field and struggled for control of it among themselves.

The War of the Pacific between Peru and Bolivia on the one side and Chile on the other from 1879 to 1884 provoked a new awareness among Huanoquiteños of their status as citizens of a nation. Those who became soldiers acquired a greater familiarity with the larger society; they also expected that, in return for defending their country, they would be rewarded with all the rights accorded Peruvian citizens, including rights to their land. Following Peru's devastating defeat, armed peasants who had participated in the defense of the new nation became a substantial threat to the landed elite, who soon realized that these weapons could be used against them (as in some regions they were) and sought to squelch any sign of rebellion among the peasants. Meanwhile, in consequence of their mistreatment by the landed elite they had defended during the war, peasants rapidly abandoned their expectations of becoming free citizens and became more circumspect about the Peruvian state's legitimacy. (See Mallon 1983 for a detailed analysis of the participation of peasants in the Wars of Independence and their changing relationships to the landed elite and the state.)

Peru's export-based economy developed in the late nineteenth century, fueled by economic liberalism. The construction of railway lines from coastal ports to highland regions was undertaken. Regional highland economies were isolated and disarticulated from the export economy, however. The construction of the Southern Railway between 1873 and 1908 restructured southern highland commercial sectors, especially the character and economy of the towns that had easy access to the railways. These new commercial circuits isolated agriculturally productive regions without railways and affected the rhythms of trade and markets (Jacobsen 1983; Tamayo 1981). Local markets were replaced by large weekly markets in towns located near the rail network.

The construction of roads accompanied the national interest in railways. The focus on exports indirectly stimulated industry and greater production of some agricultural goods and wool but destroyed the internal integration of different regions, since agricultural diversification was of little importance in the implementation of national economic policy.[10] Nevertheless, multiple roads and railways had already been built, and their effects on regional exchange networks were profound.

Between 1877 and 1961, the province of Paruro and the district of Huanoquite were greatly affected by these transformations. The roads and railways bypassed most of the province of Paruro. The result was a continuous loss of population. The district of Huanoquite experienced even more extreme isolation than provincial centers like Paruro. Cusco grew in importance to the large landowners of Huanoquite, whose properties had expanded considerably.

In addition, as Cusco's bureaucratic apparatus expanded its control over the administrative jurisdictions of districts and provinces, the status of Huanoquite declined. In 1828, Paruro became the provincial capital, which increased its political significance. Monies and services, although they were modest in comparison to those allocated to more lucrative commercial centers, flowed from Cusco to Paruro rather than to equally productive but less "important" districts within the province. Huanoquite stagnated, and its estates, although they retained immense political power within the district, could not compete with large coastal plantations or highland estates that were closer to roads and railways. Although President Augusto Leguía reestablished the existence of native communities as legal entities in 1920, "governmental indecision and contradiction virtually guaranteed the success of hacendado expansionism" in rural districts, Thomas Davies (1970:18) observes.

Huanoquite's administrative boundaries distorted the natural space and trade routes that villagers had maintained according to the course of rivers, the barriers of mountain ranges, the accessibility of valleys, and the conscious maximization of control over different production zones. Paruro's administrative status began to bring it benefits, for which Huanoquite competed. Regions far outside Huanoquite's orbit of commerce and exchange also began to affect its political status and commercial potential. Local authorities struggled to control their remaining commercial options, and the landed elite, who also served as the district's political officeholders, began to lobby for road-building projects.

The salt mines located in Huanoquite and in the nearby hamlet of Oqhupata helped to counterbalance the region's isolation. Huanoquite continued to attract a high number of travelers from the neighboring provinces of Chumbivilcas and Cotabambas. The Inca road was maintained expressly because of the salt mines and the trade they generated. One of Huanoquite's early mayors and hacendados, Daniél Galdos, repeatedly expressed concern that the road should be repaired so that the muleteers who bring salt from the mines for the salt depots in the neighboring provinces can count upon a short and safe road. . . . If the opposite occurs, this locality will remain isolated without commerce with the city of Cusco, from which it lives. In addition, it will do serious damage to the travelers from the neighboring provinces of Chumbivilcas and Cotabambas.[11]

During the late nineteenth century, an important new industry, the processing of barley into beer, developed in Cusco, with little hindrance from outside competition. Three small breweries were already functioning in Cusco in 1872, when Gustavo Adolfo Manglesdorf, one of the first bourgeois industrialists of the southern highlands, established a much larger brewery there. By 1897, six breweries were functioning in the Cusco area, and by 1903, Manglesdorf's brewery had displaced the smaller ones. Eventually sold to businessmen from Arequipa, this brewery monopolized the beer industry (Tamayo 1981:109; Kaerger 1979). Huanoquiteños began to increase their cultivation of barley for sale to the brewery, but problems of transport limited production. Not until the construction of the truck road from Huanoquite to Cusco did barley production rise significantly and come to be an important new commercial link between Huanoquite and Cusco.

In 1936, the construction began on a truck road from Cusco to Yaurisque, which ultimately replaced the Inca road as the principal transport route to Cusco from Huanoquite. The road was tortuous and indirect. At the time, engineers were paid, not by the hour, but by the kilometer, Huanoquiteños bitterly remember. They therefore designed roads that were neither the most practical nor the most direct routes between urban centers and outlying districts. Labor was not an issue, since the local inhabitants were obliged to provide it gratis, a levy instituted by President Leguía when he began his road-building campaign in 1921, which ultimately resulted in over 18,000 kilometers of new roads (Davies 1970:34–35, 82, 160).

Starting in 1950, a series of external events further undermined Huanoquite's importance as a local economic, if not administrative, center. A severe earthquake partially decimated Cusco in 1950. The Board for Reconstruction and Industrial Growth (CRIF), established in 1952 to redevelop infrastructure, devoted a portion of its funds to road construction. In 1956, the Corporation of Reconstruction and Industrial Growth of Cusco was founded, and road construction to outlying provincial and district centers began. In the 1950's, a road was built from Yaurisque to the provincial capital of Paruro.

Subsequently, during President Fernando Belaúnde Terry's first administration (1963–68), CRIF and another governmental agency, Popular Cooperation, actively sought to implement Belaúnde's dream of building roads throughout the highlands and then linking the major centers of the coast, Andean highlands, and Amazonian lowlands. This mammoth project further distorted the practical boundaries and relationships of regional space that Huanoquiteños had already forged, based on their trade networks and the geography of the area.[12] Without a radical transformation in the agrarian structure of rural areas, which were in many cases controlled entirely by the landed elite, Belaúnde's vision of national integration made little sense. Instead, it encouraged the development of primate central-place systems (Smith 1976:260).

In central-place theory, the importance of lower-level centers correlates with their political power, control over resources, and the dominant economic activities and political interests of the service sector in the marketing infrastructure (Appleby 1976; Kelley 1976; Smith 1976). Rather than creating dynamic regional economies, Belaúnde's blueprint for national development resulted in a few centers becoming dynamic economic and political nodes, while numerous highland communities remained marginalized and disconnected, both from one another and from national centers of economic and political power.

In 1961, Mario Romero, a powerful landowner in Huanoquite, became mayor and began to pressure CRIF to provide funds for the continuation of the road from Yaurisque to Huanoquite. (Map 6 shows some minor and all major roads that were built in the Huanoquite area or had some impact on it.) CRIF reluctantly allocated a small amount for this purpose the first year but gradually increased its budget as Huanoquiteños' commitment to the project became evident. By the second year, the road had almost been completed when a torrential landslide forced the laborers from all the villages that lay along its route to start all over again. Such was their enthusiasm that by 1964, the road had been finished. Many Huanoquiteños still refer to this road as their "outlet to the sea." The minimal daily wages of the laborers were paid by CRIF, which also provided the machinery and engineers for the job.

Since the road from Yaurisque to Huanoquite was badly built and lacked adequate retaining walls and drainage, however, flooding and landslides quickly made it impassable. Nevertheless, another change occurred simultaneously that led to the almost total abandonment of the Inca road and a far greater dependence upon the truck road. When the truck road was built from Huanoquite to Cusco, a number of

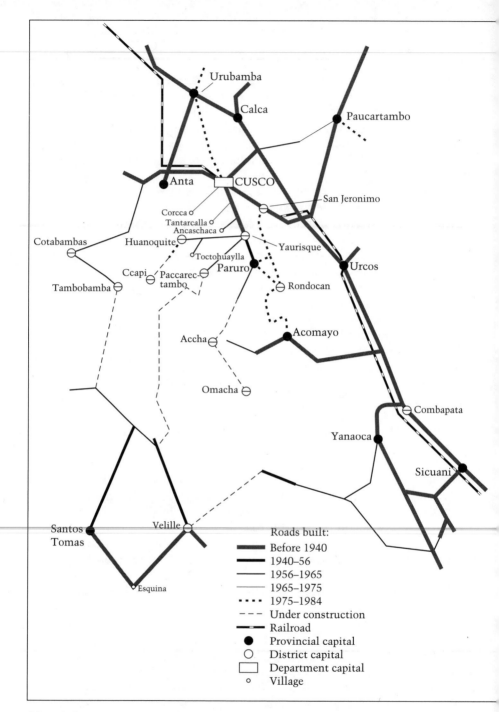

Map 6. Impact of Roads upon Huanoquite's Regional Space (adapted from Epifanio Ba●
Tupayachi, *Cuzco: Sistemas viales, articulación y desarrollo regional* [Cusco: Centro de Estudios Rural●
"Bartolomé de Las Casas," 1983])

Roads built:

▬▬▬ Before 1940
━━━ 1940–56
─── 1956–1965
─── 1965–1975
•••• 1975–1984
– – – Under construction
╪══╪ Railroad
● Provincial capital
○ District capital
▢ Department capital
∘ Village

other roads were built from villages with which Huanoquite had formerly maintained ties. These new roads did not pass through Huanoquite, and many of Huanoquite's social and economic interactions with other communities were thus permanently truncated.

In comparing maps 5 and 6, one can see how in comparison to the Inca road, the numerous truck roads gradually isolated communities from one another and created dyadic relationships between single large market centers and multiple small communities, Huanoquite among them.

Also in the early 1960's, with the assistance of Popular Cooperation, another road was built from Yaurisque to Paccarectambo, southeast of Huanoquite. Yaurisque, hardly a thriving village, suddenly expanded into a modern way station, since it became the junction of roads leading in three directions: to Huanoquite, Paruro, and Paccarectambo.

These events signaled a dramatic transformation in Huanoquite's economic and political status. Until then it had been a dynamic transit point between Cusco and communities to its south and west, via the well-traveled Inca road. It now became the terminus of a transport route and a district capital with only limited political bargaining power.

Huanoquiteños began an exceptional effort to revitalize their exchange networks. Like many other communities that had become more isolated because road construction had bypassed them, they grasped how the central-place system worked in the Andean highlands and sought to incorporate their own community into it. Thus far, however, they have had little success.

In 1980, the first peasant mayor of Huanoquite, Juan Bautista Quispe Antitupa, called a general assembly to ask if residents wanted a truck road built from Huanoquite to Cheqoperqa, which would feed into an existing road to Oqhupata, and thence to Cusco, replicating the route of the Inca road. His ideas were not new. As early as 1927, Juan de Dios Galdos, then mayor of Huanoquite, had entertained the same idea.[13] When Quispe took office 53 years later, the issue was still alive. The initial efforts of Huanoquiteños to diminish their isolation provoked outrage from Yaurisque, the existing transit point for the truck road from Cusco to Huanoquite. The new road Huanoquiteños sought to construct would bypass Yaurisque entirely. Yaurisque authorities threatened Quispe repeatedly, and records show that the Yaurisque District Council took decisive action to prevent the future loss of traffic by blockading all truck traffic from Yaurisque whose destination was Huanoquite.[14] The intensity of political opposition, corruption, inadequate machinery, and inability to come up with the necessary labor subsequently caused the project to be abandoned.

Many other changes gradually reinforced the importance of the major truck road. Hacendados built roads from their estates that fed into the main arteries. The construction of schools, a medical post, and a civil guard post in Huanoquite meant that teachers, health personnel, and police depended on the road. More recently, once peasant households had control over more of their own land and labor as a result of the 1969 reform, they also had greater opportunities to market the fruits of their labor. They found trucks more useful than llamas, mules, or horses for transporting large quantities of potatoes, wheat, corn, and barley to Cusco. Most households in Huanoquite, with the exception of the Tihuicte cooperative, do not have the capital to buy trucks. They are, however, dependent upon the trucks and truck road if they wish to compete in the Cusco market.

Following the construction of the truck road, hacendados turned their attention to the potential of participating in the commercial sector by purchasing trucks. Some did so, not because they were upwardly mobile but because their economic prospects in agriculture had gradually waned. The 1969 reform was a blow to their power. A burgeoning service sector has accompanied the development of trucking. The service sector, also primarily controlled by larger property holders, includes local stores in Huanoquite, wholesalers, retailers, and the truck owners themselves. Store owners make it possible for peasants to avoid traveling to Cusco, although they sell basic consumer goods at inflated prices. Many of them agree to barter instead of cash, but the terms of trade are usually set by the market. In addition, merchants take advantage of the bad condition of the truck road by providing their services as intermediaries and usurers, buying up peasants' produce and reselling it in Cusco at much higher prices. The trip to Cusco is indeed hazardous because, once peasants arrive there, they are inevitably besieged by hundreds of middlemen, who aggressively board the arriving truck, wheedling and haggling with the passengers in order to finalize purchases. Many of these middlemen also take the opportunity to steal what they can from passengers, since the scene is always one of real bedlam for the tired travelers.

The establishment of credit facilities for peasants through the government-controlled Agrarian Bank (Banco Agrario) in Cusco after the 1969 reform also increased dependence upon the truck road. Peasants have to travel to Cusco to apply for credit and to obtain disinfected barley seed in sacks from the Cervecería del Sur brewery, which is most easily transported back to Huanoquite by truck. Credit has become such an important factor of production for peasants that they willingly travel to and from Cusco by truck to obtain it.

The effects of the truck road upon turning wheat into baked bread were paradoxical. Several mills owned by hacendados once functioned in Huanoquite, but most of these were abandoned after the reform. Subsequently, after harvesting their wheat, peasants transported it to Cusco by truck, had it ground into flour, and then returned with the flour to bake bread in ovens in Huanoquite. They then traveled back to Cusco to sell some of their bread. This was scarcely cost-effective, and in 1989 PRODERM, a Peruvian-Dutch development agency, helped residents build a new water-driven mill in Huanoquite. The mill was a remarkable success. Besides generating important revenue for the district, it recreated many of Huanoquite's previous exchange ties with neighboring communities, whose inhabitants traveled to Huanoquite to use the mill and trade.

Economic Development?

In 1970, six years after the completion of the truck road, Huanoquite was cited in Cusco's local newspaper, *El Sol*, as one of "the villages that lives at the edge of national reality because of the inertia of its authorities."[15] This statement has a grain of truth to it, but far too simplistically characterizes Huanoquite's growing isolation, which Huanoquiteños have, in fact, been eager to diminish. They were not fully prepared for the negative consequences of the road, which they had expected would be a harbinger of development and enhance Huanoquite's reputation as a thriving commercial center. The road brought with it services such as potable water, schools, and health centers, but these have had a limited impact on Huanoquite's economic development. The health post, guard station, and a few elementary schools stand as symbolic tokens of development but have not altered the relations of production within Huanoquite or enhanced Huanoquiteños' ability to compete commercially in the national economy.

The weak integration of Huanoquite into the bureaucratic orbit of twentieth-century Peru is not entirely the result of national policies and the power of local elites. "There is nothing more difficult than to build an administration covering millions of partly self-sufficient peasant households" that differ in size, status, dispersion, self-sufficiency, local diversity, and agricultural strategies, Gerd Spittler concludes in a provocative discussion of administration in a peasant state. "The nightmare of administration is less the difference between the little tradition of one community and the great tradition of the state than that there are so many small communities which are all different from each other" (Spittler 1983:130–44). This "chaotic diversity" simultaneously prevents desired services from reaching communities like Huanoquite and staves off unwelcome intervention in Huanoquiteños' lives. They, in turn, have created their own defensive, and sometimes offensive, strategies. At times, they avoid communication with the administrative apparatus; they seemingly agree to administrative suggestions, but fail to follow them up with action; and they lie. No doubt all this began long ago, when the colonizers recruited native labor and the first censuses were taken by Spanish inspectors to calculate maximum tribute collection from different ayllus (Mayer 1972:339–66).

The positive consequences of administrative isolation have only minimally offset its negative economic and political import for Huanoquiteños, however. Huanoquite's position within Peru as a nation resembles that of other lower-level highland districts. It is separated by a great distance from a single higher-level economic and political center of power (Cusco); and it competes with a high number of lower-level nodes, all of which run the risk of losing their resources, population, and income to one or two higher-level centers that boast a more dynamic economy.[16]

Despite these obstacles, Huanoquiteños have struggled to recreate the regional space of which they were once a part, but they have had to do so under very different circumstances. They must rely upon funding from Cusco and Paruro for their projects, thus furthering their dependence upon these already higher-level economic and political centers.

The history of Huanoquite's exchange and commercial networks well demonstrates some of the fallacies of uneven and incoherent development. From a thriving agricultural region and exchange center, Huanoquite has become an isolated district whose former linkages to surrounding areas have either weakened or vanished. A number of forces have led to this, among them the cycles of the export economy, the expansion of landed estates, the declining legitimacy of native political authorities in the eyes of their polities, and the growing comparative advantage of other agricultural regions. The replacement of the Inca road by truck roads could have encouraged Huanoquite's economic growth and political clout, but the proliferation of scattered road-building projects during Belaúnde's first administration preceded far-reaching transformations in Huanoquite's agrarian structure.

The 1969 reform increased Huanoquiteños' participation in the Cusco market. Their household productivity rose as they acquired lands that colonialists had usurped from them centuries before. However, their lack of capital and the intervention of the service sector in their commercial activities have dealt severe blows to Huanoquiteños' persistent and concerted efforts to give meaning to their own visions of regional space. Truck owners, intermediaries, petty entrepreneurs, and bureaucrats have created powerful alliances among themselves, while simultaneously forging imbalanced clientelist ties with local inhabitants.

Huanoquiteños face contradictory needs. On the one hand, they seek urban services that can increase their agricultural productivity and improve their well-being. On the other hand, in attempting to secure these services, they become ever more dependent upon the Cusco bureaucracy. In trying to balance these needs, they have undertaken projects that will directly enhance their control over production and exchange. They have tried to establish a Sunday market in the village, reopen the salt mines, build roads that serve their interests, construct a local mill, and set up a rotating credit fund. They have also searched for ways to control their growing dependency upon the marketing system by imposing regulations upon truck owners, drivers, and local storekeepers, and by forcing intermediaries and truck owners to become involved in local community activities.

The national government's ostensible interest in contributing to rural development and achieving national integration is belied by the design of its commercial truck routes. Truck roads cater to urban rather than rural needs and do not follow the existing logic of indigenous space. While roads can be excellent instruments of development, their design and use, in this instance, have had little positive effect on agrarian communities such as Huanoquite. Instead, they have reinforced the urban-centered description of Huanoquite as a backwater on the edge of national reality. However, the policies of the national government are only partly accountable for Huanoquite's growing isolation. Throughout its history, Huanoquite's agricultural fertility has created opportunities for individuals to profit from local projects, agricultural production, and economic transactions.

Conclusion

The history of Huanoquite's changing status within the Peruvian nation-state demonstrates that Huanoquiteños' relationships to the state have increasingly come to depend upon their capacity to manipulate a highly paternalistic, but pluralistic, system of bureaucrats and regional intermediaries to diminish their economic and political isolation. Under these conditions, their options are limited, but they have made efforts to strengthen their community organizations and to influence the bureaucracy through suprahousehold organizations such as unions, federations, and parties (see Chapter 8).

Huanoquiteños express their experience of their changing place within different political regimes through many mediums, including oral narratives. One narrative in particular strongly conveys the Huanoquiteños' sentiments about their loss of control over the shape their regional space has taken. Many villagers, including the president of Maska, had told me of their desire for a bridge that would cross the Miska Wayku Valley, eliminating the exhausting route that the Inca road follows. Some even believe that such a bridge once existed. The following story was told to me by a young man as we sat in a field overlooking the Miska Wayku Valley. It echoes the fears, concern, and bitterness among Huanoquiteños that they have been silenced and made speechless in their efforts to communicate their needs to the government.

There are many beliefs about how the Inca empire was constructed. Some people believe that it was built by extraterrestrial creatures. In this area, we have a belief that it was the work of the *hak'akllu* [the mountain flicker, a species of woodpecker],[17] with the aid of a special herb. But we do not know what this special herb is and we continue searching for it.

The hak'akllu was the messenger of the Sun God, and he was to do the Sun's bidding. But the hak'akllu grew lazy and did not construct things as he was told. He was supposed to build a bridge of large rocks, like those of Sacsayhuaman, from Paruro to Colcha over the Apurimac River. He got as far as drawing the design of the bridge on one of the rocks with this special herb and making one of the rocks move to its proper place, when the Sun struck him dumb, made him unable to speak. You can still see the line of rocks. Now the hak'akllu only utters, "Hak'akllu, hak'akllu." He is a good-for-nothing gossip. The hak'akllu was struck dumb by the Sun because he was lazy.

This legend incorporates an idea often expressed by representatives of the Peruvian state, regional intermediaries, and members of the landed elite seeking to structure Huanoquite's regional space in their own image: that peasants' problems are simply the result of their illiteracy and laziness. The centers of political power, economic frontiers, exchange networks, and internal production units that give shape to Huanoquite's regional space are, however, the products of far-reaching economic, political, and social forces. Incorporation into the Spanish colonial regime and then the nation-state deprived Huanoquiteños of economic and political power. A great many Huanquiteños recognize that their failure to amass sufficient political power to serve their own needs underlies their inability to control their integration into the Peruvian state. They have nevertheless repeatedly struggled to restructure their relationships to the Peruvian state, challenging the images that the elite and government officials hold of them.

Huanoquiteños have taken many steps to situate themselves more advantageously in their natural and built environment, and they have engaged in diverse political activities for these purposes. As they have pursued their rights to land, political representation, and legal protection, the state has also attempted to control these processes. As we shall see in the following chapters, the passage of the 1969 reform legislation was just as much the product of the state's efforts to manage an unruly peasant population as it was of the long history of efforts by peasants to force the state to meet their demands.

The Agrarian Reform Project

From this day on, the peasants of Peru will no longer be pariahs or the disinherited, living in poverty from birth to death and viewing themselves as powerless in the face of a future that appears equally dismal for their children. From the time of this fortuitous day, June 24th, the peasants of Peru will truly be free citizens, whose right to the fruits of the earth they cultivate, and to a just place in a society that will never again treat them as diminished citizens, men to be exploited by other men, the nation will finally recognize.

> General Juan Velasco Alvarado's speech to the nation
> announcing the 1969 Agrarian Reform[1]

I became a lawyer because I saw, close up, how the peasants suffered inhuman treatment by those who had power because they controlled land. I saw this because my grandparents had their estates. Thus, as a child, I saw how they treated the peasants. I saw how [peasants] gave up their lives, served their whole lives, father and son. That's why I chose the vocation of defending the peasants. The Peruvian peasantry, especially in Cusco, is part of a very particular kind of socioeconomic and cultural order. . . . We work with a peasantry that lacks the minimum in culture; that is, to be illiterate is the worst social abuse humanity can permit. . . . It goes against all human rights. . . . This is the current state of affairs we have, and it is the fault of all the changing governments that promise so much in each election to the peasants to vindicate them, and then they forget, they totally forget, as is now occurring. Today's peasants are living their worst moment. I believe they should be sanctified, blessed, they will return as saints, given how they live. . . . The state has separated itself totally from them, and it is painful to speak of the Peruvian peasantry in this situation.

> Nerio Gonzalez, 1991

Almost twenty-five years separate the passionate oratory of Velasco and the grim appraisal of relations between peasants and the state offered by Nerio Gonzalez, an attorney who provided his legal services to peasants during the reform. How did the hopeful plans of Velasco turn into the nightmare Gonzalez sketches, in which peasants figure as saints, now living "their worst moment"? The answer lies partly in the contradictory objectives of the reform law, partly in the government's failure to understand the complexity of rural society, and partly in the reversals that have occurred in national policy, from the state's explicit support of peasants' demands to utter disregard for them. Let us turn first to the 1969 reform law itself and the history of agrarian policy that preceded it.[2]

The 1969 Agrarian Reform Law was not the first to be passed in Peru. In 1964, Fernando Belaúnde Terry, who took over power from the military in 1963, crafted a comprehensive reform law, Legislative Decree 15037, in response to land invasions and uprisings in the southern and central highlands. The violence and extent of these uprisings alarmed landlords and urban residents alike. In the Cusco area, for example, peasants blocked highways, invaded lands, cut telephone lines, took hostages, and assaulted prisons in order to free other peasants. In Huanoquite, in November 1963, peasants armed with Mausers and .22-caliber pistols engaged in a bloody battle over Mallma, an estate notorious for its abusive labor conditions (MacLean y Esteñós 1965:131–34). The landlord of Mallma, Humberto Paz, had a reputation for unusual cruelty toward peasants. Peasants claimed he had branded some of them and tried to drown others.

Victor Angles Vargas, a lawyer, and formerly a militant in the Communist Party, who has written a number of books on the history of Cusco, described the kinds of events taking place at the time:

I think it was during Belaúnde's first term in office. As usual, there was a massacre of peasants in Pampa Callasayhua, and a number of peasants had died in San Pedro. The police stopped the train there and piled up the wounded on the station platform as if they were kindling, and the people went on dying. And why had this happened? Why had they done this? Because the peasants held a meeting [*asamblea*] and they were praying before the Peruvian flag, the Peruvian flag, not the flag of another nation and not the flag of terrorists either, at that time, no, the Peruvian flag, and they were having a meeting to appoint a committee to deal with the problems they had with whomever, and as a reaction, the police started shooting and killing people. And suddenly, here in the city, they imprisoned lawyers who had defended peasants, and I, not even now am I familiar with that area, and I was never the lawyer of those peasants, but we were imprisoned. [interview, 1991]

Despite the severity of the crisis, the reform measures Belaúnde took remained primarily symbolic. They protected most of the interests of the landed oligarchy and the more conservative fractions of Belaúnde's government, while attempting to quell the uprisings.

Belaúnde began with the assumption that cultivable land, in absolute terms, was scarce in Peru, and that it was therefore necessary to expand the agricultural frontier. Rather than restructuring tenureship of existing agricultural land, he launched schemes to colonize the jungle with peasants and attempted to intensify agricultural productivity on the coast by investment in costly, large-scale irrigation projects (Albert 1983; Caballero 1981; Matos Mar and Mejía 1980a). Neither project substantially altered the agrarian panorama of the highlands, where the topography was rugged and not conducive to capital-intensive development.

Immense sugar plantations on the coast remained exempt from expropriation; the formal transfer of land required a minimum of 40 bureaucratic steps through the civil court system; and a crucial clause of the reform law permitted property owners to divide their land among the members of their families, thus causing the state less expense. Many large estates remained private, often in the hands of members of the same family (Cleaves and Scurrah 1980; Matos Mar and Mejía 1980b; Caballero 1981). According to Matos Mar and Mejía 1980b, less than 2 percent of the peasant population in need of land received any through Belaúnde's reform.

In 1965, new uprisings in the La Convención Valley were put down by the armed forces. However, the military was profoundly affected by the ongoing threat of peasant uprisings to national security and integration, and to development. It was also aware that the landed oligarchy had not contributed to national development with their agrarian earnings but rather made nonproductive and speculative investments.

The military thus began to consider agrarian policy measures that would weaken the economic and political power of the landed oligarchy, stimulate the growth of an urban bourgeoisie, lead to economies of scale in the countryside, and end the flow of rural migrants to urban areas. Many of the military officers were young. Velasco himself came from a humble background. They believed a more substantial transformation in Peru's agrarian structure was needed to ensure Peru's stability and development.

The 1969 Agrarian Reform Law

On June 24, 1969, less than a year after Velasco seized the presidency, he passed a new and far more radical agrarian reform law, Legislative Decree 17716. Known in the past as "The Day of the Indian," June 24 was henceforth declared to be "The Day of the

Peasant" to emphasize the dissolution of Indian identity and the inception of national identity among Peru's indigenous population. June 24 was already celebrated in many highland communities. On that day, El Día de San Juan, the feast of St. John the Baptist, peasants performed rituals to enhance the fertility of their livestock. Cusco's urban population had also appropriated "The Day of the Indian" over the years as a folklorized celebration of Inca heritage, since the date corresponded to Inti Raymi, one of the most important of the Inca royal festivals. For the urban population, it had become a means by which *non-Indian* identity was circumscribed and validated. At least symbolically, to the urban population, the celebration of Inti Raymi in the city also represented the "tamed" incorporation of Quechua culture into civilization.

As summarized by José María Caballero (1980), the specific objectives of Velasco's reforms were (1) to amplify Peru's internal market; (2) to transfer capital to industry; (3) to increase agricultural income for agricultural development; (4) to put an end to peasant movements; and (5) to weaken the power of the landed elite class.

In the area of agriculture, the state sought to achieve economies of scale by transforming landed estates in the highlands and on the coast into two kinds of cooperative enterprises, Agrarian Production Cooperatives (CAPs) and Agrarian Societies of Social Interest (SAISs). Peasants who had been permanent workers on estates were expected to work the newly formed CAP lands collectively. In addition to receiving a basic wage or salary, each worker would receive a fraction of the CAP's yearly profits in accordance with the number of days he had worked. Initially managed by state administrators, the CAPs were meant eventually to be run by the workers themselves.[3]

The SAISs were composed of several landed estates consolidated into a single agro-livestock enterprise—again, intended to be owned eventually by organized permanent workers. They were established primarily where extensive tracts of pastureland existed. In view of the history of injustice they had suffered as a result of encroachment upon their lands by neighboring estates, members of the surrounding communities were given the right to participate in the management of the SAIS and to receive income generated by the enterprise. Neighboring communities did not directly contribute capital, land, or labor to the enterprise. SAISs were far more common in the central highlands and coastal regions than in the southern highlands. In the district of Huanoquite, for example, no SAISs were established.

The profits the CAPs and SAISs earned were earmarked for repayment of the agrarian debt. Their members increasingly found themselves opposed to state administrators. The latter wanted to see profits either reinvested in the enterprise or returned to the government to pay the growing debt. Workers, in contrast, wanted their profits redistributed in the form of higher wages (Caballero 1981; Martínez 1980; Matos Mar and Mejía 1980a; Stepan 1978). Seventy-five percent of the rural population did not qualify for membership in these enterprises and were thus excluded from the reform, receiving no, or only indirect, benefits from it (Moncloa 1980). Many of them belonged to native communities or ayllus, or were temporary laborers who worked on a variety of estates in exchange for a portion of the harvest or a small plot of land.

The Peasant Communities Statute

The state complemented reform measures oriented toward restructuring land tenure and labor relations with the passage of Executive Decree 370-70-A, the "Peasant Communities Statute," in Februrary 1970. The statute permitted formal recognition of "Indian" communities, henceforth to be called "peasant communities," provided that they met four criteria: (1) their members had to be full-time farmers; (2) they had to reside permanently in the community; (3) all their lands had to be cultivated on a collective basis; and (4) the community's governance structure had to be reorganized into administrative and vigilance councils, whose elected members were required to be literate in Spanish.[4]

Even as it strengthened the capacity of peasant communities to pursue their legal demands, the statute created conflicts among community members over the criteria for choosing their authorities. They rapidly discovered that those comuneros who spoke Spanish and were familiar with bureaucratic logic were best able to take full advantage of the new laws being enacted. They were thus forced to reconsider the traditional criteria they had used to pick their leaders—seniority, kin ties, and knowledge accumulated over the years about agricultural cycles and the politics of negotiating among neighboring communities.

The statute also fomented innumerable conflicts between communities, and between communities and newly established cooperatives. While the statute supposedly protected the existing land boundaries of communities, once they were formally recognized, communities themselves began to argue over the legal boundaries of their respective lands. Furthermore, some community lands had been incorporated into landed estates and were then turned over to cooperatives rather than to communities during the reform. Community members thought that those lands encroached upon in years gone by should be returned to them rather than turned over to cooperatives. Community land boundaries were difficult to determine because titles were lacking or there were a number of different titles. Surveyors, in addition to being unfamiliar with the history of land tenure, were not immune from colluding with communities to expand their land bases.

José Marroquín was a lawyer who worked in the Office of Peasant Defense (Oficina de Defensa Campesina) during the reform, an office specifically concerned with defending the rights of peasant communities. The son of a "traditional Cusqueño family," Marroquín's father had been a carpenter. Marroquín had also participated in CENCIRA, the Center for Training and Research for the Agrarian Reform. Established toward the end of 1974, CENCIRA's goal was to increase the productivity of the CAPs and SAISs and encourage the use of modern technology in the countryside. When I spoke with Marroquín, he was still working as a legal advisor within the Ministry of Agriculture in Cusco. He told me about some of the problems the new statute had created:

The peasants live from their own little plots of land, which have traditionally been ceded to them by their parents. They try to preserve, to maintain, the area their parents have left them. At times, the dispute involved half a meter, and even this was huge and difficult to resolve. Instead of being able to determine what belonged to each party, we had to embark on a lengthy case to resolve ownership of half a meter. This problem was above all owing to the cultural situation. . . . There were many problems between communities, because if the authorities erred in determining the land boundaries, you can imagine the ferocity that ensued between two communities that had formerly lived in peace. That's why, when a surveyor went to the countryside to determine community boundaries and land titles, he needed to be able to resolve territorial conflicts between them without generating disputes, because, as I said, the peasants will defend their half meter of land to the death.

The statute also refused to recognize as community members any individuals who farmed their lands on a sharecropping or absentee basis, notwithstanding that subsistence strategies—determined by factors like family size, marriage arrangements, economic relationships with communities located in other ecological zones, and urban economic opportunities—often entailed the periodic absence of individuals, or even whole households, from their home communities. Intended to protect peasants from absentee landlords, the law thus inadvertently wreaked havoc with existing local adaptive strategies and social relations, discriminating against those whom it considered to be "passive" community members, even though they might be contributing a substantial income to the household.

Conglomerates of peasants called Grupos Campesinos were the last sort of entity authorized by the government to receive land. Initially, they were not recognized as legal entities that could have land allotted to them, because they were too small, did not meet the criteria of the Peasant Communities Statute, and were adamantly opposed to the kind of cooperative ownership of land that the government had proposed for the CAPs. The continued vitality of these informal entities led the government of General Francisco Morales Bermúdez (1975–80) to grant them a legal status in 1976.

The Agrarian Tribunal

The most radical measure Velasco took was to dismantle the existing court system. He dismissed all the judges of the Supreme Court and created a National Council of Justice to nominate, promote, and evaluate the record of new judges. The members of the council included lawyers who by virtue of their progressive backgrounds and idealistic support of the new regime diverged considerably from the lawyers of the civil court system.

In addition, Velasco established an autonomous agrarian or land court system (Fuero Agrario), largely independent of the civil court system.[5] The apex of this agrarian court system was the Agrarian Tribunal, whose three members were appointed by the executive branch for a six-year term, with the possibility of reappointment. Members had to have had more than fifteen years' experience as lawyers and could not own private rural property.

With the approval of the executive branch, the tribunal then selected land judges from among candidates who competed in a written examination for these posts. The land judges had to have at least three years' experience as lawyers and could not own rural private property. Based in provincial capitals, they were assigned to agrarian regions whose parameters corresponded to zones the government had targeted for land reform.

The land courts were responsible for hearing all cases resulting from the application of the reform law. The Velasco regime hoped that, aided by this novel agrarian bench, which unlike other Peruvian courts had no direct links with the interests of the urban bourgeoisie or the landed oligarchy, it would be able to realize its ambitious goals. Although the regime stressed the neutrality of the new court system, the land judges and members of the Agrarian Tribunal were, in fact, explicitly instructed to serve as an ideological arm of the state, under the jurisdiction of the Ministry of Agriculture. Their mandate was to assist peasants in following proper procedures for the transferral of property rather than to remain independent and unbiased.

The new process eliminated many bureaucratic obstacles inherent to the civil court system that had previously operated. Furthermore, it fundamentally questioned the idea of a judiciary being neutral in its application of formal norms. In 1991, I visited Guillermo Figallo Adrianzén, the first president of the Agrarian Tribunal, to ask him about his experiences. Now an elder statesman, he remained tremendously energetic, still defending peasants who could afford to pay little for legal assistance. When he ushered me into his house in San Isidro, an upper-middle-class neighborhood of Lima, a line of peasants stood in the hallway waiting to accompany him that day to the Cañete Valley, outside Lima, where litigation was in process.

In his first term as president of the tribunal, Figallo had emphasized that in ruling on cases, the judiciary had to take account of existing socioeconomic inequalities in Peruvian society in order to achieve a new social order:

It is not correct that the landed elite and peasants submit their cases before jurisdictional bodies under equal conditions; on one side is cultural level, social position, economic solvency, and remunerated professional advice; on the other is illiteracy, social marginalization, and the lack of resources. [Figallo 1970:22]

The agrarian court system sought to offset these inequalities with the introduction of a number of new procedural norms. Without doubt, the most important was the use of oral hearings. These hearings ideally required judges to have some knowledge of Quechua. Peasants were also granted free legal defense. The state attempted to diminish the possibility of submission of fraudulent evidence by ruling that judges could conduct an *inspección ocular*, in which they traveled to the site of conflict in order to hear testimony from witnesses representing each party in the dispute.

Judges were also given the legal authority to strengthen cases brought by peasant defendants, incorporating evidence and legal principles that the peasants themselves might have omitted. Nerio Gonzalez had worked as an administrator in the Ministry of Agriculture in Cusco while he was obtaining his law degree. He subsequently worked as an attorney in the Office of Peasant Communities for five years during the reform. He also worked as a judge in Cusco's First and Second Land Courts, and had served as a substitute judge in the First Land Court for the past ten years. His family was from Cusco, and his father had been a truck driver. Now a professor of agrarian law at the Universidad Andina, a private university in Cusco, he still maintained a private law practice defending peasants. Gonzalez discussed the impact of these innovations with me:

The judge, as his mission, talked principally to the parties in [a] dispute rather than with the lawyer, because lawyers generally distort the truth. We often don't tell the truth, taking advantage perhaps of the culture that we have, having been in the university, being able to read, etc., but the peasant usually and generally tells the truth. Thus, the judge would converse in their language, in Quechua. . . . The judge distanced himself from the lawyers. Often he didn't even need them. I would say that agrarian justice in our country is oral. Everything is spoken before the *pueblo* [people], and the pueblo is the best judge. It is the pueblo that, practically speaking, is cataloguing, judging, if you like, even the judge himself, how he is behaving. . . . It's not like another class of justice shut within four walls where they talk and no one listens, no one controls, and they can do whatever appears best to them, but there, no, the pueblo assists, goes to the judge, sees the witnesses, how they testify, and the witnesses are from among them, from the pueblo itself, and at times, seeing the pueblo, the witness himself cannot lie because the peasant still believes in the oath he has sworn to the pueblo, as it should be. . . . But this isn't always the norm. There are also "cunning ones" among peasants who lie. [interview, 1991]

Many judges and attorneys who participated in the new system of agrarian justice stressed that while it was far more appropriate to the needs of peasants, it entailed considerable hardship and sacrifice. The lack of transport to rural areas was frequently mentioned as a practical obstacle to implementing the new judicial process, as José Marroquín made clear:

The judicial process was so sui generis especially because the inspections of the land and the hearings took place at the site itself, not in the office of the land judge. . . . The land judge was accompanied by his secretary, who wrote down everything with his typewriter on his knees. . . . The advisor-lawyers were chosen on the basis of merit and training, but also of youth, because to perform the labor of defense of peasant communities necessarily required these inspections in the countryside, and for that you had to be young. [interview, 1991]

Judges and lawyers also informally took steps to attempt reconciliation between parties in disputes, particularly between communities or individual peasants. This was far more common in litigation between peasants than in lawsuits involving peasants and hacendados, Gonzalez observed:

Generally, we attempted reconciliation among peasants, but between a peasant and a property owner it was difficult, because the property owner necessarily behaved very forcefully . . . and the peasant, now that he had found laws that favored him, attempted to reclaim his rights. The peasant lived resentfully and didn't want to see the landlord and said so: "You have done this to me. You have abused me, my children. I am old already and have nothing. Now that the law is in my favor I will make the most of my rights." But the hacendado never recognized that, never. . . . A hacendado managed 100, 80, 200, and even more peasants for his personal servitude with no monetary recompense, social security, health, education. The peasant was even prohibited from speaking Spanish. The hacendado was thus the eternal *compadre*, the eternal godfather, the eternal one who dominated the peasant in every way. [interview, 1991]

In instances of incompliance with labor legislation, the burden of proof that he had complied with the labor laws rested upon the landowner. If a party was dissatisfied with the ruling handed down by a judge, he could appeal it to the Agrarian Tribunal in Lima. The burden of proof rested upon the party being expropriated in the event of an appeal.

The acceleration of the legal process reduced the cost to peasants. However, many cases still took three to four years to resolve, because landlords had the option of appealing the judgment in Lima. Although most decisions were upheld, the number of cases that flooded the Agrarian Tribunal in Lima meant that the final decision was often prolonged. Regionally based land judges and lawyers resented that appeal had to take place in Lima and considered it yet another unpleasant reminder of the centralizing tendency of the Peruvian state:

Many cases were appealed. It was one of the most serious errors in the administration of agrarian justice in this country to have more than sixty judgeships at the national level and only one tribunal. How is it possible that a man who lives in Huanoquite is going to have to go to Cusco, then to Arequipa, and then still to Lima when he is poor? In Lima, he knows no one, and it is a huge city where everything is commodified. There is an overt monopolization of agrarian justice in this country. There could easily be an agrarian tribunal here [Cusco], in Arequipa another, in Lima another, in Trujillo another. . . . This regional decentralization ought not be confined to the land courts; it should apply to every aspect of the judiciary, civil and penal, because for everything, we still depend on the center. I don't know why. [Marroquín interview, 1991]

The land judges played a crucial role in the decisions reached in expropriation and adjudication proceedings, as well as in any resulting litigation. The best of them were sympathetic to the goals of the reform, because they believed that both peasant culture and the economy had to change if Peru were to develop.

Prudencio Carcausto, a well-respected land judge in Cusco, was born in the province of Azángaro, department of Puno. His parents owned a small rural property of 100 hectares, Qaqachupa. He attended a local elementary school in Azángaro, then a high school in Puno, and finally the Colegio Nacional de Ciencias in Cusco. He spent seven years at the Universidad Nacional de San Antonio Abad, Cusco, where he received his B.A. in 1957 and a law degree in 1959. His B.A. thesis, which was entitled "Expropriation of the Landed Estates for Agrarian Reform," suggests that he was ahead of his time. Before becoming a land judge in Cusco, he had served in various capacities in rural areas of Puno as a judge in the civil and penal court systems. At the same time, he had opened a School of Law in Juliaca, where he provided free legal defense services to peasants for fifteen years. His view of the agrarian reform and its accomplishments was similar to that held by many others who served as legal functionaries during that time:

Because I was born and lived my childhood in the countryside, it had a great impact and influence upon the formation of my sentiments, my preoccupations, and my aims in life. I witnessed the economic inequalities, . . . the social inequalities, the landlords, overseers, and administrators on the one hand and the *colono* [tenant farmer] or servant or herder on the other, at firsthand—a depressing and disturbing vision, to say the least. . . . There has only been one social benefit of the reform in Peru. The Indian has ceased to be a pariah, the colono no longer has to eat together with the dogs behind the kitchen or to sleep below the steps together with the cattle. The Indian or the colono has begun to gain access to all the places that all free men can enter and leave. [Carcausto interview, 1991]

Over time, the reform law underwent change. In particular, the gap widened between the agrarian lawyers' and judges' explicit ideological support of the reform and the more practical concerns of technocrats in the Agrarian Reform Office and Ministry of Agriculture. The latter, at lower levels of the bureaucracy, were responsible for directly implementing the reform measures, managing new production units in the countryside, and providing technical advice to newly established cooperatives and communities.[6]

The criteria for appointment to these bureaucratic positions in the Agrarian Reform office had initially been very broad. Many of the lower-level bureaucrats who worked in the Reform Office and Ministry of Agriculture had themselves been dispossessed of their land in the countryside or had ties with the landed elite and were prone to succumb to threats and bribery from the latter. The executive branch eventually narrowed its criteria so that agronomists and civil engineers were excluded from consideration for these posts. Nevertheless, many functionaries were already firmly established in administering cooperatives. In addition, as lower-level bureaucrats, although they did not have a great deal of power, they were far more accessible to (and therefore more vulnerable to corruption by) peasants and landlords alike than lawyers and judges were.

Noé Hanco Ramírez, a judge of the First Land Court in Cusco, offered his view of the bureaucracy at that time. Hanco was from Aymaraes, in the department of Apurimac. His parents were small agriculturalists who specialized in livestock. They had saved enough money for Hanco's education in law at the Universidad San Antonio Abad del Cusco. After obtaining his degree, Hanco served as an attorney in Sicuani and then as a penal judge in La Convención. He began to work in the First Land Court in 1974 and became a judge in 1977. In Hanco's words:

Functionaries implemented the reform who didn't even know what a reform was. They weren't prepared. They were especially responsible for the disintegration of the cooperatives. The majority who implemented the reform were the children of hacendados. They were agronomists, engineers. They weren't the children of peasants . . . and even more, they were functionaries who had lived an idle economic life. They had never known poverty, especially the agronomists, children of the hacendados. Thus, for lack of training, awareness of those elements basic to an agrarian reform, the reform did not advance well. [interview, 1991]

From Hanco's point of view, then, the reform floundered because of the technical ineptitude of those who implemented it and their deep-seated resentment of peasants.

The fluidity of the law was reflected in the legal process itself. Judges were not expected to apply unquestioned norms. Rather, as Figallo noted, "agrarian judges should explicity create the law; even more ambitiously, they should elaborate doctrines of agrarian law that, in turn, might influence legislation" (Figallo 1970:19). In Luis Pásara's words, this radical interpretation of legal process meant that rather than applying fixed norms, an agrarian judge searched

for the applicable norm in order to obtain the intended result. . . . This might lead to the instrumental use—according to the case in question—of norms that had never been applied or that were considered to be declarative. . . . It is, thus, not an exaggeration to state that the agrarian reform itself generated a new kind of judicial exercise. [Pásara 1978:63–67]

Considerable debate surrounds the question of whether or not the radical measures the Velasco regime took occurred because of peasant demands or the need for capitalist development (Valderrama 1976). In reality, the reform was designed to enhance capitalist development *and* respond to peasant unrest in order to avoid social revolution. As a consequence of reform legislation, the government did succeed in restructuring land tenure and labor relations in the countryside. It immediately expropriated the sugar plantations on the coast, an act that enhanced its legitimacy in the eyes of workers and peasants. It reduced the amount of land that could remain untouched by the reform and broadly interpreted legal criteria to justify the expropriation of agricultural lands. Failure to obey the labor laws (pay minimum wages and provide social security benefits), for example, was considered sufficient justification for expropriation (Bonilla 1979). José Matos Mar and José Manuel Mejía estimate that, as a result of the reform, approximately 61.2 percent of Peru's cultivable lands that had been considered private property was transferred to peasants.[7] However, the advances the Velasco regime made in restructuring land tenure in the countryside clashed with its other goals.

Most scholars (Albert 1983; Amat y León et al. 1980) have pointed out a fundamental contradiction in the reform's objectives. On the one hand, it was intended to achieve national integration through more equitable distribution of income between the rural and urban sectors; on the other, it was to generate economic productivity in the countryside and achieve national economic growth. The equity principle required that land be transferred from hacendados to peasants. It also required that economies of scale be exploited so that a high number of peasants would benefit from the reform and productivity would increase. At the same time, national economic growth required that agriculture finance industrial development. To achieve the latter, hacendados were indemnified for their property in bonds that had to be invested in domestic industry and could be redeemed in 20, 25, or 30 years. Price controls to benefit urban consumers were imposed, thus indirectly taxing agricultural producers and keeping basic food prices low (Albert 1983).

The decapitalization of estates prior to the reform's enactment worked against the goal of increasing agricultural productivity. Galloping inflation, which began in 1974, made the bonds given to hacendados worthless. The notion of equity dissolved in the increasing differentiation between a minority of wealthy privileged peasants organized into CAPs and SAISs and the majority who were not. Finally, perpetuating the traditional bias in Peru, government credit and infrastructural improvements continued to be funneled disproportionately to the coastal zone, even though agriculture was already far more efficient there than in the highlands.

Challenges to Corporatist Reform

The Velasco regime had its moments of triumph, but its agenda created new contradictions and problems. In time, events forced the regime to change its emphases and projects. In the first phase, from 1969 to the end of 1971, the regime concentrated on breaking the power of the landed elite (Valderrama 1976:24–30). Then, starting in 1972 and continuing through the beginning of 1974, the focus shifted. As opposition to reform measures grew among workers, peasants, and the landed elite, the regime attempted to eliminate competition from parallel entities, especially unions, political parties, and grassroots peasant federations. It did so by encouraging peasant participation and state capitalism, and by trying to build grassroots legitimacy for reform ideology and objectives. The latter goal became increasingly important to the legitimacy of the Velasco regime and more difficult to achieve.

In the early years of the reform, government officials issued numerous declarations emphasizing the state's corporate ideology. On March 6, 1971, Francisco Morales Bermúdez, then minister of economics, described the Velasco regime's vision of national integration to a group of North American businessmen as follows:

We are attempting to disassociate ourselves from a liberal industrial society and identify ourselves instead with a purely communitarian society, with whose ideology we sympathize because we consider it to be revolutionary. The social order ushered in by our revolution respects the fundamental orientation of human nature. We wish to create a society that is different from both capitalism and communism.

We ought not to permit international communism to establish itself. We respect its ideology but we neither share it nor do we want to share it. Neither should we permit imperialism to gloat over the difficulties that a free and sovereign people encounters as it stumbles to discover its own path.[8]

The minister of energy and mines, General Fernández Maldonado, also sought to specify the new path upon which the military junta had embarked: "The revolutionary ideology of Peru . . . is

Christian . . . and profoundly humanistic and socialist. This is, in reality, the first revolution in the world that, simultaneously and inseparably, is trying to be Christian, socialist, and libertarian" (quoted in Pease and Verme 1974:521).

The ambiguity of specific tenets of the reform law and, most important, the radical nature of the measures the state took—socializing property, enforcing labor legislation, and expropriating the subsidiaries of multinational corporations—incited resistance from powerful unions, federations, and political parties along the entire spectrum of civil society. It also created fissures within the regime itself, particularly between wealthier, more conservative naval officers and working- and middle-class army officers, including Velasco himself.

Between 1971 and 1974, the government authorized the creation of a number of new political organizations. The powerful National Agrarian Society (SNA), which had traditionally been the lobby of the landed oligarchy, was abolished by executive decree, and the National Agrarian Confederation (CNA) was established in its place. Irrespective of whether they were members of state-established cooperatives, peasant communities, landless peasants, or property owners unaffected by the reform, all rural workers were now incorporated into a network of approximately 150 agrarian leagues, linked to departmental federations. About 2,500 base organizations had become members of the CNA by 1974.

On June 24, 1971, the state announced the formation of SINAMOS, the Sistema Nacional de Apoyo a la Movilización Social (National System in Support of Social Mobilization). (SINAMOS is a brilliantly conceived acronym meaning "without masters" [*sin amos*].) SINAMOS was responsible for organizing peasants into leagues that would become part of the national membership of the CNA.[9]

In announcing the creation of SINAMOS, Velasco specifically addressed the regime's concern to incorporate all Peruvians into the revolution:

We have had to confront the difficult problem of the people's participation in the revolution. To resolve this problem, we have passed the Law of Social Mobilization. It is not our intention to encourage the formation of a political party loyal to the Revolutionary Government. We want to contribute to the creation of conditions that will stimulate and encourage the direct, effective, and permanent participation of all Peruvians in the development of the Revolution. This participation will discover its own, wholly autonomous organizational modalities and mechanisms of action, out of the reach of corrupt traditional political leaders who in invoking the name of the people, only serve to eternalize the power of a vile oligarchy. [quoted in Pease and Verme 1974:279–80]

Many peasants did not find their voice in either SINAMOS or the CNA. The CNA did not represent the majority of agricultural producers who had been excluded from the reform. SINAMOS agents also tended to be more radical than the technocratic agents of the Agrarian Reform Office and the Ministry of Agriculture. From Marroquín's point of view, "the orientation they gave SINAMOS agents was mistaken and differed from that which Velasco himself had envisioned. Velasco wanted to concentrate on development, improving production, but it appears that SINAMOS agents were trained only to be politicians" (interview, 1991).

Peasants who did not identify with either SINAMOS or the CNA turned instead to the Peasant Confederation of Peru (CCP), a grassroots peasant organization founded in 1947. Its popularity had grown as a result of the reform's failure to meet the demands of many of Peru's peasants. The CCP's objectives specifically included demands for more land for all peasants and support for land invasions of private property and state cooperatives.

Pásara describes the regime's effort to achieve corporate control and depoliticization as a strategy of failed sectoral and functional integration. For peasants and landlords alike, it was no longer possible to deny that class issues were at stake, and that the state was taking deliberate steps to suppress them. In addition, bureaucrats and legal personnel working within the regime itself differed in their interpretations of the reform legislation depending on their class backgrounds, training, concerns about status, and personal histories.

In the most extreme manifestation of its efforts to eliminate political opposition to its objectives and retain legitimacy, the state passed executive decrees eliminating all unions within cooperative enterprises and promoting a paramilitary force known as the Revolutionary Workers' Movement, which specialized in military operations against combative unions (Pásara 1978:156–62).

Liisa North accurately sums up the immediate results of the state's well-intentioned, but floundering, efforts to establish its own organizations in order to resolve all labor and political conflicts and demands:

Precisely because the military government was not tied to any one set of class or sectoral interests and was oriented toward national and popular interests, its reform measures, considered one by one, satisfied no organized interest, and its policies appeared inconsistent, indefinite and contradictory. As a result, the traditional party organizations, the associations of urban and rural propertied classes, old and newly created workers' and peasants' organizations—in short all factions of civil society—began to struggle and maneuver to impose their definition of desirable goals on the regime. [North 1983: 266]

In the longer term, the state's efforts in this direction inadvertently fueled far more radical resistance, which took the form of active and violent questioning both of the model of reform itself and of the state by both peasants and fractions of the dominant classes, including the military. The state had carefully crafted an ideology intended to gain the support of all peasants, while struggling for national legitimacy by proclaiming the judicial branch to be unaligned with the interests of any social class. In practice, although the tenets of the reform did not take account of the needs of all peasants, it was clearly poised to break the hold that the landed oligarchy had always had on the judicial system. Nevertheless, the political topography of agrarian production could not so simply be engineered to achieve this goal. Reform of the judiciary was crucial to restructuring relations of inequality in the countryside. Alone, however, it could not eliminate other focal points of political, economic, and cultural power and conflict that counterbalanced the protection offered by the new legislation. Hector Bejar, an ex-combatant of the 1965 guerrilla offensive who became a functionary of the Revolutionary Government, warned of this danger:

One part of the Peruvian bureaucracy is constituted by public employees and another by the political authorities—prefects, sub-prefects, mayors and governors. At the local level throughout Peru, the heads and representatives of ministries as well as the political authorities are recruited among the most influential families of each locality. Throughout the country, they form a social sector integrating thousands of persons which make up an important part of the system of internal domination which served the oligarchy and is related to a large number of officers from the armed forces. Replacing this sector would not only involve breaking up thousands of small provincial fronts, but it would also involve attacking the entire complex of family relations of the members of the armed forces. [quoted in North and Korovkin n.d.:93]

In 1975, the Velasco regime's "unrealizable project" (Pásara 1978: 37) culminated in a military coup whose participants were closely allied with the urban bourgeoisie and capitalist interests. It was headed by General Francisco Morales Bermúdez, who had been minister of economics in the Velasco regime. Morales gradually turned back the tide of the reform. Although his military government achieved immediate results through repression, the popular expectations, demands, and conflicts among peasants that the agrarian reform law had unleashed could not be squelched or diverted so easily. The reform had also sufficiently threatened the hegemonic interests of the more conservative sectors of the military and the bourgeoisie that, once having regained access to the state apparatus, they had no intention of relinquishing their power base. The state had accrued a substantial debt because of its experiments in expropriating, and then nationalizing, foreign companies. In addition, it had effectively prevented the development of Peruvian capitalist enterprises by creating a monopoly over crucial national industries.

The year 1975 represented the beginning of the end of efforts to restructure rural production and exchange relations on behalf of peasants. Between 1975 and 1991, three other presidents came to power. While their policies differed, all of them ignored the economic and political needs and demands of peasants. During a second term in office (1980–85), President Fernando Belaúnde brought in a new law (D.L. 002) legalizing the reprivatization of rural property.

President Alan García became the first candidate of the APRA party (Alianza Popular Revolucionaria de América) to be elected to the presidency (1985–90). Confronted by a growing national political and economic crisis, he focused far more on the passage of emergency laws to support the military and paramilitary in their battle against Sendero. García also nationalized the banks and refused to pay Peru's foreign debt. These extremely unpopular measures lost him the support of the Peruvian bourgeoisie and foreign economic aid from the international community.

President Alberto Fujimori (1990–95), an independent who had formed his own party, Cambio 90, which had no affiliation to Peru's traditional political parties, announced "the reform of the agrarian reform" in July of 1991 through two pieces of legislation, D.L. 011 and D.L. 018. In Fujimori's words, this legislation represented "the final disposition expressly repealing Law 17716, the Law of the Agrarian Reform."[10] He authorized the total liberalization of the purchase and sale of rural land; permitted corporations to buy and sell land; eliminated the right of peasants to seek credit from the National Agrarian Bank (Banco Agrario) without interest; privatized natural resources such as forest land; and raised the amount of land that could remain exempt from expropriation. In addition, in an effort to deal with Peru's economic and fiscal crisis, Fujimori passed severe austerity measures (popularly known as the "Fujishock") and authorized a 57 percent reduction of administrative personnel in the agricultural sector.

One of Fujimori's symbolic acts in 1991, the continuation of an "invented tradition" (Hosbawm and Ranger 1983), was to declare June 24 a holiday for the first time. Garbed as a Quechua peasant in poncho, knitted cap (*ch'ullu*), and finely woven vicuña scarf, Fujimori danced with peasants in the central highlands of Huancayo after announcing his new agrarian policy. He then traveled to Cajamarca, where he turned over weapons to civil defense patrols composed of peasants (*rondas campesinas*) so that they could defend themselves against Sendero.

Conclusion

The gradual reversals of the 1969 reform, culminating in Fujimori's agrarian policies, created serious confusion and resentment among all peasants, regardless of their membership in communities or cooperatives. Especially destructive was the constant frustration peasants experienced in scrambling to adjust to conflicting and contradictory legislation. The juridical and bureaucratic process operated at a far slower pace than the passage of legislation by executive decree.

The state also failed to realize the immense efforts made by rural inhabitants to understand and take advantage of new legislation. Even as new laws pertinent to agrarian policy that contradicted one another were passed in rapid-fire succession, peasants were still deeply engaged in responding to previous measures. For example, many peasants in the 1980's were still pursuing litigation they had initiated during the 1969 reform. Furthermore, with each change of national administration, chaos intensified within the offices of the Ministry of Agriculture in Cusco. The judges of the land courts and the higher administration of the ministry offices were periodically replaced by personnel sympathetic to the policies of the new regime, while lower-level civil servants who had been sympathetic to the Velasco regime remained in their jobs. Under these conditions, peasants grew increasingly hesitant to use legal channels to press their demands.

Even more important in undermining the success of the reform was the failure of the state to take into account the varied productive, social, and political relationships that already existed among peasants. Even in cases where the Velasco regime successfully expropriated landed estates and adjudicated them to peasants as cooperatives, it attempted to maintain firm control over their management, especially over the revenues generated by these enterprises.

The state also attempted to stifle the voices of peasants who had organized themselves into political federations and unions. Its hostile reaction to the existence of unions within cooperatives and its desire to maintain control over them are apparent in its insistence that since there were no longer any "masters," there were no longer any labor disputes. Consequently, there was also no longer any need for unions. In seeking to establish a base among all social classes, the state eventually undermined its capacity to achieve legitimacy and to maneuver among the conflicting demands on the agarian court system.

The failure of the state's novel juridical apparatus to take sufficient account of ethnic and class differences within Peruvian society are central to the following chapters. W. W. Borah has written in great detail of the history of legal codes in colonial Mexico and the need for "accommodation and adjustment between differing ideas and provisions of law, equity and morality" when two peoples come into contact with each other, a need that becomes even more pronounced "the longer the period of contact." He points out that once substantial European settlement had taken place, the problems of the intersection of European law and legal procedures with those of native societies took on new forms, which "exhibit characteristics of class differences within a common social and political structure, but with residues of cultural differences retained from a differing past" (Borah 1983:5).

The case of the 1969 Peruvian agrarian reform and how it unfolded in Huanoquite, one rural district dominated by haciendas, is instructive of the kinds of problems that beset peasant communities and a nation-state when the state attempts to impose its own visions of human categories, ideology, and law without careful consideration of the weight of deeply entrenched differences. Unlike Borah, however, I do not consider these to be residual cultural differences. The history of ethnic and class relations in the Peruvian Andes has created heterogeneous communities. The identities of Quechua peasants are forged out of a recognition of their subordinate position within a national society, their incorporation into dominant models of interethnic relations, the class differences among them, and their struggles to maintain local autonomy.

The Velasco regime succeeded in dismantling the formal power of the landed elite, but the political and economic topography that emerged after 1969 did not eliminate inequalities or relations of subordination. In tracing Huanoquiteños' experiences of the agrarian reform, we shall see that new, but not altogether different, kinds of relationships came to characterize political life in rural communities. The neat categories of mestizo and campesino had long ago burst their seams in the small efforts of Peruvians from all walks of life to cross socially defined boundaries, or even to imagine how they might cross them. Nevertheless, the reform was a weapon that set in motion the resuscitation of numerous land claims among peasants. Hand in hand with revisions in land and labor regimes came struggles over corporate identities, cultural knowledge, and economic resources. In turn, these struggles became central to the efforts of Huanoquiteños to perpetuate their communities.

- 3 -

Contesting Meanings of Labor and Territorial Control

> It is essential to know in what terms people think about basic moral and legal issues. Yet, however elegantly such ideas may be described, presenting the "traditional" categories of legal discussion without the context of discourse offers statements without speakers, ideas without their occasions, concepts outside history.
>
> Sally Falk Moore, "History and the Redefinition of Custom on Kilimanjaro"

The sun had barely risen and the early morning air was chilly. Tomás Chaparro, the young president of the formally recognized community of Maska, threw his poncho over him and slipped outside, thinking about the day ahead, the long trip, and the Maskakuna who would anxiously be awaiting his return. Chaparro had attended high school at the Colegio Nacional de Ciencias in Cusco, spoke Spanish fluently, and was a skillful negotiator of consensus. Now his skills were being put to the test in his efforts to regain some of his community's lands, which had been taken from them so long ago.

Chaparro began readying himself for his journey. Maybe he would buy some sugar and noodles, maybe some fruit for the children, if he had time. Irena was already cooking breakfast. He sat at the table and slurped his warm soup. Then he dressed. His fiesta shirt was a little worn, as were his trousers, but they would do. He combed back his hair, put on his black rubber sandals, and hoisted up his pants with an old leather belt. He checked to make sure that all the documents were there and carefully wrapped them again in the yellowing newspaper. Irena handed him a woven carrying cloth (unk"uña) in which he placed the newspaper together with the freeze-dried potatoes (ch'uño), boiled lima beans (habas), and roasted corn (hank'a) that Irena had prepared for his snack. The morning was still young as Tomás quietly made his prayers known to San Miguel, Wataqasa, Ch'uspi, Wanakauri, and Yachakauri, the guardian mountain spirits (apukuna) surrounding Huanoquite. The mist was rising, a good sign.

He left. Four hours later, the great city came into focus below him. It had been an easy walk, clear and dry. He hurried the last hour into Cusco, slightly amazed at the number of trucks and buses, the noise, and the flood of people rushing down the sidewalk.

He reached the by-now-familiar building that the Velasco regime had designated as the Agrarian Reform Office. His heart fell when he saw the long line of people already waiting, but he also could not help but be excited. Perhaps now the tables would be turned, and he would be able to help make it happen. Perhaps the ones above would finally listen to the voices of the people, his people, who worked the land and understood what it meant. Perhaps it would become theirs forever. Perhaps this would be the government his children would remember. He got in line. He saw Pedro Mamani and Juan Coasa from Acomayo and greeted them. They must have come on a similar mission. He had gotten to know them in the federation. It had taken them a long time, but they were among the lucky ones. They still had their titles. They hadn't been misplaced, burned, or taken away from them. Now it was a question of gaining the sympathy of the *técnicos* who had spent so much time last year talking about cooperatives. Cooperatives were fine but the *comuneros* deserved their rights too. Could he make it happen?

The sun was setting. The supervisor finally called Chaparro into his office. So many others had slipped in ahead of him, friends of this técnico or that one. Now in don Zamalloa's office, he felt uncomfortable in his country clothes as he unwrapped the documents from the newspaper and explained. At least he spoke Spanish. He was afraid don Zamalloa would rip the documents, the way he was rustling through them so rapidly. And then he waited to hear what don Zamalloa would say.

Now it was dark. The office had closed. He would have to stay at his uncle's tonight. It was too late to start back. He did not have good news. The Bejars had begun their own proceedings. That same small piece of land was once again going to be a thorn in their side. Would anything ever change? How much money would it take? How many days of not working in the fields? How much blood? Zamalloa had laughed and slapped him on the back when he told him. He thought it was a small thing, easy to fix. His last words had been to reassure him, encourage him to fix it up with Bejar, come back, and everything would be all set. Tomás was tired.

In the southern Andean sierra, before the passage of the reform, the state had rarely responded positively to peasant demands. It had not hesitated to siphon revenue from peasants in the form of tribute, forced labor, and taxes, however, and had almost always backed the landed elite in peasant uprisings. In addition, even where avenues of justice had existed in formal terms for peasants,

> the establishment of a working system of justice, which sometimes ruled on behalf of the natives to the detriment of their exploiters, did not vindicate or somehow balance the colonial legacy. Rather, colonial justice played a crucial—perhaps indispensable—part in the subjugation of the natives to an exploitative society that lasted for centuries. Far from vindicating an exploitative experience, "justice" rooted it into the fabric of colonial Andean society. [Stern 1982b: 291–92]

The agrarian reform represented a turning point in the relationship between justice and exploitation for Quechua peasants in the highlands. As the balance of power between the landed elite and peasants shifted in the countryside, peasants found land court judges more receptive to their claims against landlords. Landlords were less able to manipulate state authorities with impunity or exercise their power illicitly. When Velasco proclaimed the reform law, his denunciation of powerful, unproductive landlords served as an incentive for many peasants to revive old claims to land, directly resist the abuses of landowners, and invade lands they considered their own before they were targeted for expropriation by the government.

It is impossible to determine the distribution of landholdings among peasants and estate owners in the district of Huanoquite before the reform with any precision, because no reliable census data exist. We do know that the disparity in holdings between peasants and estate owners was extreme. Out of a total estimated land base of 37,000 hectares (1 hectare equals 2.47 acres) in Huanoquite, the state sought to expropriate 28,374 hectares from twenty-nine estates with a view to adjudicating them to 767 peasant households (the average household was composed of five people). In the course of the reform, 22,920 hectares were successfully expropriated, adjudicated, and transferred to four CAPs, five Peasant Communities, and three Peasant Groups. Fifty-nine percent of the land went to the CAPs; 19 percent to the Peasant Communities; and 22 percent to the Peasant Groups. Thirteen estates remained partially intact after the reform, with control over 19 percent of the land that the state had attempted to expropriate (see Appendix B for details). After the reform, the CAPs controlled 48 percent of Huanoquite's cultivable land base; Peasant Communities 15 percent; and Peasant Groups 18 percent. These figures correspond closely to national-level statistics on post-reform land-tenure structure (see Chapter 2), although the latter do not document the continuing and active presence of the landed elite in the countryside.[1]

The Mosaic of Legal Codes

During the reform, Huanoquiteños drew upon various principles in order to defend their land and regain access to lands they believed rightfully belonged to them. In reading the multilayered written texts of their claims, one discovers valuable indicators of peasant interpretations of the reform. These written texts are nevertheless a challenge to interpret. They are often silent precisely where one wishes peasant voices would take over the page. In contrast, the defenses of landlords are far more clearly enunciated and textualized. Still, interesting patterns emerge that reflect the complex relationships that were developing between local communities and the Peruvian state during this period of time.[2]

On the one hand, almost all peasants wanted to take advantage of the new law. In participating in the legal process, they heeded the logic of the reform law. On the other hand, they felt compelled to force the state to recognize the legitimacy of land titles they already held, many of which dated from the colonial period. They also had to confront the ingenious and strategic defenses of members of the landed elite who were striving to use the reform law to their own advantage. Finally, while peasants shared a desire to reclaim their lands and control over their labor, they were already enmeshed in quite varied socioeconomic relations of production.

The latter fact proved to be one of the greatest stumbling blocks for peasants and the state alike in transforming land-tenure structures. The official slogan "Land to the Tiller" implied that those who worked land directly had legal rights to it. However, by giving priority to the expropriation of large private estates worked by permanent laborers, the government ignored the multiple labor regimes and land-tenure patterns of the countryside, which had their own hierarchies and logic.

The assumptions the Peruvian state made were greatly influenced by modernization theory stressing the advantages of economies of scale. "Ideologues all too often conceive peasants and workers as aggregations of similarly situated individuals, not as persons closely tied into networks and groups through previous social commitments," Sally Moore remarks of similar assumptions on the part of the Tanzanian state about the disjuncture between modernizing legislation in Tanzania and the workings of the indigenous Chagga society (1986:314).

In Huanoquite, as in so many other highland regions, the rugged and broken topography impeded the development of economies of scale; sharecropping predominated; and at least nine communities had maintained their corporate structures. Communities with collective control over some of their lands thus coexisted with peasants who worked permanently as sharecroppers on estates in order to gain access to land, and with peasants who worked periodically for wages, but also had access to small amounts of collective land from their communities.

Bitter conflicts developed among these groups as they sought to justify their respective rights to land in the eyes of the state. Just as the differences in socioeconomic relations among peasants confounded state efforts to arrive at a comprehensive and equitable reform law, in a more subtle manner, so did the history of legal principles that had already influenced existing tenure patterns in Huanoquite. The reform law respected the validity of colonial titles to land, leading to the proliferation of unexpected "paper battles" in which distinct corporate entities and individuals fought over the validity of land titles that dated from different periods of time.

The legitimacy granted by the state to colonial titles led to much forgery of fradulent titles. The case I describe in Chapter 5 between Maska and Inkakuna Ayllu Chifia is representative of the problems reform personnel encountered when faced with what appeared to be equally valid titles to the same piece of land. Manuel Aparicio Vega, a paleographer who had been the head of the Archivo Departamental Histórico del Cusco, suspected that the documents both parties in the dispute were using had been falsified.

Nerio Gonzalez also describes a typical paper war that took place in the province of Paruro, one not necessarily involving fraudulence, but rather the multilayered stratigraphy of colonial rulings granting title to the same land to different communities at different times:

There were boundary problems where they would say, "This is ours, this is not ours," and both would have property titles. In that kind of case, the battle between peasant communities was terrible. There was one between the peasants of Collana Yaurisque and Acopata where they made competing claims over the same piece of land for two, three, four, five years in the courts. Unfortunately, neither party won. The litigation was not resolved, and I believe they became fed up with the duration of the litigation. This was one of the problems created by the reform. [interview, 1991]

Colonial law had changed over time in terms of the validity it had attributed to native principles governing land and labor rights. Bernard S. Cohn (1989:136) and Joan Vincent (1989:163) offer examples of how particular codes of "customary" or "traditional" law were selectively embraced by colonial regimes and by native inhabitants in India and Uganda respectively. If native principles governing land-tenure rights were not incompatible with the goals of colonial regimes, they were tolerated. The same was true in Peru. While on the face of it, this practice might appear to protect indigenous rights to land at least partially, it created innumerable legal problems once peasants could use the law for themselves. With changes in the colonial and Republican regimes over time, new titles were issued to some inhabitants, and others were no longer honored. Thus, colonial "rights" dating from the sixteenth, seventeenth, and eighteenth centuries to parts or all of the same piece of land were brought before the land judges by different groups of peasants during the reform.

Furthermore, colonial administrators and jurists had often obtained their knowledge of these principles, not from the native population at large, but rather from those individuals or ethnic groups who had already been considered of a higher status in precolonial society. In Uganda, the legal decisions and codes colonial officials arrived at often depended upon information gathered from "those empowered to codify the 'tradition' they had invented" (Vincent 1989:163).

In the context of Velasco's reform law, these colonial titles reflected a status hierarchy that other inhabitants desperately wanted to overturn. The case in Chapter 5 exemplifies the anguish inflicted by a colonial legal decision about land rights in favor of Inkakuna Ayllu Chifia, a moiety composed of higher-ranking Inca nobility, rather than Maska, a lower-ranking moiety composed of autochthonous inhabitants of Huanoquite.

While colonial legal codes shaped peasant defenses during the reform, the folk categories that peasants relied upon to guide their routinized social relations were equally important in how they determined land and labor rights. Unlike the selective principles of customary law that had been incorporated into colonial jurisprudence, these folk categories had not been ossified in written form. Rather, they were integral to people's daily practices. Of most importance were the efforts of households and ayllus to gain access to multiple microecological zones in order to maximize resource diversification and minimize risk, and the weight that distinct kinship networks carried in determining access to land and labor.

Just as peasants in Huanoquite responded in various ways to the passage of the reform law, so did the landed elite. In the midst of the dramatic policy changes wrought by the reform law, Huanoquite's landlords developed their own ideas of how to maintain a comparative advantage, and they often succeeded in moderating the effectiveness of peasant initiatives. At the same time, their diverse strategies prohibited them from acting as a united front. As we shall see in the following pages, they rarely resorted to physical violence against peasants during the reform. Instead, they attempted to influence the bureaucrats who were crucial intermediaries in the reform process. González stresses, for example, that a principal loophole in the way disputes were resolved lay in the adeptness with which hacendados worked the administrative networks of the Ministry of Agriculture (and the money they paid out to judges and reform personnel), so that cases would be thrown out before they ever came before the land courts.[3]

Landlords also tried to take advantage of local patron-client ties they had established with Huanoquite's peasants. Both peasants and landlords were especially aware of the value of the protection patron-client ties offered peasants. It was not easy for peasants to relinquish these kinds of ties, and the relationships of domination and subordination that characterized peasant-landlord rapport. For many peasants, these ties were habitual, convenient, even desirable, and therefore, at a fundamental level, less threatening than the potential upheaval that a rupture with hacendados would signify.

Vicente Suni Jacho, Francisco Tacuma Ima, Exaltación Gutierrez Chura, Martín Ramos Quispe, Lorenzo Puma Chura, and Julia Condori Quispe, for example, who were permanent workers of Quishuares, pleaded with reform officials not to expropriate the estate of Braulio Grajeda Challco, because: "We have a spiritual kinship with the property owner and have lived without any problems in a harmonious way with no labor problems with our families and we have occupied houses that the property owner has provided to us free."[4]

Many property owners attempted to present themselves as peasants rather than landlords. The creative imagery they used in defense of their lands included the contentions that they spoke Quechua, engaged in reciprocal exchanges with peasants, worked the land directly, and were permanent residents of the countryside. Some even claimed poverty, illiteracy, and kinship with native inhabitants. The artful legal defenses landlords employed during the reform are discussed in greater detail in Chapter 4.

Convergence and Reconciliation: Intermediaries and Bureaucrats

Despite Velasco's radical proclamations predicting the disappearance of ethnic discrimination and economic inequities, and the emergence of just social relations among Peruvians, conciliation became a central feature of dispute settlements during the reform. As observed in Chapter 2, the state itself strove to eliminate the volatility that class conflict could incite. It did so by seeking to structure itself into a corporate entity whose ideology, organizational form, and legal measures would satisfy the demands of all Peruvian citizens.

Avoidance of class conflict was also initially the aim of reform bureaucrats and legal personnel, many of whom were agents of the state. Public defenders who assisted peasants in crafting their claims in the land courts injected their own points of view into the testimony, sometimes neutralizing the more extreme and polarized positions of peasants and landlords. In the words of Noé Hanco Ramírez, "In my case, I always tried to encourage litigants to reach a happy medium, a conciliation, a mutual agreement. In most cases, I was able to make them reach a compromise, to make them negotiate" (interview, 1991).

Reform officials also stressed reconciliation in order to hasten legal proceedings. Some of them moderated the meaning and implications of aspects of the law simply because they did not agree with them. The law specifically declared that the officials who staffed the regional reform offices and land courts should defend and protect peasants. Nevertheless, usually by no fault of their own, most of them had only the vaguest idea of the details of individual and group biographies. This meant that they rarely had all the evidence they needed to judge a case, especially when it involved confrontations between two groups of peasants. They inferred evidence as best they could from superficial clues and from visible differences between the claimants. But they were guided by their prejudices and did not have available to them the full histories of the disputes brought before them. Their solutions were thus frequently conventional. Rather than interpreting the law in accordance with the particularities of each case, they tended to stay close to the most obvious and simple interpretation of the reform law's articles and statutes.

The dispute between two groups of peasants on the estate called Huancacrara in Huanoquite, described in more detail in Chapter 4, is a case in point. One of the groups consisted of the estate's overseers and their extended families; the other of the actual workers. There was great bitterness between them, and during adjudication, the conflict became extremely heated. In the end, Huancacrara was turned over to all of the peasants. Regardless of how the overseers had exploited the other peasants, they all fell into the category of permanent workers on the estate according to the reform law. Subsequently, one of the overseers was mysteriously murdered.

Who Is the Tiller? The Case of Llaspay

In making the steep ascent from the river to Huanoquite, the last leg of the long journey from Cusco, one glimpses off to the side a stunning patchwork of maize and wheat fields, a complex of adobe buildings, an old orchard, and a rivulet of water flowing through an irrigation canal. This is Llaspay, a lush property of 1,535 hectares. A site of busy activity, every time I visited the place, it nevertheless always seemed to be cloaked in a special kind of silence. At the time of the reform, it was a private estate owned by Benigno Pacheco, an engineer and munitions manufacturer. The story of the expropriation and adjudication proceedings that took place at Llaspay gives us a far better idea of what peasants had at stake and in mind as they attempted to defend their land and labor rights. True, the claims they made were shaped in part by the reform law itself. But there was room for them to interpret the law, to draw upon different kinds of evidence, and to organize politically in order to pressure reform officials to reach conclusions they might otherwise not have considered. The defenses they devised reveal how they were thinking about power and political authority, what criteria they were using to determine the value of their labor, and why it was so difficult for them to reach consensus.

Unlike some of the other landlords in Huanoquite, Pacheco was a relatively progressive and farsighted man. He did not have a keen interest in farming but had a managerial instinct for organizing and maintained a productive estate. Aided by his inventive bent and the labor of his workers, he had built a road to his property. He also had a thresher and bellows on Llaspay and a rustic shower, constructed out of parts from an old Model T Ford. When word of the reform reached Huanoquite, the peasants who labored permanently on Llaspay responded quickly to the news. They began to organize themselves into what they called the "Pre-Cooperative Tupac Amaru II" and started to negotiate with Pacheco to turn over his estate to them. They offered him a down payment on the property collected from those who had joined the Pre-Cooperative. They even designed their own letterhead, which they used for all their missives to the reform office. Pacheco astutely realized that he would probably be forced to give up his estate. He therefore reached an informal agreement with the permanent workers of Llaspay to turn over the property to them according to the payment schedule they had established.

Had the matter ended there, it would have caused everyone far less pain, but temporary wage laborers who worked on Llaspay but lived in nearby communities immediately contested the agreement, demanding that reform officials organize them into a Peasant Group in order that they might be allotted land, not only from Llaspay, but from Poqestaca and Qotawana, two other estates where they also worked. They spoke eloquently of the injustices they had suffered in the course of working "for more than fifty years on the estate, subjected to the most iniquitous exploitation by the owner, who obeyed none of the existing labor laws and never paid us a salary but rather only our *ch'akipa*, a thirst quencher of two glasses of maize beer [*chicha*], alcohol, and sometimes coca leaves."[5]

In demanding that they also be given land from the other two estates, they explained, "it is necessary for us to have more land given that we are increasing [in number] day by day." Finally, they launched a frontal attack upon the permanent laborers:

We would also like to bring to your attention another group of peasants, led by Gerardo Vera Rojas, who, together with others, are trying to take advantage of us by forming a so-called Agrarian Cooperative. They are charging sums of money in accordance with the possibilities of each permanent worker. We are thus not in agreement with their behavior and for that reason we demand that you put an end to it and adjudicate the land to us as a Peasant Group.[6]

The permanent workers responded by pointing out that they, too, had received no wages, and that it was even less likely that Pacheco would be able to pay them their back wages, which would amount to a far greater amount than those of the temporary workers. Secondly, they stressed that their formation into a cooperative was well under way, with assistance of the National Office of Cooperative Development (ONDECOOP).

Their letter to the reform office is of considerable interest, because it shows the difficulties peasants encountered confronting the bureaucracy, the negotiations they pursued, the pressure they independently exerted upon landlords, and their precise grasp of the reform law:

On August 10 of last year [1970], we presented a request asking that Llaspay and Poqes [Poqestaca] be expropriated immediately since the owner, Engineer Benigno Pacheco S. has not complied with paying salaries in addition to particular benefits that correspond to us by law as workers from remote times. For these reasons, supported by the Superior Resolution 184-0 of June 31 of last year, our request has been in various offices, especially in the

Ministry of Labor, where the owner has been cited several times through the intervention of the police chief of Sapi. In the end, we did not get to talk to the assistant director of the Ministry of Labor but rather directly to the owner in the following manner. The owner has left us his property, given that he does not have the money to pay us and given also that we are organizing ourselves into a cooperative with ONDECOOP's knowledge. And the workers in a meeting, agreed to reincorporate the owner [into the cooperative] after much pleading on his part that he would live there with his family, and that what we were doing to him was not just. From what was said, Sr. Director, [it should be clear that] the estate is already in our hands, and the Cooperative will manage it. We have eighty associates, ex-workers from the estate.[7]

President Gerardo Vera and Secretary Narciso Huamán, selected leaders of the permanent workers of the Pre-Cooperative Tupac Amaru II, also demanded, as had the temporary workers, that other lands be turned over to them. They, too, wrote the reform office that the families represented by the Pre-Cooperative were "so large, each consisting of more than seven children, that Llaspay would never be enough land for them." They added that the community members of Toctohuaylla who worked on Llaspay periodically were unjustified in claiming rights to Llaspay because they mainly worked on another estate, Pumawanka. They also asserted that the lands of Pumawanka should be expropriated because the owners were "ruining the terraces of the two Inca sites on the property and not exhibiting the proper respect due to archaeological monuments that are part of the nation's patrimony." They concluded that "the logical solution would be to expropriate Pumawanka," and said they would be pleased to collaborate with the temporary workers in making this possible, with the understanding that the temporary and permanent workers would divide the Pumawanka lands among themselves.

A number of patterns emerge from a review of the claims presented by the temporary and permanent workers of Llaspay. Most important, peasants were calculating their rights to land and the value of their labor in ways that sometimes differed markedly from how the state was calculating them. There was considerable sensitivity among peasants to the cultural meaning of labor, as well as to the different ways in which land values could be equated with the past labor invested in the land.

The initial statement that the temporary workers made called attention directly to the use of liquor and coca leaves in exploitative labor relations in the Andes. Their reference to the fact that their work had been remunerated solely with a ch'akipa (thirst quencher) highlighted the prevailing attitude among the landed elite that alcoholism was the reason landlords had such difficulty obtaining labor from the resident Indian population. Their contention, still commonly expressed after the reform, was that in order to get Indians to work, they had to be given drink, and that they paid them no, or very low, wages because of the quantity of alcohol they were obliged to supply.

Catherine Allen (1988) has shown that the same attitude prevailed among the landed elite with respect to coca chewing. The "power games" built into these kinds of exchange appear as a kind of reversal of the "forced ritual feeding" between Andean highland peoples and the natural and supernatural forces that surround them. In the latter instance, ritual feeding in excess helps bring into equilibrium the various forces that make constructive life possible for Andean communities. For example, in fertility rites for livestock, llamas and alpacas would be force-fed maize beer in order to ensure their future fertility. In the former instance—landlords who force excessive amounts of alcohol or coca upon native inhabitants without paying them in any other form, and then justify it as being necessary to make them work—create even further imbalances of power in the natural and social system.

In the case described above, the temporary workers actively attempted to challenge the dominant ideology by showing that they understood the manipulative ways in which the landed elite had used alcohol and coca exchange for labor. In short, they claimed that the coca and alcohol they had received over the years from Pacheco as "a wage" in no way compensated for the labor they had invested in his estate.

References to "growth" often appeared in peasant claims to land. I would argue that although growth was expressed in these statements in demographic terms, peasants attributed other meanings to it, specifically aspirations for power, especially political and cultural power vested in the expansion of their rights over land and labor. Peasant households, communities, and collectivities suddenly had room to grow, to acquire land for their kin. In turn, these possibilities meant an increase in political power and well-being.[8]

A third pattern, one that peasants resorted to more frequently with time, was the effort to organize themselves *informally* into corporate entities that resembled those the reform office had formally authorized. The temporary workers at Llaspay, who did not share a common territory, tried, for example, to organize themselves into a "Peasant Group." Individually, the temporary workers had no legal status under the reform law. They were excluded from consideration altogether. Yet they were numerous, and by organizing themselves into Peasant Groups, they forced the state to at least recognize them as a legal entity. The permanent workers, who did reside on the same territory, represented themselves as a "Pre-Cooperative," obviously mimicking the state-run CAPs.

A fourth pattern was the use of reconciliation by peasants themselves. Peasants recognized that the reform office would respond favorably to conciliatory actions. In the case of Llaspay, the permanent workers agreed to integrate Pacheco into the Pre-Cooperative. Many members of the Pre-Cooperative may also genuinely have felt that Pacheco should be given some rights. Patron-client relationships always entailed a certain degree of sympathy, and even complicity, between peasant and landlord.

One also finds a number of cases in which peasants attempted to strike their own bargains with landlords prior to state expropriation. Many groups of peasants such as the temporary and permanent workers on Llaspay encouraged landlords to turn over their property to them in lieu of back wages they had not received. This strategy occurred as an important means of resisting state control. Although they ran the risk that reform officials would not validate their informal contracts, peasants pursued this alternative as a way to avoid becoming part of the state-managed cooperative movement. They also formed themselves into "pre-cooperatives" for the same reason, since, as the permanent workers of Llaspay explained, they, not state administrators, would manage these kinds of productive units.

Finally, the statements made by landowners and peasants alike during the reform process frequently invoked symbols of nationalism as a way to gain sympathy from the state for their claims. Inca archaeological monuments and terraces (as in the Llaspay case), the Peruvian flag, festivals celebrating Catholic saint days, other acts of Catholic religious devotion and faith, and respecting the power of written documents such as colonial land titles all served as strategic means that peasants manipulated to gain the sympathy of the state during the reform process. The way they used some of these references, such as Inca monuments, called attention to an idealized Inca past with which peasants may have identified. At the same time, Inca architecture was integral to Peruvian national identity, in part because of the international recognition it received, in part because it pertained to an age of empire.

Peasants did not invoke symbols of nationalism during the reform solely for strategic reasons, however. They also attributed meanings to the symbols and conventional rhetoric of state- and elite-promoted nationalism that were important to constituting their own identity as they sought to rupture the artifice of "superficial" Peru.

The artifice, described at length by Enrique Mayer (1991), shows how the Inca roots of Peru have been essentialized as fundamental to Peru's identity by the dominant classes and the state, whereas it is, in fact, the Hispanic overlay that has really become entrenched in the Peruvian nation, closing off the majority of institutional channels to the indigenous population. In turn, these realities have contributed to the hostility, resentment, and fear that more accurately (and with far more deadly consequences) characterize Peruvian society. Mayer's observations coincide with those of Alberto Flores Galindo, who comments on how peasants attempted to use images and ideologies of nationalism on their own behalf during a land invasion he documented:

The nation and nationalism depend upon the class that acts upon the problem. It is understandable that nationalism and the "old bourgeois symbols," such as flags, ended up being redefined in the mobilization of peasants, and in this way acquired a whole new radical impetus, precisely because of the scarce (or nonexistent) nationalism of the dominant classes. [Flores 1978: 184]

In contrast, while the state and landed elite often made reference to the same glorious and idealized Inca past, they did not actually wish to trace their ancestry to the Incas. Nor did they find in contemporary Quechua culture any relic, except perhaps a degraded one, of this magnificent past. More commonly, they considered contemporary Indians to be a race altogether different from the Incas.

The ideology of national integration and nationalism, narrowly defined by the state, was perhaps more pronounced under the Velasco regime than at any other time in Peruvian history. In the course of reviewing hundreds of statements issued by state officials, I found not one that entertained the possibility of multiple ethnic groups or religions or cultures coexisting. A speech made by Prime Minister Mercado Jarrín, upon his inauguration into the Pro-Navy National Association in March 1973 provides a typical example of the ideological orientation of members of the Velasco regime:

This Revolution is neither a stage nor a step toward another, ultimate system of governance. What we want is to use what we have always used in Peru: not forget our traditions and to follow our own form of life as it has always been in Peru. We are a Christian, western country; we have a culture, and that culture is what we will continue defending. For that reason, I beg of you confidence, confidence in ourselves and confidence in the destiny of our Nation. [cited in Pease and Verme 1974:492]

That the state itself was eagerly promoting a nationalism in which Quechua peasants would ideally play a fundamental role made it all the more likely that peasants, out of both moral conviction and strategic manipulation, would invoke the Inca and colonial symbols that embodied the regime's nationalist rhetoric.

The temporary workers of Llaspay lost their case. The state had an interest in hastening the expropriation process, alleviating the burden on the courts, cutting administrative costs, and exploiting economies of scale. Notwithstanding that the negotiations between Pacheco and Pre-Cooperative members had been private and informal, the government therefore ruled in favor of the Pre-Cooperative in August 1975. All that was necessary for its implementation was for the state to authorize the agreement formally.

Moreover, although the permanent workers, over the years, had received small plots of land from Pacheco in return for their labor, the land judge who interpreted the reform law used his failure to pay the workers wages as a justification for turning over the lands to them. Failure to obey the labor laws, regardless of the amount of land peasants had received in exchange for working on an estate, was perhaps the state's most common means of justifying expropriation and determining to whom lands should be adjudicated, so long as the amount of land involved was fairly extensive. Peasants rapidly came to grasp the logic of such rulings and started using them in their own interests, as the case below demonstrates.

Chanca was an immense estate of 10,000 hectares owned by a powerful commander of the Peruvian Air Force, César Mendíburo Romainville. The permanent workers demanded the estate's expropriation, declaring, "Our ancestors have worked here; now we work here. We are paid nothing, we are charged for pasturing our animals, and we have never known vacation."[9]

Temporary workers in general were far more exploited than the permanent ones. At Llaspay, they had received no land but rather only food, alcohol, and coca leaves for their labor. Although the reasons the permanent workers wanted the estate adjudicated to them differed from those of the state, they reached the same conclusion.

It is highly unlikely that peasant concerns with the national patrimony (invoking the preservation of Inca terraces) or demographic expansion played a significant role in the judge's ruling. These kinds of claims reflected peasant efforts to construct an alternative social order and to persevere in demanding their historical rights, but they carried little weight in the courts because of the way the law determined the ideal recipients and parameters of new kinds of socio-economic production units that would lead to economies of scale and cohesive organizations that could more easily be managed by the state.

Conclusion

The Llaspay case is representative of many that came before the land courts. Despite the success of the permanent workers in having Llaspay adjudicated to them, the legal ruling led to further conflict between the permanent and temporary workers. In some cases, such conflicts resulted in land invasions, and in large areas of land remaining uncultivated because of ongoing disputes. This was particularly true of conflicts between CAPs and Peasant Communities.

In other cases, and this was true of most of the CAPs established in Huanoquite, CAPs uncannily began to resemble the estates of old, relying upon the temporary labor of neighboring communities. A singular difference was that violence grounded in terror and servility, which had been inherent in the relationships between estate owners and workers in the past, was replaced by domination and subordination based on economic differentiation. Some peasants were able to accumulate land for themselves; others were not.

Velasco's reforms thus brought into focus the disjuncture between the peasants' ideas of morality and practical notions of justice and the state's legal scaffolding. The ways in which peasants defined just rights to land in their claims confused and frustrated reform agents and attorneys, who often failed to understand their logic. The testimony presented to the land judges frequently reflected conflicts among peasant groups rather than conforming to the aims of the reform law. The reform measures provided peasants with the opportunity to challenge land claims validated by colonial titles and overturn existing patterns of stratification, but inegalitarian hierarchies of a similar type, reborn within state-managed cooperative structures, ultimately created precisely the cleavages that Sendero Luminoso proved able to manipulate to its own advantage.

Double Visions: Images of Peasants, Technocrats, and Landlords

When we study the relationship between legislation and legal change, we must investigate power and meaning. . . . the forms that laws take and their impact on the local level are each shaped by political struggle, which can be understood in terms of the historically located class relations. At the same time, legislation shapes the context and trajectory of such struggle. . . . the significance of legislation is always greater than the meaning intended for it. Legislation never speaks for itself. Its meaning is a matter of interpretation and contention. It must be understood in the cultural terms with which individuals experience and interpret it in relation to their goals and objective interests.

George A. Collier, "The Impact of Second Republic Labor Reforms in Spain"

Landlords and peasants differed among themselves in the defenses they created to retain their lands during the reform. As did peasants, landlords invoked growth, territorial control, progressive development, and nationalism in their claims. However, their reasons for doing so, and the meanings they attributed to these notions, differed from those of peasants. One of the most common stances they took was to present themselves as marginalized peasants and to invoke the principle of reciprocity in their negotiations with peasants. In presenting themselves as peasants, they drew upon multiple images of peasants—prominently including the figure of the peasant as a downtrodden, uncivilized being who, once given the appropriate economic resources and education, could become a respectable Peruvian citizen, which coincided with the image promoted by the Velasco regime.

Indianness was seen as a contaminating quality, but one that could be purified by the right treatment, in which landlords could assist. Still, a good many landlords did not confine themselves to the belief that Indians could be transformed into Peruvian citizens with the proper training. Their image of peasants had also been constructed from their long history of having exploited peasant labor, their scarcely sublimated fear of Indian reprisals for having done so, and their great dependence upon peasant labor for their livelihoods, status, and even identities.

In his ambitious book *Shamanism, Colonialism, and the Wild Man*, Michael Taussig discusses "the colonially construed image of the wild Indian" as "a powerfully ambiguous image, a seesawing, bifocalized and hazy composite of the animal and the human." The brutality of rubber extraction in the inaccessible reaches of the Putumayo jungle perhaps created greater extremes than those found in the Peruvian highlands of the twentieth century, but similar dynamics were at work, creating a reality composed of an "ambiguous multiplicity of signs," which, as Taussig points out, could not be "straight, monochrome, and flat" but was rather a reality of "equivocation, possibility, shadow, and murk." The views of Indians as simultaneously (or alternatively) wild and terrorizing beasts and "grown-up children" were "tenaciously linked and covertly complicit, the one feeding off the other" (Taussig 1987:82–83, 85):

> In their human or humanlike form, the wild Indians could all the better reflect back to the colonists vast and baroque projections of *human* wildness. And it was only because the wild Indians were human that they were able to serve as labor—*and* as subjects of torture; for it is not the victim as animal that gratifies the torturer, but the fact that the victim is human, thus enabling the torturer to become the savage. [Taussig 1987:82–83]

In Peru, the real terror would come later, but at the time of the reform, it was sublimated, channeled, yet apparent in the legal discourse that hacendados elaborated to represent Indians and themselves to the courts, to themselves, and to the "Indians."

Don Quixote

The example of Amadeo Grajeda, son-in-law of a powerful family of landlords who were descended from the illegitimate daughter of a priest in Huanoquite, illustrates how landlords used images of peasants to defend their land rights during the reform. Grajeda began by telling state officials why Casa Blanca, his family's estate, appeared to be unproductive:

> I do not work the land. Rather, my wife, doña Margarita Cárdenas de Grajeda, and my children work it directly. Working in such an environment is the task of giants, because not even the peasants want to live or work here. . . . The means of communication are infernal. . . . The peons cultivate what they can and what they want, but, as I say, there are dozens of *topus* [approximately

one-third of a hectare] that remain uncultivated because of the lack of man-power, the lack of peons. The banks of the Apurimac River are totally rough terrain. I would hope that someday a highway reaches them, but for the moment, this remains a myth. Who knows if fifty years from now, with the advances of modern technology, it will be possible to build a road?

Grajeda continued by stressing his courage and the valor of his father in having undertaken farming in such a rugged environment:

It is necessary to colonize, but in order to colonize in these times, one must have the philosophy of a genius like don Quixote, and only my father, don Rosendo P. Grajeda, was [in] everything a genius in the art of agriculture . . . making the crops grow from the very rocks and rugged pastureland. I myself farm various topus of land and, notwithstanding my tenacity, my capacity to adapt, my traditional attachment to the land, and my physical strength, I find it difficult to ride horseback by day and night, because all that exist are footpaths, and if God's servant, the horse, becomes tired or dies in this service, it becomes necessary for me to walk on foot, thus competing with the Inca *chaski* [Inca foot messengers who traversed the empire].

Finally, Grajeda concluded, "We are in agreement with the philoso-phy of change and transformation of structure that the Revolution-ary Government is implanting."[1]

Grajeda's defense focused upon the lack of peasant labor because of the wild, untamable nature of the terrain. He described his estate as a frontier that he was conquering as a pioneer. His improvement of the terrain constituted a "civilizing enterprise" and was thus in accord with government policy. He failed to note that the reluctance of peasants to work his estate might have been the result of the exploitative relationship it entailed. Instead, he depicted his father as a kind of hispanicized Inca hero who had performed miracles, "making the crops grow from the very rocks" (a magical power that present-day Quechua frequently attribute to the Incas).

In claiming past rights to the land, that his kin had occupied it for years, and that he himself had worked it, he stressed three consider-ations that were persuasive to reform officials in their decisions about whether or not to expropriate property. In conclusion, he drew attention to the fact that he had on occasion been reduced to the equivalent of an Inca foot messenger because of the lack of modern technology—a scarcely veiled reference to the age of modernity the Revolutionary Government would usher in.

The peasants who worked on Grajeda's estate rallied to disprove his assertions. They claimed they had inherited the land from their ancestors and had been responsible for cultivating it since "time immemorial." Grajeda rejoined that since such a small number of peons were involved, they had no need for all the land. The workers, in turn, demonstrated that the land they had was insufficient for their subsistence, and that, as was true of the workers on Llaspay, they had only received liquor, coca, and food for their labor. Finally, they showed that neither Grajeda nor his immediate family worked the land directly. Grajeda was in fact a schoolteacher in a nearby town who owned real estate in Cusco worth twice as much as Casa Blanca, and his children lived elsewhere.[2] This evidence was damning, and in 1975 the state expropriated Casa Blanca and turned it over to the workers.

The Landlord as Peon

Landlords went to great efforts to depict themselves in terms of the "peasant model" embedded in the reform law. For example, Juana Calancha, a wealthy, powerful widow, insisted to reform officials, as did many other property owners trying to save their lands, that she was "a true peasant, illiterate."[3] Similarly, Braulio Grajeda described himself as "a child" and "a temporary laborer";[4] and Alberto Astete Acurio depicted himself as "a poor soul who worked the land in good faith."[5]

One of the most interesting cases was that of Enrique Bejar, who insisted that he was a "peon" who merely rented land from Estela Vizcarra, the owner of Miska Pata A, a property the state was considering for expropriation. The case demonstrates the kinds of conflicts that arose among landlords who, despite their efforts to retain their oligarchic hold over the rural peasantry, often fought bitterly among themselves during reform proceedings. Bejar explained that, as the workers of Llaspay and Benigno Pacheco had done, he and Julio Pacheco, Estela Vizcarra's nephew, who was representing her, had drawn up an informal bill of sale to facilitate reform proceedings, and Vizcarra had agreed to turn over the land to him.[6]

Bejar was unprepared for the angry response from Julio Pacheco, who reported to reform agents:

Señor Bejar would like to appear as no more than a simple peon in accordance with the declarations he has made to Reform engineers, which are totally false. I would like to add that Señor Bejar, as a property owner, has already sold part of his property called Molino for S./40,000. In the eleven years during which he has rented out this property, he has garnered fat profits, with which he has built houses [and] acquired more land and a truck. . . . Thus, I beg of you to take into account what I have exposed for your benefit, so that it will come as no surprise to you that Bejar is no tenant but a property owner.[7]

The reform agents agreed. Bejar was not only prevented from purchasing Miska Pata A but also lost most of his other land. However, long after the reform, he continued to reside in Huanoquite. He farmed his land directly with a zeal rarely found among landlords. Day after day, he would head out to his fields as the dawn broke and return, exhausted, late in the afternoon. More and more he came to resemble the peon whose image he had conjured up for himself.

The Dynamics of Kinship and Control over Territory

As we have seen, a number of Huanoquite's landlords preferred to negotiate directly with peasants in the hope of receiving some compensation rather than being expropriated in exchange for risky long-term bonds that had to be invested in industry. Still others, to avoid court costs—and calculating that given the Andean tradition of reciprocity and patron-client ties, they would get something back, whether in the form of land or labor—shrewdly turned over portions of their lands to communities as "gifts."[8]

Andean terms of exchange were frequently inegalitarian. In Huanoquite, local ties, founded on the negotiated exchange of mutual obligations, were often transformed into asymmetrical interdependent relationships in which collectivities with different statuses became bound to one another through the exchange of goods and labor. Centralization was offset by asymmetrical horizontal links among collectivities ranging from large polities to moieties to ayllus to household domestic units (Alberti and Mayer 1974; Allen 1988; Salomon 1985:511–31).

These same dynamics were manipulated effectively by landlords and peasants alike before and during the reform. By "generously" offering their lands to communities instead of engaging in prolonged litigation, landlords deflected the animosity of community members, strengthened their paternalistic ties with them, and incited factional strife between peasant communities. In the future, so long as they maintained the proper flows of exchange, they were assured of a status similar to that which they had enjoyed before the reform, and, most important, of a supply of labor to work their remaining lands. The repeated willingness of landlords to give up their lands prior to the reform also reflected their weakness. It resulted from the impact that a longer-lasting peasant offensive, accelerated by the reform, had made on the political security of the landed elite in the highlands.

Some landlords sought membership in communities or even

claimed kinship with community members in order to retain usufruct rights over a portion of their lands as community members. At
the same time, if landowners claimed kinship with peasants, the
latter could force them to comply with the corporate obligations that
assertions of kinship entailed. Communities were selective about
the kinds of "outsiders" or "fictive kin" they would admit and opened
their doors only to landlords who would remain under their scrutiny
and authority, fulfill their collective obligations, and contribute significantly to the needs of the community. These obligations included
sowing, harvesting, cleaning irrigation canals, contributing labor and
resources to infrastructural projects such as repairing or constructing
public buildings, bridges, or roads, and activating ties with bureaucrats and other well-placed individuals in Cusco, Paruro, and Lima.
Community members could fine or throw out individuals if they
did not comply with their obligations, and they sometimes did so.
Equally frequently, however, they found themselves unable to exercise their legitimate collective authority against these hacendado
community members because they felt constrained by the prior history of patron-client relationships that had characterized peasant-
landlord exchanges and were grateful for the kinds of services these
new kinds of community members could assist them with. During
the time I was in Huanoquite, hacendados turned community members only rarely helped in collective labor tasks. They might assist in
writing letters to bureaucrats in Cusco, offer advice on the best prices
for seeds or building materials, or even send one of their "male
servants" in their stead to clean a canal. They might work their own
fields held in usufruct, but they would hardly ever take the final step
of participating in communal manual labor. Nonetheless, hacendado
community members had an important impact upon the authority
structures that evolved in Huanoquite after the reform.

Land Invasions

Extralegal land invasions and counterinvasions by peasant groups
in Huanoquite occurred frequently during the reform. For example, a
series of recurrent invasions, termed "a bloody abusive battle" by the
police chief of Paruro, took place as three groups fought over the estate of Huancacrara: the community members of Tantarcalla, the
permanent workers on the estate of Huancacrara, and the overseers
of the workers on the estate, who were also peasants. Simultaneously
with battling among themselves over rights to the estate, they were
also fighting with the owners of the property.

(*above left*) The truck road from Cusco to Huanoquite during the rainy season
(*above right*) Repairing a landslide on the truck road from Cusco to Huanoquite

3. An abandoned estate surrounded by intensively cultivated fields

4. The district capital of Huanoquite

5. (*left*) The Inca road from Huanoquite to Cusco

6. (*above*) Inca thrones (*Inkaq tiyanan*) in Huanoquite alongside Inca road

7. Cusco, former capital of the Inca empire, the nearest city to Huanoquite, and site of all state offices concerned with agrarian questions

8. Peasants waiting outside an attorney's office in Cusco for advice on a land title (photo taken by Gabino Quispecondori)

. Terraced fields of maize, wheat, and early potatoes

. The estates of Llaspay and Cotahuana

11. (*left*) Fiesta. Note truck drivers in drinking competition. To the left, two members of the landed elite, Osc Bejar and Humberto Paz, conversing with each other

12. (*above*) Transfer of sponsorship of the pilgrimage of Qoyllur Rit'i from Mario Laymi, c of Maska's authorities, to Rafael Ttito, owne of Llulluch'ayuq

13. (*left*) Tomás Chaparro, president of Mask with his wife and four children

14. (*above*) District capital with the flat pampa of the cooperative of Inkaq Tiyanan de Tihuicte in the background

15. (*left*) Celebration and blessing of Tihuicte's second-hand tractor after the original one had been blown up by members of Sendero

16. (*above left*) Embrace between Roberto Alqa, "compadre" of tractor blessing, member of the landed elite, and prior school supervisor, and Tihuicte socios
17. (*above right*) Cirilo Mora, "father" of Evangelical Protestants in Huanoquite

18. Silvestre Alvarez, Catholic catechist, carrying his Bible

19. (*right*) Leonardo Herrera, a respected peasant leader and officer of the cooperative of Tihuicte, with his family

20. (*below*) Uproar at the fiesta of the Virgin of the Assumption because priest did not appear to bless the holy image

Extralegal invasions increased the probability that reform officials would act upon particular cases, since violence was almost sure
to result if they did not. Although they were terrified of peasant
"uprisings," landlords also took strategic advantage of them in order
to play upon the growing divisions among peasants. The reform law
condemned extralegal invasions in no uncertain terms. Landlords
thus sometimes even encouraged peasants to invade as a means of
strengthening their *own* positions and excluding invading peasants
from having their land claims considered by the land courts. In the
Huancacrara case, the owners began laying out their case by claiming
that the peasants on the estate had not "risen up" but rather had
"massively invaded" the property; and they concluded their defense
stressing:

The Agrarian Reform Law states that those who invade or usurp rural property or try to possess it will be excluded from the Agrarian Reform. Perhaps
those who prepared the technical report are biased, marginalizing the property owners. Paradoxically, the Agrarian Reform is not punishing peasant
invaders but rather the property owners.[9]

Peasants, in contrast, used invasions as a way, not only to get the
attention of reform officials, but also to reassert what they considered the appropriate order of things suppressed by the state, the
landlords, and the overseers. Gavin Smith (1989:189) describes, for
example, how once they had invaded lands, the peasants of the
central highlands of Huasicancha reconstituted their ideal of social
relations and defended themselves against the hacienda overseers,
the army, the civil guard, and political authorities by building residential structures of "fire-scarred stones and old thatching straw,"
establishing lookout posts, creating a defensive political organization, and herding together their sheep with those of the hacienda.

The Knowledge of *Técnicos*

Landlords and peasants also focused upon government *técnicos*
and their qualifications in the claims they made. The "engineer,"
"surveyor," or "technician" became the target of considerable slander
from landlords. These individuals were responsible for determining
the boundaries and description of the property in dispute and the
kind and number of workers on it. This information was crucial to
deciding whether or not a property should be expropriated, to whom
it should be assigned, and its value, including the value of any improvements. A higher property value meant greater indemnification

for the landlord (and increased debt for the cooperative). A greater number of peons left less land protected from expropriation (and more territory for new cooperative members).

Landlords therefore often sought either to discredit these government agents or to collude with them. Peasants also sometimes tried to make allies out of them, but more often they simply ignored them, preferring rather to sidestep officialdom by reaching negotiated solutions to conflicts with other peasants or landlords through the direct mediation of their own communal leaders.

Not unlike the *ladinos* of colonial society (see Adorno 1991:232–70), many of these representatives of the state spoke Spanish and had some education, but came from peasant backgrounds. The power of the ladinos had arisen from their performance of straddling functions—interpreting, Christianizing, or facilitating the resolution of lawsuits—in mestizo society. As intermediate social figures, they were functionally important, but they were distrusted because of their lack of clear loyalty to one social class and culture or another. They had abuse heaped on them by mestizos and campesinos alike.

During the reform, técnicos acted as intermediate social figures, and estate owners angrily expressed their distrust of them. Take the protestations of Teodicia Ruíz Caro de Lovón, the owner of Qeñaparo:

The worst part is that we are arguing about a series of falsehoods that have nothing to do with reality. It is said that the "expert" in this case hasn't even traveled to the rustic property. . . . I should add that those señores responsible for making inspections of property that is being expropriated aren't even familiar with the property whose value they are calculating, and the worst of the matter is that they determine its value from their work posts without ever having visited the property. I can confirm that many cases like this have occurred.[10]

María Carmen Ayerbe Calancha, owner of Roccoto was even more pointed in her criticism:

Reform surveyors have failed to take account of the property's forest areas or fruit trees, which are the estate's principal capital. They have made an indiscriminate list of peons that does not correspond to who actually works on Roccoto. I demand that the reform office communicate with me directly and not through third parties who are functionaries or subalterns of the agrarian reform.[11]

Peasants, especially those who belonged to communities, also questioned the knowledge and leadership qualities of técnicos and the ease with which they could be corrupted by landlords or other groups of peasants. As we shall see in the next chapter, they engaged in intense debate over whether it was best for them to place their faith in state bureaucrats or in their own indigenous leadership, particularly when they were admonished that "the official recognition of an indigenous community is solely authorized by legal personnel, not by the recognition of control over lands that the community considers its own."[12]

In many cases, communities opted to sustain their faith in indigenous leadership, but they gradually became more astute about couching their customs and history in a language that would appeal to reform officials. Rather than making reference to issues of justice or class conflict that might be involved, they would stress the steps they had taken to reorganize their communities, collect data, reform their finances, and control their resources, all activities associated with the tinkering of técnicos. For example, the community of Huanca Huanca, in order to justify its demand for formal recognition, issued the following statement:

We comuneros have the right to use these small plots of land and family orchards in a direct and personal way.... We have held assemblies, filled out registration forms for the community, conducted a general census, provided our map, verified the absence of opposition from our neighbors and from neighboring *feudatarios*, and we have a title dating from 1579.[13]

They also began to select leaders adept at fostering good relations with the government and building a consensus between state officials and community members.

Conclusion

In the competitive interpretations of the law described in the preceding two chapters, we can see how the 1969 reform legislation collided with a dominant political order and the heterogeneity of socioeconomic relationships in the countryside. Despite the difficulties in determining the individual authorship or veracity of some of these documents, they nevertheless illustrate the specific discourses that emerged from the contradictions and opportunities with which the reform law confronted different sectors of Huanoquite's rural population.

The claims that fill the reform archives do not reveal a "true" or "false" unitary response to the reform on the part of Huanoquite's peasants or landlords, or, for that matter, the ranks of Cusco's bureaucracy and legal apparatus. Rather, as William Hanks argues for colonial Maya texts that he describes as "hybrid" and "ambivalent," they serve as "artifacts of communicative actions performed in a complicated, changing context" (1986:726–27). In these claims, the voices of Huanoquite's community or ayllu members, workers with no affiliation to a community, and mestizo landlords and their families come to life as they offer conflicting testimony over rights to land and labor.

Evaluations of the reform have often failed to take into account the multiple vantage points of those who participated in it. Yet the existence and effects of these multiple vantage points became crucial motivations for the totalizing projects of both Sendero Luminoso and an increasingly repressive state after the reform.

Local interests, memories, and perceptions colored the claims peasants submitted to the land courts. At the same time, these claims arose from the reform law, which represented a particular political, economic, and social order, the history of the social relations of production in Peru, and the meanings peasants read into these ongoing relationships and processes.

Underlying the peasants' claims, too, were their long experience of agricultural adaptation through control of multiple ecological zones, their strategic accommodations in the face of the Spanish invasion and conquest and the rule of landlords, and the Velasco regime's rhetoric of national integration. They attempted to build on these, often for purposes other than those specified in the reform legislation.

The archival sources may appear chaotic, but their logic is more easily discerned once it is understood, first, that these documents were crafted in large part out of materials supplied by the dominant society; second, that for peasants one of their purposes was to evade the dominant society's total control; and third, that they were necessarily inconsistent. As Joan Scott has pointed out, language itself reveals systems of meaning or knowledge that are constructed through differentiation; meanings are therefore "multidimensional, established relationally, directed at more than one auditor, framed in an already [discursive] field, establishing new fields at the same time" (1988:58–59). I would add that the "discursive" fields that made their appearance during the reform were also firmly anchored in existing material conditions that had a significant bearing upon the form and content of meaning and knowledge that was produced. That is, the language of political struggle itself mediates between objective conditions and ideological systems or consciousness.

In reasserting their claims to land under the reform law, Huanoquiteños were confronted with new challenges to their capacity to establish and sustain a united political front. Class stratification, alternative sources of local prestige and power, and the changing policies of the national state exacerbated factionalism among high-land peasants. Many of the conflicts that began during the reform did not remain confined to land or the interpretation of the law. They became a principal vehicle through which peasants sought to shift the meanings and locus of political authority in their communities.

Shifting Political Fields

Every interaction contains within it elements of the regular
and elements of the indeterminate and both are "used" by
individuals. This is true not only of small scale face-to-face
encounters. It can also be said of plans and actions on a large
impersonal scale, as in administrative action and legislation.

Sally Falk Moore, "Uncertainties in Situations,
Indeterminacies in Culture"

Recurrent struggles over the meaning of legitimate authority
took place in Huanoquite during the reform. These struggles
were among the primary vehicles that Huanoquiteños used to
redefine their relationships to the state; they altered local hierarchies
of status and prestige and shaped Huanoquiteños' views of their
history and of their class and ethnic identities. Not surprisingly,
contests over the control of land frequently served as the primary
focus of these struggles, and Huanoquiteños rapidly took advantage
of judicial institutions and legal personnel in order to make their
respective cases.

These struggles did not occur as mechanical reactions to the
passage of agrarian reform legislation. Many of them had been under
way since the Spanish conquest, but they flared up with a remarkable
intensity during the reform. Colonial judicial institutions had provided the means for native inhabitants to resist encroachment upon
their lands and to temper exploitation at the hands of their own
authorities, who had been compromised by the colonial administration. In similar fashion, the reform law provided the means for peasants to fight back against the long history of abuse they had suffered
at the hands of state officials and the landed elite. However, their
use of the tenets of the new law also pitted peasants against one
another as they sought to shift existing status hierarchies within
their communities.

These status hierarchies were founded in control of land, labor,
knowledge, and ritual powers that together formed a complex political field of economic, political, and symbolic capital. "Political
fields" are sites "of struggles in which individuals seek to maintain or
alter the distribution of the forms of capital specific to them" (Bour-

dieu 1991:14). They consist of the positions particular agents occupy and the relationships among them as they are determined by the distribution of different kinds of resources or "capital." Capital, for Pierre Bourdieu is not only economic but also cultural and symbolic. One of the principal means of maintaining or challenging the status quo within and across political fields is through the transformation of one kind of capital into another. I find the concept "political field" preferable to "infrastructure" or "ideology" because it does not artificially separate and institutionalize economic, cultural, and political domains; it forces one to consider the culturally informed ways in which people make calculations between economic, symbolic, and political capital. The parameters that create political fields are, by definition, the empirical face of social processes.

Two questions in particular intrigued me as I followed some of these struggles. Under what circumstances and whose direction did Huanoquiteños come to challenge existing authority structures? In turn, what were the dynamics that led particular individuals or groups to occupy positions of power after the reform? These questions, which arose during my initial field research in 1984, became ever more compelling in trying to explain Sendero's ability to root itself in highland communities.

In a book on the history of peasant intellectuals in Tanzania, Steven Feierman recommends that we attempt to understand "the contest of society over whose discourse is to become authoritative, whose practice will be accepted?" (1990:31). It is not my intention to provide a history of peasant intellectuals in Huanoquite here, but rather to show, in a more modest fashion, how and why particular individuals came to challenge existing political fields in the district following the passage of the reform legislation, what their relationships to different collectivities were, and why they were able to come to occupy positions of power at that particular juncture in time.

Old Forms, New Content

We saw in the preceding two chapters that Huanoquiteños involved in land disputes during the reform often invoked earlier land rights and titles, some of which dated to precolonial times. The uses of customary rules in land disputes were particularly important as one way in which peasants relied upon continuity of form while attempting to force changes in the meanings these forms carried. Sally Moore succinctly characterizes this interplay between traditional form and meaning: "Emphasis on the sameness of form over time has often been important in both the strategies of individuals and in the policies of governments. . . . Context, content and meaning shift, even as familiar forms are repeated for new reasons" (1989:277–78).

This is one way in which *habitus,* which Bourdieu defines generally as a set of dispositions or habits that inclines agents to act and react in certain ways (1977:72), undergoes change. Many of these changes result in unintended consequences. Bourdieu argues that the dispositions that compose *habitus* generate practices, perceptions and attitudes that are "regular" without being consciously coordinated or governed by any "rule." They are "inculcated, structured, durable, generative, and transposable" (72, 78). Bourdieu's model focuses almost exclusively upon practice itself as the locus of activities that may either reinforce or shift political fields. Discourse constitutes "explanations." Explanations, while they may be more accessible to the anthropologist, because they are proffered as social and public guidelines and customary knowledge, are not given primacy by Bourdieu in orienting actual cultural practices. In fact, Bourdieu's model suggests that, practically speaking, discourse is almost irrelevant to explaining with any precision why one person rather than another may take the initiative in instigating social change.

I find Feierman's model, which addresses the relationship between discourse and practical activities on the one hand and the creation of fields of power and emergence of authority on the other, more convincing. His proposition, summarized below, knits together discourse and practical activity with contests over authority in a more dynamic and open-ended manner than Bourdieu's:

> The central unresolved question is about who invests a form of discourse or practical activity with authority. Who authorizes it? Who succeeds in defining a set of issues or course of action as the appropriate one, preempting the space of opposed utterances or alternative practices? Each person has a sphere of competent knowledge, but not all knowledge is equal in its weight within society, in its capacity to move people toward collective action, or to create authoritative discourse. [Feierman 1990:31]

More detailed examination of the ways in which political forms have acquired new meanings in the Andean highlands, and why and when people situated in different social positions actively engage in tranforming customary manners of behavior in their daily lives, enables us better to specify, not only the conditions under which political changes take place in the Andes, but also some of the reasons why certain kinds of changes do not occur. Many communities have similar stories to tell of feuds that resemble the one described below—interminable, almost, but not quite, repetitive, and passionately involving a far-flung network of people. A functionalist explanation for these feuds would be reductionist. They tend to keep matters sufficiently unresolved that the hope that they will eventually reach their objectives never dies among the principal parties. Just as important, the struggles themselves allow groups to perpetuate the idea that "community" is still possible. At the same time, the historical context in which these feuds take place results in slippage between discourse, action, and consequences in ways that are never wholly predictable. The resulting instability creates a number of opportunities for various groups or individuals to vie for control of political space.

Individuals sometimes acted alone and sometimes with the consent of the collectivities they represented in order to fortify the political solidarity of their communities through the instrumental use of reform legislation. In doing so, however, peasants from similar sociopolitical units often found themselves in opposition to one another. The exacerbated factionalism between different communities following the reform legislation was a product, on the one hand, of the uneven implementation of the reform. On the other hand, it also resulted from the ongoing struggles between particular individuals who sought to take advantage of new opportunities that the reform helped to make possible in order either to accumulate personal power or to strengthen the power of their collectivity and, in doing so, their personal power. Thus, "agency" itself interacted with state policies, shaping the direction, limitations, and content of political struggle.

The first few years following the passage of reform legislation were especially turbulent and exciting times. Huanoquiteños, like many other peasants, paid close attention to the strategies that peasant leaders were elaborating in other parts of the rural highlands in order to pursue their rights to land and labor. In addition, the discourse and actions of particular individuals encouraged and persuaded Huanoquiteños to pursue particular disputes. For example, Hugo Blanco Galdos, a native son of Huanoquite, had served as a principal leader in the early 1960's in the peasant uprisings in La Convención. Although he did not directly assist Huanoquite's peasants in their litigation, he became a symbol of radical resistance that groups of peasants either invoked or decried.

In these negotiations, a third actor, sometimes less obviously, and frequently without being physically present, also played a critical

role—the government. Ironically, the adeptness with which Huanoquiteños could manipulate the law for their own purposes exacerbated cleavages among them and prevented them from arriving at a
coherent notion of legitimate authority that could serve them in
defending their political interests. The state thus played an important role in transforming the political topography of rural communities, but individual actors at the local level were also exceedingly
important in redefining political fields in Huanoquite, in challenging
the existing criteria upon which ethnic identity was founded, and in
contributing to the growing weakness and instability of rural communities after the reform.

Although the reform legislation provided the broad framework
for land disputes to be activated and pursued, these disputes also
arose because of the memories that Huanoquite's communities retained of their former social organization and prior land claims.
Particular conditions provoked their memories to come bubbling to
the surface. The interplay between memory, discourse, strategic action, and the tenets of the reform law thus led to a substantial degree
of jockeying and negotiating among Huanoquiteños, since they did
not share one and the same history.

After the reform, power in Huanoquite primarily came to be
exercised, not by the landed elite, but rather by new kinds of figures
who had roots within Quechua society as well as valuable ties to
mestizo society. While it might be easy for Huanoquiteños to point
to individuals who were powerful, it became far more difficult for
them to draw distinctions between those who had power and those
whom they recognized as legitimate authorities. In distinguishing
between power, authority, and influence, I follow Max Weber (1947).
Michael G. Smith elaborates: "Authority is, in the abstract, the right
to make a particular decision and to command obedience. . . . Power
. . . is the ability to act effectively on persons or things, to make or
secure favourable decisions which are not of right allocated to the
individuals or their roles." He adds that whether power is exercised
through influence or force, it is inherently competitive, whereas authority entails a chain of command and control. Although the idea of
authority implies positive actions and duties, the exercise of power
has no positive sanctions, only rules that specify "the conditions of
illegality of its operation" (Smith 1960:18–19, 20). In short, the exercise of power can occur without legitimacy, whereas authority
necessarily depends upon it.

The dispute recounted below was first documented in the mid-
seventeenth century and continued to preoccupy Huanoquiteños in

the years that followed. Over three centuries later, when the reform was passed, it resurfaced, although it may not have been far from people's minds in the interim. For the people involved, it became a frame through which they attempted to revise a history not yet put to rest in order to create a different outlook upon the future. Because the case had been recently revived, I was able to obtain a wealth of archival materials relevant to it, which I found in the Agrarian Reform Office, the Peasant Communities Office, the Second Land Court, the private property register at the Palace of Justice, and one lawyer's private archives. Coincidentally, one of the lawyers whom I interviewed, Nerio Gonzáles, was responsible for representing the principal defendant in the case. I was therefore able to obtain his point of view as well. The case was well known to bureaucrats in Cusco who in one way or another worked with agrarian policy. Most of them shook their heads in despair and astonishment whenever I mentioned "the Tito litigation."

Huanoquiteños also offered their own accounts of the events that had transpired, and I was able to interview most of the principal actors in the dispute. In the pages below, I synthesize the dispute, which was remarkable in its complexity and longevity. What impressed me most about the case were the multitude of details that participants in the dispute mastered and the tangled, layered quality of the defenses they presented. That the dispute has been sustained in different forms since the Spanish conquest suggests that it is a central mechanism that communities in Huanoquite were using to define and differentiate themselves.

The Dance of Fraternal Twins

This dispute began with a conflict over moiety lands. One ideal form of Inca-imposed social organization was a structure in which smaller ayllus (minimal ayllus) were embedded in larger ayllus (maximal ayllus), which, in turn, formed moieties. These moieties existed in a complementary, hierarchical relationship to one another. They were similar in form and function, but their status differed in accordance with the resources they controlled, whether or not their members were original inhabitants of the region, and the nature of their alliances and exchange relations with the Incas. Bernabé Cobo offers an early description of moiety organization:

Thus, they [the Incas] divided each town and *cacicazgo* into two parts known as the upper district and the lower district; or the superior part or faction, and the inferior; and even though these names denote inequality between these two groups, nevertheless, there was none, except for this preeminence and advantage, which was that the group of *hanansaya* got preference in seating and place over those of *hurinsaya*. . . . In everything else they were equal, and the Hurinsaya people were considered to be as good as the Hanansaya people. The object the Incas had in dividing the towns and provinces this way into factions and tribal groups was so that . . . in some measure the will of his vassals would be divided, so that they would not join together to promote uprisings, and if some rebellion or insurrection occurred, the people of one group would not agree and unite with the other, since they were men of opposing factions and opinions. [Cobo [1582–1657] 1979:211, ch. 24]

In records dating from 1656 to 1731, two moieties of Huanoquite, Maska-Urinsaya and Inkakuna-Anansaya, appeared repeatedly as principal adversaries in a long-standing land dispute.[1] The Incas had accorded the Maskas a special status as "Incas of privilege" because they constituted a local pre-Inca population that had accompanied the original founders of the Inca empire from the region of Paccarec-tambo to Cusco. The Maskas were reported as wild barbarians wandering around Cusco in the time of Inca Roca, and the Incas adopted the *maskaypacha* as their royal insignia, pointing to the primordial character of this pre-Inca ethnic group. As *Incas de privilegio*, the Maskas were considered members of the lesser Inca nobility, and they were given honorific titles (Zuidema 1964, 1982; Sarmiento 1960:119–220).

The Inkakunas, in contrast, were "the nobles of the commoners," the offspring of non-Inca women and higher Inca nobility (Poole 1984; Zuidema 1982). The Incas encouraged these intermarriages as a strategy of empire-building in order to create political alliances out of kinship ties (see Silverblatt 1987). In Huanoquite, the Inkakuna were considered actual royal descendants of the ruling Incas Wayna Kapaq and Yawar Waqaq, and they occupied maize and pasture lands there, as well as in other regions in the province.[2] The presence of In-kakunas in outlying regions of Cusco as cadres of pacifying colo-nizers was intended to instill notions of Inca hegemony in the rest of the native population.

In Huanoquite, the Inkakuna held a higher status (*anan*) than the members of Maska (*urin*) within the Inca model of social stratifica-tion. From the time of Inca occupation onward, rivalry characterized relations between the two moieties. Both Maska and Inkakuna re-tained their own ethnic lords, but the lord of Inkakuna, Felipe In-quiltupa, was considered the principal lord (*kuraka principal*) during the latter half of the sixteenth century.[3]

Rivalries between the two moieties revolved about many issues, including the appropriation of land by Inkakuna from Maska and Inkakuna's use of local labor (see Moore 1958 for a general discussion of this practice under the Incas). Questions of political status and the imposition of Inca law fueled this rivalry. Following the Spaniards' arrival and the consolidation of Huanoquite's multiple ayllus into a *reducción* in the latter half of the sixteenth century, the members of Inkakuna were relocated further up the valley and nearer to Maska. At that point, questions of status between the two moieties became thoroughly entangled with questions of territoriality and land rights. In pre-Inca and Inca times, while control over territory had been linked to status, the two were not synonymous. Inkakuna's relocation brought its people far closer to Maska's potato-growing area, to which they had no customary rights, and much further away from their own maize fields, to which they did have rights.

By 1656, Maska's monopoly over potato lands had caused resentment among the members of Inkakuna, even though the latter continued to control valuable maize lands. At that time, Fray Domingo de Cabrera y Lartaún, inspector of *composiciones de tierras*, was sent to Huanoquite on a *visita*, or household census, to determine the lands that each moiety could hold from the Crown by purchase of title (see Chapter 1 for a detailed explanation of the policy of composiciones). In the dispute between the two moieties, Cabrera y Lartaún, one of the more enlightened emissaries of the colonial government, ruled that Inkakuna should receive:

A moderate composition of potato and puna lands . . . because my clients have neither potato lands nor puna where they can keep their cattle, and so that my clients will have and possess [potato lands and puna] as do the rest of the Indians of the other sector. His Very Reverend Paternity ought to give my client a moderate settlement of . . . potato lands because the sector of Urinsaya Mascas has more than 200 and does not permit them to herd or sow on them even though they all live together in one village. . . . For that reason 20 *fanegadas* [approximately nine hectares] were presented and shown to Don Felipe Inquiltupa, principal lord and governor of this village of Huanoquite of the sector of Anansaya of the Ingas and his Indians because they do not have what the Urinsayas possess, and their boundaries should be marked so that there will not be conflicts between them.[4]

Herein lies the earliest written evidence of the dispute between the two moieties. A portion of Maska's lands was turned over to Inkakuna, thus enhancing its higher status. Upon handing down his decision, Cabrera y Lartaún called attention to a Crown decree protecting ayllu lands, which Inkakuna—that is to say, its authorities— would nonetheless soon ignore. He warned several individuals who

claimed to have title to portions of land being turned over to Inkakuna that:

There ought not be other rights to lands distributed to the Indians. Even the
previous lord of these ayllu lands should not have sold them, and if I find any
titles of sale I will declare their dominion null and void and without value
and meaning, for the Indians' community lands ought not and cannot be sold
to anyone.[5]

Cabrera y Lartaún's position of defending Indian ayllu lands was
unusual. In the years that followed, Huanoquite's ayllus lost most of
their land to the expansion of colonial haciendas. In 1723, at the
behest of Inkakuna's cacique, Melchor Sutiq Huaman, Inkakuna's
rights to its potato and puna lands were reconfirmed in a general
inspection conducted by don Pedro de Minaur, the colonial governor
and inspector.[6]

By the twentieth century, six powerful haciendas had taken over
the majority of Huanoquite's lands, and most ayllu members worked
on these estates part- or full-time in exchange for plots of land or
grazing rights. Under these conditions, it became progressively more
difficult for ayllu members to defend their lands, especially since
landlords persisted in coercing and pressuring ayllu authorities to
relinquish them. Ayllu authorities, as was true during the colonial
period, also often found it easiest to deal with landlords by exploiting
their own polities (Guerrero 1990; Spalding 1984).

At the beginning of the twentieth century, two brothers, Santos
and Gerónimo Wallpamayta, were considered to be the local authorities (*cabecillas*) of Inkakuna. Without his brother's knowledge, Gerónimo Wallpamayta sold part of Inkakuna's remaining lands, including a piece called Llulluch'ayuq, to Daniél Galdos Alvarez in
1902.

Galdos was one of Huanoquite's most powerful landlords and
active politicians. Regardless of whether or not Gerónimo Wallpamayta had acquired valid title through earlier composiciones to
some of the lands he sold, his brother and most of the other members
of Inkakuna regarded the lands as theirs. Whether or not Galdos paid
Gerónimo Wallpamayta is unknown, but he made sure to document
the transaction in writing in the property register at the Palace of
Justice in Cusco.[7] Much later, in 1973, when the lands were again the
focus of bitter dispute, Inkakuna claimed that Galdos had seized the
land outright and "miraculously" caused the original title to it to
disappear during his tenure as mayor.[8] Inkakuna's members enjoyed
a brief moment of revenge by ostracizing their own cacique, Gerón-

imo Wallpamayta, who left Huanoquite, accompanied by a small group of loyalists, and moved to Chifia, an estate located far below the colonial center of Huanoquite on the north side of the Molle Molle River. Ironically, this was where many of Inkakuna's original maize lands could be found. Some descendants of Inkakuna had maintained residence there, working on the hacienda of Chifia and cultivating some of the maize fields that still belonged to Inkakuna. After the loss of their lands to Galdos, many of Inkakuna's members eventually left Huanoquite and joined the rest of the moiety on the banks of the Molle Molle River. They also renamed their moiety Inkakuna Ayllu Chifia (IAC). Thus it came to pass that Inkakuna physically abandoned the place of residence to which it had been relocated as part of the colonial resettlement plan.

However, matters did not end there. Maska began to encroach upon IAC's few remaining puna lands. When members of IAC protested, Maska's authorities pointed out that they could not possibly have rights to lands separated by such a great distance from their village—that is, two valleys beyond the "new" home of IAC on the lands surrounding the Chifia estate, separated from the puna lands by the Corcca River and the immense pampa of Inkaq Tiyanan de Tihuicte.[9] Although Maska's defense was plausible, it was deliberately couched in terms of Western principles of consolidated property rather than Andean principles of holding rights to land in regions often located at great distances from home villages (see Murra 1975). As long as the members of Inkakuna had remained within Huanoquite proper, their land claims had made sense, but once they departed to their precolonial home, much further away, their rights were called into question.

The initial dispute between Maska and Inkakuna was hardly unusual. Such conflicts formed part of the daily fabric of social life and were an outcome of the customary rivalry between moieties whose relationship to each other could most aptly be characterized as one of asymmetrical complementarity. The ideology that undergirded these sociopolitical arrangements inevitably led to periodic outbreaks of conflict. Ritual battles (*tinkuy*) had taken place year after year in Huanoquite, expressing the nexus between the ideology of balanced equilibrium between seemingly like social units and the reality of controlled inequality. Until the government had prohibited it, human sacrifice or, at the very least, the shedding of human blood, had been an expected part of the dance of "fraternal twins."

The dispute between Maska and Inkakuna spilled over the boundaries of choreographed ritual because of the intervention first of colonial and then of national law and policy in determining land claims. These policies affected real claims to land, and peasants used them against one another (Stern 1982a). In the Cusco area during the period of reform, attorneys and judges repeatedly referred to the decisions that Cabrera y Lartaún had made in his visita almost 400 years before as the baseline for determining the just rights of peasant communities to different pieces of land.[10] The disruption of traditional residential patterns because of the colonial resettlement policy, the permanent alienation of moiety lands by the rural landed elite, the dissolution of communities, the arbitrary redefinition of their boundaries when they were granted legal status, and the conflicting loyalties of ethnic lords to their polities and to colonial authority and wealth made this kind of dispute far more confusing to resolve in terms of Andean principles of status and land control. At the same time, people's memories of their land rights remained alive, making it almost impossible for bureaucrats predisposed to the logic of Western legal traditions to understand the stakes involved in the litigation. Disputes of this kind throughout the highlands beset bureaucrats' patience after the passage of the reform.

Rafael Tito Lezama: Landlord, Entrepreneur, Peasant

I know Tito. He is an authentic campesino, a hard worker. This señor resided on an estate called Llulluch'ayuq. I believe the señores Galdos left it to him. Señor Tito Lezama is an authentic campesino. . . . The Galdos sold the property to him. He gave them cattle, he gave them money. Then they didn't want to turn it over to him. His only recourse was the land court. . . . He's no longer a member of Inkakuna. Where he lives now is far from Inkakuna, very far. "Very far," he says. "No! What am I going to gain there? I don't even go to the *asambleas* [meetings]. I don't do anything. I am disconnected, and anyway these men recognize me as an owner of an estate." Then he didn't want to be part of Maska, because Maska didn't like Tito. They said, "You're with Inkakuna, you have nothing to do with us." Thus he had to turn himself into a private property owner. . . . But this didn't go over well with the members of the communities. They said, "No, you've become a private property owner with so much land." That's the problem.

Nerio Gonzalez, interview, 1991

During the expansion of hacienda lands in Huanoquite, large propertied families had carefully sought to ensure that their lands remained with their heirs. At their deaths, hacendados usually left detailed wills with instructions as to how their property should be divided. Daniél Galdos was no exception. He left most of his land to his numerous sons and daughters, who, in response to the changing times, made their own decisions about what to do with it. Eventually, in 1963, two of his daughters sold part of their land to a couple, Mariano Velásquez Baca and Leonor Mendoza de Velásquez. The land included Llulluch'ayuq, one of the properties that Galdos had presumably bought from Wallpamayta of Inkakuna. Other pieces of Inkakuna's lands passed down to three Galdos grandsons.

Kin ties between the Galdos and Mendoza families went back at least three generations. Daniel Galdos's father was Juan de Diós Galdos Mendoza, and his mother was a Mendoza too. Kinship ties among families of the landed elite through marriage were desirable. For example, the Galdos, Bejar, and Paz families in Huanoquite had numerous affinal ties among them.

Velásquez died shortly after purchasing the land. His widow then sold the land only a year later to Rafael Tito Lezama. Tito was an enterprising man from IAC who would succeed in making everybody's life miserable for the next two decades.

Before obtaining Llulluch'ayuq, Tito had served as IAC's official spokesperson (*personero*) and commanded respect as such among ayllu members for the services he had performed to facilitate IAC's formal recognition as a community in 1963, roughly the time of Belaúnde's agrarian reform.[11] Once Llulluch'ayuq was in his hands, however, he abandoned IAC, moved to his estate, and took on two defining characteristics of a landlord: he used unremunerated labor from IAC and Maska; and he refused to comply with collective labor obligations to IAC, his community of origin. At the same time, he proved adept at enhancing his leverage over community members through his activities as a cattle dealer and his strategic purchase of a truck, the services of which were greatly needed in the district.

Tito stands out as a powerful example of the manner in which ethnic and class identities shifted during the reform. He actively sought to construct a new identity for himself, in which he continued to present himself as a "campesino," but one who had the same access to economic and political power as the "vecinos" and could command the latter's respect. Although aspiring to similar economic and political standing, other peasants had refused to abandon their loyalties to their communities or the reciprocal and collective obligations that being a community member entailed. They thus sanctioned Tito harshly for his aberrant behavior and took advantage of the reform legislation to do so.

Tito became the proud owner of Llulluch'ayuq, a beautiful estate whose land extended in all directions. Galdos had built an irrigation canal that meandered through the property. Tito and his family proceeded to farm the land and market its produce. Of both Quechua and Hispanic descent, he prided himself on his toughness, his capacity to survive in isolation, his entrepreneurial skills, and his stubborn refusal to speak Spanish. He communicated only in Quechua. He dressed in loose-fitting homespun wool (*bayeta*) trousers and jacket, typical of colonial Indian fashion, even as the men around him embraced the occidental tastes of the Cusco market, purchasing shirts and sweaters of synthetic material and cheap shiny trousers.

Despite the visual image he presented as a humble man of the earth, his choice of clothing attested to his economic power. The labor invested in homespun wool clothing made it far more expensive than manufactured synthetics. It is not entirely clear how Tito accumulated enough money to buy his estate. It is likely that between his cattle dealing and his success as a farmer and IAC officer, he had been able to save enough to make a down payment on the property. Members of IAC and Maska believed, however, that he had made a pact with the devil that had allowed him to find a "nest egg" of gold in the mountains. Tito's vicious dogs, his two sons and daughters, and his in-laws protected him. He felt he could rely upon the labor of peasants in the area, including those from his natal community, who had little land, and that of his sons-in-law, who were from Maska. Until the 1969 reform, he had considered his land reasonably secure from expropriation.

Preparing for Battle

"Get off this estate."
"What for?"
"Because it's mine."
"Where did you get it?"
"From my father."
"Where did he get it?"
"From his father."
"And where did he get it?"
"He fought for it."
"Well, I'll fight you for it."
Carl Sandburg, *The People, Yes*

While Tito and the members of IAC and Maska prepared themselves for the reform, the slow wheels of the bureaucracy turned. In 1973, Tito first heard that his property might be expropriated. He responded by trying to persuade reform officials that he worked the land himself and had improved it, thus complying with the Revolutionary Government's slogan "Land to the Tiller." He also claimed that he had a title to his land dating from February 1802, and that he had given permission to members of IAC to graze their cattle there.[12] Tito subsequently testified that he had a contract of sale dated August 1, 1967, from the widow Velásquez. The titles never materialized.

By 1975, Tito's prospects began to look grim. As a last resort, he tried to persuade IAC to reincorporate him as a member of their community. He reasoned that if he reincorporated himself into IAC, Llulluch'ayuq would no longer be considered the property of a private landowner and therefore subject to expropriation. Rather, according to the precepts of the Peasant Communities Statute, it would be considered part of the holdings of an indigenous community, which were supposed to be protected.

Tito also promised IAC that if they agreed to the arrangement, he would give them permanent control over his property. Julián Quispe Ccaro, the president of IAC, consented, and sent a letter to the reform office telling them that they no longer need concern themselves about Llulluch'ayuq's status, because it now belonged to IAC. Quispe added that those who would farm the estate were all "community members by birth" of IAC.[13] Tito also wrote reform officials that he was "illiterate and a native-born member of IAC."[14] It is not entirely clear why IAC's membership agreed to this arrangement, but I conjecture that it was simply out of desire to regain control of lands that had once been theirs. Also, they were well aware that even though Tito was powerful and might not be trustworthy, the agreement itself might give them further leverage both with the reform officials and with Tito himself.

Unexpectedly, Maska's members began to wage their own battle against Tito and IAC. The conflict rapidly shifted from one between Tito and the state to one between Tito, an upwardly mobile peasant-entrepreneur-hacendado, the state, and two native communities. The agreement Tito had made with IAC pitted Maska against both IAC and Tito. Maska entered the arena with a vengeance, trying to prove to the land court that the land in question was a private estate, and that Tito had either usurped it from Maska or purchased it from the Velásquez couple. They argued that, in either case, it should be expropriated and judicially assigned to them, since the land had originally belonged to them before Cabrera y Lartaún turned it over to IAC so long ago.

Tito protested. He was, he declared, "an illiterate peasant with a small property," and the peasants who labored in his fields "were not my peons but rather my relatives within the fourth degree of consanguinity" (that is, they were all members of the same ayllu). He stressed that "the fruits my relatives gather from my fields are their only source of subsistence."[15]

Maska responded by declaring that Tito left nothing to the members of IAC but rather "was the sole beneficiary of the harvest from his property." Furthermore, they reiterated their earlier argument that "Inkakuna ought not make a leap of three leagues to our community and, as the law says, no community member should administer two or three properties when there aren't enough people to work them, whereas Maska, because of its large population, should take over these lands under orders from the land judge. In reality, we have been working these lands for more than fifty years."[16]

Tito then asserted that he had never owned Llulluch'ayuq. Because of the owner's sudden death, the sale had never been finalized, but he had continued to rent the property as a member of IAC. Even more confusingly, he produced a title of sale from Daniél Galdos to a member of IAC, dated 1962, to prove that the land belonged to IAC. Maska demanded to know how he could claim the land had always belonged to IAC if it had been sold to them again in 1962.[17]

In 1975, Maska's president, Raimundo Galaretta Ccasani, wrote reform officials:

Llulluch'ayuq is in the hands of an element that is clearly not a peasant but rather one with the soul of an exploiter, since he works the entire property for himself, using the services of IAC in an abusive fashion. . . . In addition, Tito is a livestock dealer and therefore prevents, in every way imaginable, our pasturing our livestock on this property so that his cattle alone can take advantage of it. He is a neocapitalist, fattening himself on the dispositions of the agrarian reform, to the detriment of the majority, we the peasant community of Maska.[18]

Later, Maska added that "eight peasants served as his peons," and that "the sales he made to wholesalers of his livestock amounted to an income of three or four million soles per year" (Archivo Reynaldo Alviz).

Huanoquiteños regarded cattle dealers with great ambivalence. Those who dealt in cattle but continued to work the land as community members were tolerated, whereas those who were simply merchant capitalists were envied, resented, and even hated (see Marc Edelman's "Landlords and the Devil" [1994:58–93], a fascinating account of community members' views of cattle dealers and their pacts with the devil in Costa Rica). Gavin Smith observed the same kind of attitude among Huasicanchinos in the central highlands:

Livestock is, in effect, the commodity face of the village households. . . . They become commodities the moment the *carnicero* digs his fingers through their fleeces to feel the meat on the ribcages. The activity of the carnicero was therefore seen to be incompatible with the social relations among members of a confederation. [Smith 1989:131]

Smith's reference to a confederation aptly describes the loose (and often tenuous) interconnections between different corporate units and individuals who coordinated productive, commercial, and political activities among themselves. The overwhelming self-interest of entrepreneurs such as Tito threatened these important, but fragile, links between economically differentiated units after the reform.

At the lower levels of the land court system, it was rarely possible to determine with any clarity the validity of claims made by disputants, and often equally difficult to determine the legitimacy that community members granted to their representatives. Shyster lawyers, hired by individuals and communities, served their own avarice more than justice, and the proliferation of titles made the judicial process ever murkier (see also LeGrand 1986 for similar examples from Colombia). Furthermore, traditional authorities were often ill prepared to wade through the intricacies of the reform legislation. Without the ability to speak Spanish and political savvy, they were also likely to become lost in the hallways of the land courts and reform offices.

In 1975, Maska's members took matters into their own hands. Four hundred of them, led by their president, invaded Llulluch'ayuq and the Galdos lands, where they turned over the earth to prove that it belonged to them. They did not regard their act as one of invasion or occupation but rather as one of reclaiming what had been theirs (Flores Galindo 1978:177). As tensions rose between the two communities over the historical revisions they were attempting, members of IAC, led by their president, Julián Quispe Ccaro, also invaded the same lands. Violence erupted between the two communities, and the land judge made a hurried trip from Cusco to Huanoquite in an effort to encourage reconciliation. He recommended that Tito's property be divided into two parts, one for Maska, the other for IAC.[19] Maska rejected the arrangement, and for their "insolence," several of its members, including the president, were arrested, fined, and sent to jail.

Another long trial between the two communities began with IAC staunchly supporting Tito.[20] In 1982, IAC testified:

Maska's denunciation of Tito is unnatural. Its members are being incited by Hugo Blanco Galdos, who has appeared in the district of Huanoquite and resolved that those from Maska ought to take over Llulluch'ayuq immediately. Inciting acts of invasion and violence, in this manner they have proceeded to turn over the earth in different places, boasting that the aforementioned had ordered them to take this stance, possibly because of his own frustrations, which are influencing the present case. . . . The controversy is in the hands of agrarian justice, which cannot be manipulated or altered by the behavior of "personages" who also have an interest in the lands of Llulluch'ayuq. . . . Even his [Hugo Blanco's] brother, Oscar Daniel Blanco Galdos, has started judicial proceedings against Rafael Tito.[21]

Hugo Blanco Galdos: Peasant Revolutionary, Son of the Elite

It is unlikely that Hugo Blanco or his brother Oscar directly incited Maska to invade the contested lands. Nevertheless, Hugo Blanco was from Huanoquite and had spoken out repeatedly against the abuses of the landed elite. He himself was the grandson of the powerful landowner, Daniél Galdos, and his father had been a lawyer who defended peasants. Blanco, when he reached college age, had gone to Buenos Aires to study agronomy. There he became a Trotskyist. He returned home periodically and had many relatives in Huanoquite, some of whom had become members of Maska. The police chief of Huanoquite, despite his displeasure over the ongoing violence between Maska and IAC, confided to me that Blanco was "charismatic" and had the capacity "to cause the people to rise up."

What was this capacity? Blanco's political philosophy differed from that of many other leftist intellectuals who have come before and after him. He had close ties with peasants, spoke Quechua, and rejected the assumption that a military cadre without mass support (*focoísmo*) could successfully lead a revolution in the name of the peasants. He also believed that worker-peasant alliances were essential to the success of any resistance movement. Following the 1960's uprisings in the La Convención valley, where Hugo Blanco had served as one of the principal leaders, members of the district of Huanoquite established the "Hugo Blanco Agrarian League," a subsidiary of the provincial "Pachacutec Agrarian League," in his honor. The La Convención uprisings had hastened the passage of reform legislation. After being imprisoned, tortured, and threatened with execution in 1963, Blanco had become an international cause. Recognizing his appeal to peasants, the Velasco government took the risk of releasing him from prison in 1970 in an attempt to co-opt it. Rather than supporting the regime, however, Blanco once again became the spokesperson of the many peasant communities excluded from the reform and therefore invading lands. In 1971, the Velasco regime deported him to Mexico.

In his book, *Tierra o muerte* (Land or Death), Blanco speaks explicity of the abuses hacendados committed in Huanoquite. One of his most powerful sketches of political life in Huanoquite, included in the book, is found in a letter he wrote from El Frontón prison in Lima in 1969 to the famous Peruvian writer and ethnologist José María Arguedas:

We call fried mustard leaves *nabos hauch'a*. We like them enormously, although the silent and pervasive reason for their existence evokes death: hunger.

When hunger comes, it devours broad beans, corn, potatoes, freeze-dried potatoes; it leaves nothing to the Indian . . . except for these leaves, without butter, without onions, without garlic, even without salt.

After more and more of these leaves, death comes: they are its "green heralds." Death comes under different pseudonyms in Spanish and Quechua: tuberculosis, anemia, pneumonia, sickness from springs, from the wind, from sorcery. They call it by pseudonyms because its real name is an evil word: HUNGER.

But the mustard leaves are not to blame for this; that is why we like them so much. I'm not saying they are delicious. I don't understand those things. I already made that mistake once with freeze-dried potatoes. I said they were delicious, but those who are knowledgeable claimed they were insipid. Because of that, I will only say that we like them very much even though they remind us of periods of hunger.

Those periods of hunger when sometimes the gringos (They are so good!) send us corn with weevils and powdered milk, which come to the church, to the mayor, or the governor, and from there are destined for the hacendados' pigs.

I don't ask that they distribute this charity to us. I demand that they return to us what is ours so there won't be any more periods of hunger. It was my first cousin, Zenón Galdos, who demanded that the charity be distributed to us. It cost him dearly. For what he did, Sr. Araujo, mayor of Huanoquite, killed him with a bullet. Sr. Araujo is not in prison. He comes from a good family. [Blanco 1972:139–40]

As symbolic figure and recognized kin of Huanoquite, Blanco thus encouraged Maska in its battle against Tito and IAC. IAC and Tito, in contrast, used Blanco's reputation and notoriety as rabble-rouser in order to gain the sympathies of reform officials and draw attention to the illegitimacy of his, and therefore of Maska's, actions.

The Resolution

IAC finally realized that even if Tito won the case, he would never in good faith share his property with them. This was a turning point in the dispute. IAC withdrew from its alliance with him and turned against him. Tensions ran high in Maska because of the inordinate debt its authorities had incurred. In addition, Tito's two sons-in-law, who were members of Maska, found themselves in an awkward position, at once on the verge of being ostracized and considered crucial mediators by Maska. They chose to mediate between Maska and Tito, but to no avail.

In 1981, Maska's treasurer, Demetrio Pantoja Bejar, and its president, Juan Roque Chaparro, discovered that Velásquez, whose widow had sold Tito the property in dispute, had a daughter, Vilma Josefa Velásquez Mendoza, who was living in Lima. After poring over the reform legislation and inheritance laws, they made an expensive journey to Lima to find Vilma. They persuaded her to testify that she was the legitimate heir to Llulluch'ayuq, and that the property should never have been sold to Tito. Furthermore, Vilma agreed to turn over the lands to Maska.[22] Maska's leaders chose a strategy that demonstrated their understanding of the logic of the reform process and of the legal weight that inheritance law carried in the courts. Vilma testified in court in 1982. At that point, Tito had no way to exit gracefully. Shortly thereafter, Maska elected new community authorities, who reached an out-of-court settlement with Tito in May 1983, fourteen years after the reform. Reform officials formally authorized the settlement after the fact. Tito turned over half his lands to Maska and remained with the other half. IAC received nothing.[23] When the litigation came to an end, Tito had lost most of his savings. Maska and IAC were at least twelve million soles ($2,400 at that time) in debt, having long since depleted the reserves of their modest communal treasuries.

Ambivalent Figures of Authority

Whatever else a legal proceeding may be—an encounter between contending parties seeking confirmation of their respective claims, a carefully staged ritual aimed at the exorcism of potential chaos, a life-threatening confrontation with the manifest power of the state—it is not a simple recapitulation of a past occurrence. It is never really possible to reconstruct exactly the actions or utterances that gave rise to the case at hand. . . . Faced with such uncertainties any legal system must cope with the problem of

defining as well as discovering facts. . . . By deciding how to assess facts—indeed by deciding what shall be regarded as fact—a legal system may create what shall be taken as so.
Lawrence Rosen, *The Anthropology of Justice*

It would be far too simple to suggest that this dispute boiled down to a series of transformations and permutations of the repressed, yet perpetual, conflicts between the original moieties of Maska-Urinsaya and Inkakuna-Anansaya. Particular individuals played significant roles in shaping the course that the dispute took. Tito, the son of a humble peasant, turned shrewd entrepreneur and powerful landlord, and Hugo Blanco, grandson of one of Huanoquite's most powerful landowning families, turned peasant activist and revolutionary, both used Maska and Inkakuna, native communities with long-standing land rights, instrumentally. In turn, guided by their leaders, Maska and Inkakuna sought to take advantage of these alliances for their own purposes. It is also worth noting that Hugo Blanco, directly or indirectly, was assisting Maska in reclaiming lands that had been taken away from it by his grandfather, who had "stolen" them from Inkakuna. Likewise, Tito, who had fought hard to gain IAC's formal recognition as a community, was now asserting private rights to collective lands IAC believed had been unjustly seized from it.

The main protagonists in this drama were not pitted against each other in purely adversarial relationships. They sought to represent themselves as allies, stressing what they had in common with each other in order to further their own interests. They manipulated the knowledge, economic resources, kinship ties, and power available to them to that end. They drew upon particular cultural and axiological principles in order to make their respective cases. On the one hand, they did not hesitate to invoke moral sentiments and "common sense," grounded in cultural assumptions, in order to gain the support of various individuals and factions. They pointed out the precedence of kinship ties, compliance with collective labor obligations, and the exploitative nature of labor relations and community service built around the dynamics of merchant capital, rather than reciprocity and subsistence, in order to assert their rights to collective lands.

On the other hand, they also invoked novel cultural principles embedded in the reform legislation, such as the priority of nuclear family membership in determining property rights, the equation of invasions with illegal activity, and the supposed neutrality of the officials of "agrarian justice." In the course of combining these contradictory principles, they further fractured any semblance of ethnic or class unity among communities in the district.

The "arts of resistance," which arise hand in hand with domination, and so often serve as the foundation for subordinates and subalterns to fight back or protect themselves from the state or dominant classes (Scott 1990), proved, in Andean society, to be a double-edged sword. Andean highland peoples relied heavily upon compromise and negotiation as "adaptive resistance" (Stern 1982a) and as a means of building consensus to preserve a measure of relative autonomy from the state, bureaucratic officials, and the legal codes imposed by different regimes.

Compromise, used in this way, became the core of resistance and strength within Andean society, but it also provided the opportunity for individuals such as Tito to establish themselves in authorized and authoritative niches, thus leading to a gradual, progressive erosion of the very autonomy that Huanoquiteños had sought to maintain.

The case in Huanoquite presented all involved with new and darker lenses through which to view the future. A process of increasing class formation, encouraged unwittingly by the reform legislation itself, was giving rise to new kinds of local powers, which were able to alter existing hierarchies of status and prestige between communities.

The dispute meant far more to the participants involved than is immediately apparent from reading the documentation relevant to it. It was about territorial boundaries, about how different collectivities would represent themselves to each other, and, most fundamentally, about restructuring community identity and existing hierarchies of legitimate authority.

Characters such as Tito did not fit the existing categories of native political authority based on age, status, and the performance of communal obligations. The conclusion to the dispute reflected these stances. Built upon existing cultural principles of customary, colonial, and national law, these stances turned out not to be ephemeral; rather, they led to the emergence of new, but not entirely different, kinds of political figures. The legitimacy of such authorities was not endorsed unanimously across different sectors of the peasantry. Maska, in particular, showed a great capacity to fight against exclusion from the reform. In the end, however, it was Tito who succeeded in most adeptly fusing new and old principles for his benefit.

A year after the settlement, Tomás Chaparro Bejar, president of Maska, extended reconciliation to Tito. Chaparro, whom we encountered taking his community's titles to the Agrarian Reform Office in Cusco in Chapter 3, was representative of a new, younger generation of leaders who emerged during the reform. They had gained the respect of native inhabitants because of their knowledge of the bureaucracy, their refusal to succumb to corruption, their formal education, and their consumate skills in seeking compromises between communities and landlords, and among landlords and communities. Chaparro's father was a well-to-do peasant; his mother belonged to the Bejar clan of landowners. Chaparro worked all his land himself and conscientiously participated in collective labor obligations. In contrast to Tito, he exhibited humility and idealism, which he channeled into sustaining and strengthening collective resource management. He foresaw that an absolute resolution to conflicts such as those between IAC, Maska, Tito, and the state would deplete the energy and resources of community members and weaken their capacity to unite around constructive causes. Chaparro thus proposed to Maska's members that Tito be invited to become a member of Maska and put his truck back into service. Maska's members agreed, and Tito wisely accepted their invitation.

Tito had lost less than either Maska or IAC in the battle. He had retained over half his land; the amnesty Maska granted him allowed him to rely upon Maska's labor in exchange for grazing rights he granted it; and he earned additional profits with his truck service, upon which both Maska and IAC depended. Maska was still repaying its debt ten years later and had gained only half of what it had sought. IAC did not recover any of its land and had to contend with the hostility of Tito and Maska.

In reluctant, but strategic, recognition of Tito's power, Maska invited him to assume one of its most prestigious and traditional ritual offices, that of sponsor for the regional pilgrimage to the sanctuary of Qoyllur Rit'i, a festival that drew hundreds of thousands of people from the department of Cusco to the glacial peaks of Ausangate. Many Huanoquiteños went on the pilgrimage every year. Given Tito's interest in gaining legitimacy in the eyes of Maska's members, he had no choice but to accept the burden of sponsorship. He expended vast sums of money on elaborate costumes for the dancers, food, drink, firewood, musicians, and the use of his truck for the arduous journey. Maska's invitation and Tito's acceptance of it represented an acknowledgement by Huanoquiteños of Tito's personal power. However, it was also an aggressive effort by Maska to tap into his power and defuse it. In order to do so, however, it had to incorporate him into its existing authority structures.

Conclusion

The reform represents a crucial "frame" through which to view shifting political fields in the Andes. It provided the economic, political, and symbolic material for the construction of the qualitatively different political fields in which characters such as Rafael Tito, on the one hand, and Tomás Chaparro, on the other, came to occupy front stage as potent new economic and political forces. The reform created avenues for Huanoquiteños to assume local leadership roles, but the contrasts in the character and behavior of the leaders who emerged reproduced, to a large extent, the contradictions inherent in the reform law itself. After the reform, these new kinds of authority figures existed in a remarkable tension with one another, as well as in the eyes of the state and community members. They became the repository of old values and practices, but displayed an acute understanding of contemporary legal systems and bureaucracies. They also often took to an extreme traditional notions of labor, reciprocity, and kinship, but used them in order to take advantage of markets, the bureaucracy, and the acquisition and exchange of commodities and private property.

While few would argue that political factions, ethnic divisiveness, and economic stratification are not, as a matter of course, at work in rural highland communities, this chapter has tried to show the complex roots that generated these divisions and debates as the reform proceeded. Differences among inhabitants over ideal leadership qualities and the uneven application of the reform law led to great political instability in the district. They also resulted in deepening economic cleavages and differentiation within and between communities and cooperatives, setting the stage for Sendero's intervention in Huanoquite's political struggles.

Epilogue

Sendero Luminoso has focused its efforts in the countryside most intensely upon the destruction of entrepreneurial and ambiguous postreform authority figures like Tito. Even though members of Sendero in rural areas also occupy ambiguous intermediary positions—as teachers and merchants, for example—because of their ideological position, they regard themselves as facilitators of peasant demands. For them, Tito represents precisely the archetype of those who have used the peasants to advance themselves. From their point of view, Tito is exacerbating economic differentiation and political conflict among peasants, and, perhaps less obviously, serving functions that they themselves wish to serve.

Five years after "the end" of the litigation, Tito suddenly announced the sale of his property. Most Huanoquiteños conjecture that Sendero's threats upon his life accounted for his doing so. Tito himself claimed the sale was necessary because of debts he had accrued in yet another lawsuit, with a competing truck driver.

– 6 –

Changing Landscapes in Huanoquite
after the Reform

> In modern societies based on class—as opposed to traditional
> societies based on caste—identity and status are *achieved*
> rather than *ascribed*, *fluid* rather than *fixed*. Individuals are
> allowed—and therefore expected—to create their own identi-
> ties. Because class boundaries are less rigid than caste ones,
> individuals are expected to move across them as if there were
> no boundaries at all. The more society assumes the appear-
> ance of a *continuum* rather than of *discrete* classes, the greater
> is the gap between social mobility as a norm and its avail-
> ability in practice. . . . For each boundary that is blurred or
> ironed out, new ones arise or old ones are revived; for each
> new boundary across an old continuum, a distinction is abol-
> ished elsewhere. But the rules regulating the new boundaries
> which divide the world are more elusive than the old ones.
> They are made and re-made elsewhere, and they change too
> fast for people to keep up with them. . . . Social mobility and
> cultural change, then, are not to be seen as a transitional
> process from one identity to another, but as a permanent
> condition.
>
> Alessandro Portelli, *The Death of*
> *Luigi Trastulli and Other Stories*

A dynamic tension characterizes the relationship between the
formation of internal hierarchies and the construction of
collective cultural identity in the agrarian societies of the
Andean highlands.[1] In the two decades following the 1969 reform, a
new economic and political geography gradually emerged from the
wars of paper and words in Huanoquite. No longer composed primarily of peasants subordinated to the landed elite, rural society
experienced growing economic stratification. Existing political hierarchies based on age, gender, traditional knowledge, kinship ties, and
the successful performance of religious and communal obligations
were also affected by these processes of economic differentiation. As
hierarchies changed, inhabitants confronted the challenge of arriving
at new kinds of crosscutting ties able to create consensus among

households and communities. The economic transformations in household production and exchange thus directly affected political struggle in the highlands. This chapter examines a wide range of data obtained through formal interviews with peasants in Huanoquite in order to analyze the effects of reform policies upon economic and political activities in the district.

The reform structured the options available to peasants as they attempted to enhance their access to economic and political resources. Some Huanoquiteños showed more skill than others in drawing upon new resources and knowledge that became available to them after the reform. Even when peasants appeared to be of similar economic standing, inherited family privilege, kin ties, personality, age, the experiences of migration, and the meanings people attributed to community shaped the paths they pursued. Many reflected at length upon the negative consequences of the unequal distribution of land, striving to balance their loyalties to their communities with their aspirations to upward mobility.

Huanoquiteños engaged in various kinds of tenure arrangements in accordance with their developing relationships to the market economy and with the array of labor relations they were capable of mobilizing. Generational conflicts appeared in new forms and for new reasons. Arriving at the "correct" mix of private, usufructuary, and corporate (here referring to the collective land rights of both communities and cooperatives) tenure rights impelled community and cooperative members to question and experiment with tenure arrangements. For example, relationships between the cooperative of Inkaq Tiyanan de Tihuicte and the community of Maska became strained because of the differences that developed in their tenure arrangements and agricultural practices. Nevertheless, common problems and shared historical memories created crosscutting ties between the two organizations, tempering conflict and dissension. The often bitter conflicts that unfolded between Maska and Tihuicte were typical of the kinds of cleavages that appeared in highland regions throughout the Andes after the reform. Most obviously, the greater attention that reform officials devoted to cooperative organization and management marginalized communities. Community members recognized that, comparatively speaking, they had received less land and fewer state resources (such as credit and machinery) as a result of the reform than cooperative members. As James Howe has observed of Kuna cultural practice in Panama, in Huanoquite "agreement about what mattered underlay sharp disagreement about what should be done" (Howe 1991:33).

As Huanoquiteños gained greater freedom over the use of their own labor, they began to take advantage of a wider range of relationships in order to improve their economic and political standing. However, many of them found they were unable to comply with the divisive demands and expectations that resulted from their participation in these networks. In turn, their inability to do so prevented them from attaining the economic and political power they sought, sometimes as individuals, and sometimes as collectivities.

Peasants tapped into, and attempted to exploit, networks of individuals who composed communities, cooperatives, the district council, extended families, fictive kin networks, formal political parties, agrarian leagues, extension agencies, marketing links and intermediaries, and educational and religious institutions in order to gain greater political and economic leverage for themselves. Some peasants were able to meet these challenges better than others and eventually rose to positions of power in which they could represent other peasants in their demands. Ascent to such positions required skillful use of both exogenous and indigenous knowledge and bargaining strategies, and sufficient economic resources to devote the time and labor needed to forge consensus among increasingly differentiated households.

While individual peasants sought to use these channels to enhance their personal economic and political power, district councils, cooperatives, and especially communities made multiple labor demands upon all peasants. Many, overwhelmed by the amount of work required of them, refused to comply with the demands of their authorities. As a result, severe conflicts ensued among district, community, and cooperative authorities, and between leaders and their constituents, over the requisitioning of labor for public work projects.

Peasant participation in formal political arenas was a relatively new phenomenon. It had not substantially increased political power for the district as a whole, but it had become an important mechanism used by particular individuals to enhance their status and influence. The proliferation of political positions at the district level, counterposed to the relative lack of power available to local authorities, was reflected in the failure of local leaders to exert substantial leverage on the regional bureaucracy to meet local demands. In turn, this paradox made Huanoquiteños more aware of their subordinate position within the national society despite the passage of the reform.

Cooperative and Community in Comparative Perspective
Inkaq Tiyanan de Tihuicte

> There are conflicts between the cooperative and community. The cooperative authorities are corrupt. People don't want to work. We don't have the machinery we need. Relationships between the cooperative and community are strained. There is disunity. The community have always hated us. They don't work and they are lazy.
>
> Arístedes García, co-op member and tractor driver

> There is little organization. A few cooperative members work community lands. . . . Most of the community's herd is grazing on cooperative land.
>
> Santiago Cruz, agronomist and honorary co-op member

> With the agrarian reform, now we are a community. The hacendados worked well, but the community works even better. Now the hacendados can't herd us. We work for ourselves.
>
> Gerardo Pérez, community member

Although community and cooperative members alike in Huanoquite were mostly delighted that the hacendados no longer ruled the roost, severe conflicts came to characterize relationships between cooperatives and communities. Long after the reform, many of these conflicts would be astutely used by Sendero in its efforts to establish itself in the countryside. Below, I discuss the origins of some of the most salient of these local conflicts and their far-reaching consequences in the light of Peru's growing political instability.

In 1968, the Urioste family, a group of absentee landowners, leased Tihuicte, their estate of approximately 800 hectares, to the Agrarian Research and Promotion Service (SIPA), a branch of the Ministry of Agriculture, as an agricultural experiment station.[2] Tihuicte's topography was unusual for the highlands. The result geologically of a tectonic uplift, it consisted of a great plateau and had ample irrigation water. Under SIPA's direction, Tihuicte flourished. Extension agents introduced chemical fertilizer, insecticide, and new potato varieties on a grand scale. Rape (*Brassica napus*), a cultigen entirely new to the highlands, was planted with successful results. The oil was extracted from the seed and exported. Its leaves served as feed for hogs and sheep. The enterprise relied upon permanent workers from the estate and paid them a wage. It also periodically used temporary labor of up to 400 workers from neighboring communities during peak labor times. Often the workers were paid in agricultural products rather than cash, or in a combination of the two. In turn, the workers experimented with new potato and seed varieties they received in exchange for their labor and also tried out on their own land some of the new agricultural techniques they saw being used on Tihuicte.

SIPA's control of Tihuicte signaled the advent of agricultural production and commerce on a grand scale by and for the members of Tihuicte alone. For many of the members, SIPA revolutionized the understanding of farming that they had originally acquired from working with their families. In the words of Mayor Fortunato Eguilúz, a co-op member: "Working we lived, my uncles, my brothers. Little by little, working we learned. Also, agronomists from the Ministry of Agriculture, from SIPA, taught us how to use insecticide, spread chemical fertilizer, sow. They introduced new potatoes: *compis, mariva, renacimiento, yungay.*" A simple story told to me more than once by people who were not members of Tihuicte captured how they perceived the transformations in production and social relations that were occurring on Tihuicte: "A poor man from the community of Toctohuaylla traveled to Tihuicte to trade his eggs for a few potatoes. No one would trade with him."

Another story was labeled "the great potato burning." The first version was told to me by a member of Maska: "One year, an enormous number of potatoes were burned on Tihuicte. We did not understand why they burned them. Maybe they had too many but did not want to share them." A few peasants from Maska said that Tihuicte burned the potatoes because they were diseased and would have contaminated the rest of the harvest. One hacendado commented that the destruction of Tihuicte's tractor years later had been "God's revenge," because "the potatoes had been burned in the midst of so many poor people." She added that her son had told her "SIPA burned the potatoes because otherwise they would have glutted the market and the price would have been too low."

Landed estate owners made such comments because they felt threatened by the growing economic power of cooperative members, who were nightmarishly coming to resemble the landed elite more and more closely. To draw attention to the fundamental differences between landowners and Quechua peasants, the rhetoric of the "vecinos" had repeatedly denigrated the "Indians" as lazy. Now, quite suddenly, "Indians" were showing every sign of being hardworking, capable of capital accumulation, and of pursuing the logic of supply and demand on the market. The differences between Indians and vecinos were not only blurring; at least some among the former threatened to replace the latter.

Peasants excluded from SIPA's operation made such comments for other, but not entirely different, reasons. *Envidia*—jealousy and resentment—was their underlying motive. They too wanted the resources, credit, and capital to be able to do what workers on Tihuicte were doing. At the same time, they were suspicious of the metamorphosis taking place before their eyes as peasants turned into landowners and began to value quantity and impersonal market exchange more than small-scale barter and the intimacy of social relations that accompanied the latter. During the harvest, three or four commercial lorries per day made the long journey to Huanoquite for the express purpose of buying Tihuicte's potatoes.

SIPA's control of Tihuicte ended with the passage of the 1969 reform legislation and the active efforts of permanent workers to transform Tihuicte into a cooperative. It was ideal terrain for a cooperative, and the Velasco regime restructured it into a CAP in 1974. While basically the same membership existed, workers no longer regarded themselves as eternal tenants or employees, but rather as future owners of the enterprise. Under SIPA, labor discipline had been strictly enforced, and workers could be fired and replaced at will by SIPA extension agents. Now that workers were officially cooperative members, they no longer feared losing their jobs. They felt that the dignity of their ancestors had been restored to them. In the words of Basilio Roque:

They gave us this, the Ministry of Agriculture, to create a cooperative. We were great, trucks, machinery. The hacendados had exploited all the *chakareros* [field workers]. Like ranchers, they had herded us, making us work. The hacendados wanted their desires satisfied without ever working.

In the administrative office of the co-op, *socios* (as co-op members referred to themselves) hung a painting of Tupac Amaru, the eighteenth-century Indian resistance leader, who had served as an inspiration for the Cusco departmental agrarian league, Federación Agraria Revolucionaria Tupac Amaru (FARTAC). They also hung a painting of a prototypical Inca and an emblem emblazoned with the new name they gave to Tihuicte to reflect the prestige of its members' Inca roots, "Inkaq Tiyanan de Tihuicte" (The Inca Throne of Tihuicte). An odd resemblance began emerging between socios as the new landed elite and socios as Incas. In throwing off the yoke of the hacendados and regaining a measure of autonomy over their land and labor, socios came to consider themselves members of a very different kind of state than that to which they had previously belonged. For them, it was the dawning of a new age. At the same time, the state was paying socios far greater attention and offering them far more resources in the form of credit and purchasing power than it was according communities. It is not surprising that comuneros (as community members called themselves) came to perceive the socios as the nouveau landed elite.

The problems that accompanied Tihuicte's evolution from a landed estate to a CAP resembled those experienced by many other estates-turned-cooperatives established during the reform. Government administrators brought in to assist members initially in running their new enterprise were guilty of corruption and mismanagement. Socios preferred to farm the majority of their lands on a household rather than collective basis. SIPA had already parcelized some of Tihuicte's lands into household lots, and when it became a CAP, each member was given at least one hectare of the more hilly, unirrigated land to work on a household basis.

In 1982, members of Sendero Luminoso blew up Tihuicte's tractor.[3] The CAP went into an economic downspin. With bankruptcy looming, the Inca symbols Tihuicte had adopted began to lose their inspirational significance for socios.[4] While the socios struggled with their predicament, Maska's *comuneros* did not hesitate to take advantage of it. Tihuicte had possessed considerable capital in the form of trucks, tractors, harvesters, and threshers; a large amount of pastureland, which it rented to comuneros; forests of eucalyptus trees; and agricultural lands planted in maize, wheat, and potatoes, which were among the most important highland commercial crops. The rapid succession of disasters the CAP suffered—the total breakdown of its truck, the discovery of corruption on the part of Ministry of Agriculture administrators and accountants, the inability of the CAP to accumulate dividends to distribute to socios, and the dynamiting of its tractor—eventually demoralized the socios. They failed to participate in cooperative labor tasks and let much of the CAP's land lie fallow. Many of them gradually retreated into producing only for purposes of subsistence.

The problems of Tihuicte's financial management and the physical destruction of its tractor were compounded by economic differentiation among socios, notwithstanding their assertion that "all of us are equal." The distribution of land among households was skewed, ranging from 2.5 to 25.25 *topus* (3 topus equal approximately 1 hectare).[5] Socios with expertise in particular areas—making budgets, handling and repairing machinery, acquiring marketing knowledge and contacts, and wielding political clout—held higher status and received additional lands in usufruct in exchange for sharing their skills and resources.

Generational conflicts also emerged. Tihuicte's land was limited, and older and younger socios had different ideas about how it should be farmed. The optimistic ideals of "growth" and "equality" voiced by many Huanoquiteños at the inception of the reform were offset by the fact that older socios who had more land and had contributed "more service" to the co-op preferred to farm "according to their own criteria" (that is, they did not feel compelled to produce much more than they needed for subsistence). Younger socios, by contrast, with less land, more obligations, and more ambition, sought to produce a surplus to sell on the market.

The use of tractors rather than plows, and mechanical harvesters, threshers, and trucks rather than human and horse power, alarmed older members. The latter relied heavily upon drinking and ritual libations to the earth to maintain the proper circulation and balance of energy (*sami*) between natural, human, and supernatural forces. Younger members, more interested in increasing production and taking advantage of the market, and also more sensitive to discrimination against Indians who drank, attempted to abandon drinking rituals. Many became Evangelicals. (See pp. 151–53 below for discussion of why many Huanoquiteños converted to Evangelical Protestantism.) They also turned to sports, particularly soccer tournaments, as a valid excuse for retiring from co-op gatherings at which heavy drinking was the norm. Soccer teams proliferated in Huanoquite after the reform among both communities and cooperatives. They became an alternative form of political and social organization that, almost de facto, excluded older men, while simultaneously playfully replicating the tensions and conflicts between different groups in the district.

The older men's alarm at the technological and economic changes they were witnessing was not entirely misplaced. Tihuicte encountered serious environmental problems as a result of the overuse of fertilizer. Productivity diminished, and many socios talked about "how worn out" the soil had become. One deeply religious Evangelical commented that chemical fertilizer had to be applied to Tihuicte's soils to produce, but that "all the plagues would come and the land would not produce as before. It needed to rest." Socios responded variously to the long-term destructive effect of chemical fertilizers upon productivity. The younger ones felt that the only reasonable solution was to purchase another tractor. The older ones believed that the soil simply had to rest. In the meantime, without a tractor, the land lay fallow, and kikuyu grass, which has relatively poor nutritious value for livestock (see Daubenmire 1972), rapidly began to overtake the plateau, forcing socios into alliances with comuneros in order to gain access to community pasturelands in the puna.

After the succession of disasters Tihuicte suffered, Maska proposed that Tihuicte be dissolved and incorporated into the community. Together, they would then proceed to repay Tihuicte's debt. Tihuicte's socios rejected the proposal outright. At that point, socios and comuneros began to use the word "invade" rather than "repossess" or "reclaim" to describe the action Maska had in mind. In the words of Jesús Castillo, a socio, "when they are drunk, the comuneros say bad things about the socios: 'We want to invade their land. They have abandoned their lands.' " The people of Maska were well aware that Tihuicte had not illegally seized community lands. Rather, they felt that Tihuicte's rights to the lands should be rescinded because socios were not working the land. Younger comuneros were most vocal about invading co-op lands and had formed a committee for that purpose.

Maska

The hacendados took from the community before. Now, the community has taken from the hacendados. It's good that they have. The hacendados hid the titles to the community land. I was helping Maska get recognized. Now the titles have reappeared.
Braulio Mora, community member

With potatoes, we have changed. We work with credit. We have lawsuits. We've taken land from Tito. I spent ten days in jail. Before we were lazy, before the road arrived. We got *compis* potato seed from SIPA.
Silvestre Alvarez, community member and catechist

There's animosity between the cooperative and community; resentment, because the community doesn't want to give the cooperative land in the puna.
Felipe Herrera, co-op member

The structure of tenure rights within the community differed from that of the cooperative. Once they reached the age of eighteen and had demonstrated their commitment to the community by regularly attending communal labor projects, men were given community membership and some lands held in usufruct. Each member began with a minimum of 1.5 topus but received differing amounts of land "according to his ability to till it." This criterion discriminated against younger comuneros and thus perpetuated, and contributed to, increased differentiation among households. Comuneros held from .5 to 23 topus in usufruct, the average holding being 7 topus. The total amount of land of all kinds that each member held ranged from 1.5 to 35 topus—that is, from a little over a third of a hectare up to almost twelve hectares. The ideal espoused by comuneros—that community lands would be redistributed annually to households "according to their labor capacity"—masked the long-term retention of lands by households, a practice that was pre-Columbian in origin and had been repeatedly misunderstood by Spanish colonial administrators and reform officials. In reality, the annual redistribution of land occurred only in the case of migration, death, or as compensation to officeholders who had performed additional duties for the community. Each year, lands were allocated first to the communal fund, then to the treasurer, and then to the president; finally, some adjustments were made among individual comuneros.

Younger and poorer members did not have the labor power older and wealthier members had at their disposal. To be older did not *necessarily* mean one had access to more labor, but it did mean that one's extended family was usually larger; older men had usually passed through several festival sponsorships that had led to additional permanent reciprocal obligations. They had to meet these obligations but could also demand like services in the future. Also, older members tended to have accumulated more private land through inheritance, giving them greater access to the market, higher status, and the ability to take more risks. Although members did not progressively purchase more land as they grew older, the domestic cycle of inheritance meant that comuneros under the age of 30 generally had no inherited private land, while older ones had from .5 to 9 topus.

On community lands, crop rotations and fallow periods meant that although in general land-tenure patterns might remain the same for households and the community as a whole, the crops they cultivated would vary, and they would not cultivate the same piece of land continuously.[6] Cooperative members sowed the same land year after year without a fallow period, alternating early potatoes, corn, and wheat. Fallow periods had once been observed, permitting cooperative lands to recuperate, but the interest in marketing agricultural surplus of hacendados, then of SIPA, and finally of the socios themselves had led to their omission. A measure of collective control remained, however, since all socios sowed the fields they held in usufruct in the same crop within a single sector each agricultural season.

Maska's members pressed one another to maintain the customary law of communal control over grazing lands. During the rainy season, most community livestock remained in the puna, but during the dry season and great potato harvest, comuneros brought their livestock down to the cooperative's pampa and to the fields on its flanks. Most of the lands sloping down from the pampa had either been purchased or inherited by comuneros or were owned by the Catholic Church, but rented by community and cooperative members. There, livestock grazed on the stalks that remained in fields after the harvest. However, since scheduling was not perfectly coordinated, tension and pressure built up to keep livestock out of still unharvested fields. Complaints of damage done to fields by livestock appear repeatedly in district council, community, and cooperative records. The district council had primary responsibility for fining farmers whose livestock wandered loose or invaded fields.

Maska's members had private properties that sometimes dated back to the colonial period. Community members had purchased some of these lands from large landowners. The church had ceded others that lay sodalities (*cofradías*), and then individual festival sponsors, rented in perpetuity. By 1984, the lay sodalities had vanished and been replaced by individual festival sponsorship.

Land inheritance practices differed among households. Some divided their land and property equally among their children. Others reserved the house for that male (usually the youngest son) who had remained at home to take care of his aging parents. Residence of married children varied. It was biased virilocally in the general vicinity of the husband's family. Life cycles made inheritance ambiguous (see Lambert 1977). Widows returned to live with their aging parents. If the youngest son still resided at his parents' home, conflict between siblings was likely to ensue. Some households divided their land and property when their children married; others did so at the death of the parents. Parents took into account three principal factors in distributing their land and property to their children: the residence of the children; their willingness to contribute labor to their parents; and the initial wealth of the parents. If a family were "fat" in land and animals, parents could provide children with a subsistence base and the seeds of reciprocity by gradually turning over resources to them, first shortly after a child's birth, then ceremonially at baptism and the hair-cutting ceremony, and again at the child's marriage.

The practice of partible inheritance caused the integrated land base of a family to shrink, and reunification of parcels was rare. Other factors entered into it, but this form of inheritance, disparaged because of the way it breaks up land into smaller and smaller plots (*minifundios*), also had a regenerative dimension, in that younger farmers quickly began to participate in reciprocal labor exchanges. Moreover, as genealogical maps spread horizontally through affinal ties, so did the links between different and disparate plots that had once belonged to a single family. (That is, although the same family might not have access to its original land base, children might through intermarriage once again be able to amass a similar amount of land.)

Partible inheritance did not, however, obviate intergenerational conflicts between the aged, who sought security, and young people seeking autonomy, marriage, and more property. It remained, instead, a painful source of intergenerational tension. The old refused to give up their lands in order to retain their children's labor, and their children sought land and independence from their parents to win a wife or husband, to establish their own families, and, in the case of males, to obtain formal membership of the community as adults. The system also generated conflicts among siblings wishing to migrate in search of employment opportunities elsewhere. One of them usually had to stay at home or return, since family land without an heir would eventually be sold or reincorporated into the community.

Although opportunity factors greatly determined the decision to migrate, many recognized that the land base in their community underwent its own cycle of expansion and contraction. Migrants therefore returned to their communities when they knew they would be able to obtain sufficient land, or at least have a better chance of doing so. While demographic pressures pushed people to migrate, the availability of cash occasionally permitted migrants to return and purchase land to expand their subsistence base.

Renting and Sharecropping

Land and labor were intimately intertwined in determining tenure patterns and social relations among comuneros, socios, and those members of the landed elite who remained after the reform. The land market in Huanoquite was small, albeit growing, and land sales were uncommon. Even unproductive private lands were regarded as a safeguard against risk. Sharecropping was the preferred method of acquiring additional land or income. Maska's members occasionally rented land. Some rented private land in exchange for labor they performed for the owner. The labor might include herding livestock, helping to construct a house, or assisting in the fields. Some private landowners, particularly members of the landed elite, had land within the village that they did not use, which community or cooperative members were occasionally able to rent for cash.

A far greater number of Maska's members relied upon sharecropping arrangements. They differed in their reasons for doing so. Structurally, sharecropping relations were not unlike the colonial practice of *yanaconaje*, in which serfs (*yanakunas*) performed inordinate labor in exchange for small pieces of land (see Matos Mar 1976; Matos Mar and Fuenzalida 1976:15–52). The practice had developed as a way to avoid paying tribute, but it persisted, particularly in the case of peasants who were not members of communities or cooperatives, or who held little corporate land in usufruct. For some, sharecropping was a way to make ends meet. For many more, it had become a major and enduring means of obtaining maize and wheat lands to which they otherwise had no access.

Sharecropping contracts varied from more or less equal partnerships to highly asymmetrical ones. Peasants entered into them for different reasons. They contributed most or all production factors except the land. Poorer sharecroppers did not apply chemical fertilizer to the fields, because they bore its entire cost and reaped only half the benefits, the harvest being split evenly between sharecropper and owner.[7] Landowners had various reasons for encouraging these contracts. If they were members of the landed elite, their dependence upon an unreliable temporary labor force often forced them into sharecropping arrangements.

It has been argued that such sharecropping contracts should be understood as a preferred method of appropriating surplus labor in the following contexts: (1) where class relations are such that decisions concerning the nature of the contract lie with landowners, but where the costs of supervising production are potentially large; (2) where the tenant is in a position to have a decisive influence upon the contract, and where the tenant is also insufficiently endowed with resources to allow him to discount income variance as a decision variable; (3) in contexts where class relations are less obviously determined and both landlords and tenants are existing close to the margin of survival (see Pearce 1983:65). These contexts indeed existed in Huanoquite and help to explain the predominance of sharecropping. Nationally, highland landlords and peasants were marginalized. At the same time, the high demand for labor meant that landlords were not in a position to command or supervise it easily. Finally, although some landlords had surplus land, they might not have the kind of land they needed for purposes of subsistence. For example, Tihuicte's members were willing to establish sharecropping arrangements, exchanging some of their land for labor and capital from members of other communities. Maska's members specifically wanted access to more maize and wheat lands, which they could obtain from various private landlords and from the cooperative. They could sell maize and wheat for a surplus. With maize, they could also prepare beer (chicha) to consolidate reciprocal labor contracts, and with wheat they could bake bread for purposes of sale or personal consumption.

Most of the members of the landed elite, although they used wage labor, depended heavily upon sharecropping arrangements, because they could not obtain labor otherwise. While cooperative and community members had many resources to share—family ties, labor, pasture, and draft animals—private landowners, even when they did have some of these resources, shared them only reluctantly, since to do so was to admit to a further reduction in their power and status. Where the landed elite rejected sharecropping, they were often at a frantic loss for labor, especially at peak labor times.

One striking example of this was the case of a woman, an outsider, who had bought a piece of land in Huanoquite from another private landowner. In desperation, she doubled the going wage, inciting a backlash from other private landowners, who rapidly and successfully exerted pressure on peasants to persuade them not to work on her land. One can see here how local members of the landed elite manipulated their clientelist and fictive kin ties by invoking boundaries between "insiders" and "outsiders" in order to prevent peasants from taking advantage of the higher wages offered by this new kind of entrepreneurial landowner from the outside.[8]

Both cooperative and community members turned down wage-labor offers for several reasons: the declining value of Peru's currency—money was fast becoming worthless—meant that farmers preferred goods or labor rather than cash in exchanges; the lack of embedded reciprocal obligations in a wage-labor relationship (no debt remained); the greater degree of exploitation in wage-labor relations; and the habit of setting wages without allowing for exceptional circumstances or the closeness of kinship ties.

Almost all peasants preferred to work for others on the basis of *ayni*—labor exchange, but to obtain labor for their own fields on the basis of *jornal*—wage labor: "I prefer to work with ayni because wages [*jornal*] aren't even enough to buy bread, but I prefer to pay people and not use ayni in my fields because it's hard to get eight or ten people for ayni. One loses time. With jornal the work advances" (community member Lucio Callañaupa). Thus, a perpetual tension existed in meeting labor demands across households. Peasants could sell or consume the products they received through sharecropping. In contrast, the wages they received rarely covered the cost of their labor. In theory, they could use their wage earnings to obtain labor in the future for their own fields, but few preferred this method of payment.

Poorer and younger community members, especially those who had obtained loans from credit agencies at low interest rates, relied upon sharecropping in order to obtain all the marketable harvest they needed to repay their loans. In contrast, wealthier peasants turned to sharecropping less out of need than out of a desire to expand their options.

Tenuous Ties

Despite the animosity that had grown between them since the reform, Tihuicte and Maska depended upon each other. The reform had created greater opportunities for community and cooperative members alike to participate in the market and expand both their farming and their off-farm enterprises. Maska often provided part-time labor to Tihuicte or lent the co-op draft animals for plowing and threshing[9] in return for access to Tihuicte's maize and wheat lands. The ties between the community and cooperative were fragile, however. Angered by the reform's failure to arrive at an equitable distribution of land between cooperative and community, and emboldened by the sight of fallow co-op lands after the destruction of Tihuicte's tractor, members of Maska plotted a takeover of the co-op.

Maska and Tihuicte controlled almost the same average amount of land. Maska's comuneros had an average of 4.06 topus, and cooperative members had about 3.19 topus apiece. The location and tenure of their lands differed markedly though. The most glaring disparity in landholding patterns between Tihuicte and Maska was that in addition to the lands each corporate entity distributed in usufruct to its members, Tihuicte had about 200 hectares of collective land, whereas Maska had approximately ten hectares and a communal flock of 22 sheep.[10] Therein lay the reason for the extreme tension between Tihuicte and Maska.

Seventy-five percent of co-op members' land formally belonged to Tihuicte, whereas only 57 percent of community members' land formally belonged to Maska. In addition to relying upon the usufruct of community land, Maska's comuneros thus held more of their land through sharecropping, rental, purchase, and inheritance. Both community and cooperative members rented and had inherited about the same amount of land. However, comuneros had bought an average of 13 percent of their land and had made sharecropping arrangements for 16 percent, whereas Tihuicte's members had only bought 3 percent of their land and controlled only 7 percent of it through sharecropping contracts.

Another salient difference between community and cooperative was that the proportions of irrigated and unirrigated land they controlled mirrored each other. Sixty-eight percent of Tihuicte's land was irrigated, in contrast to only 36 percent of Maska's. The crop complexes of cooperative members also differed from those of community members, given where their lands were located and their access to irrigation water. Cooperative members farmed 20 percent of their land in wheat, 20 percent in potatoes, 39 percent in maize, 13 percent in barley, 3 percent in early potatoes, 1 percent in broad beans (*Vicia faba*), and 3 percent in *tarwi* (*Lupinus mutabilis*, a legume high in nitrates) and various tubers. Maska's comuneros, in contrast, planted 17 percent of their land in wheat, 34 percent in potatoes, 18 percent in maize, 19 percent in barley, 5 percent in early potatoes, 3 percent in broad beans, and 3 percent in tarwi and various tubers.

If we assume that socios and comuneros held shared conceptions of the optimal composition of landholdings in order to cover their subsistence needs, maximize their ability to participate in the market economy, and spread their risks as evenly as possible, we may conclude that pragmatic reasons existed for socios and comuneros to bury their differences and attempt to cooperate.

Socios, for example, wanted more potato-growing lands; comuneros sought more irrigated maize and wheat lands; and socios, although they farmed in a less risky microenvironment, could not spread their risks as evenly as could comuneros. Indeed, socios actively tried to obtain community puna lands to grow potatoes, which they considered "the mainstay of nutrition." Potatoes were an excellent, although risky and labor-intensive, commercial crop. In similar fashion, comuneros sought cooperative lands for pasture and to cultivate more maize. Maska's authorities made a formal request to the cooperative for maize land in 1983, specifically stating that they wanted to grow more maize in order to be able to offer community members maize beer during community labor projects.[11] The cooperative granted them the land, and, in exchange, the community turned over some of its potato land in the puna to Tihuicte.

Two important and related factors continued both to create tension between cooperative and community members and to control conflict between them. The first was labor supply and demand. Tihuicte's labor needs led its members into alliances with Maska. While comuneros were in a subordinate position in sharecropping arrangements with Tihuicte's socios, the former continued to use these arrangements to gain control over maize, wheat, early potato, and pasture lands. Many cooperative members had close relatives who belonged to the community. Often they were brothers. The artificial boundaries between Tihuicte and Maska partially dissolved when relatives informally recreated sounder ecological control over multiple production zones that was to their mutual benefit. Many peasants thought that tenure regimes should be restructured so that their access to land would range from the valley bottoms to the high pastures of the puna. In the eyes of the state, this form of tenure was not conducive to the economies of scale required by the market. Nevertheless, it made peasants more self-sufficient outside the market and, in the longer term, provided them with greater stability, given the unpredictability of market prices and the natural risks peasants encountered in farming in such a harsh environment.

The Meanings of Work

Cooperative and community members continued to draw upon a shared repertoire of mechanisms to offset the forms of inequality that began to structure the organization of production after the reform. However, the needs of peasants, especially of poorer ones, perpetuated inequalities. Huanoquite's peasants also found it difficult to escape their long history of working primarily for the landed elite.

Economic practicality and pragmatic necessity alone did not determine peasant forms of land tenure and labor practices after the reform. Ideas about work also informed these relationships. One peasant told me starkly of his experiences with the landed elite, and how Huanoquite's peasants "had cowered before the hacendados, completely frightened." In almost the same breath, however, he acknowledged, "the hacendados taught me to work. They woke me up. Even though they whipped me, I learned."

Peasants belonging to both the community and cooperative spoke often of "a lack of labor." When I queried them further, they explained that they did not mean there was an absolute shortage of labor, but rather that they were accustomed to being ordered around. Unless told what to do, they did nothing. They did not make these comments about themselves but rather directed them at other peasants, particularly cooperative members. Some peasants discovered that they could be more successful if they ordered their companion laborers as the hacendados had ordered their peons.

Here, then, the dynamics of manipulation, subordination, and deference came into play. Many peasants in Huanoquite had fought against the hacendados and their abusive behavior, and they had won some of their battles. At the same time, faced with a recent autonomy that was neither complete nor secure, most peasants found it difficult to organize their own labor and resources. They also confronted a frustrating lack of support from the government when they tried to market their products at decent prices. The lack of good roads and the government policy of subsidizing the cost of imported food for the cities contributed to peasant decisions not to be particularly enterprising. These policies simply reinforced peasant beliefs that the national society and the government did not recognize the value of agricultural labor.

Household Differentiation

Any single path model or factor analysis would obscure the diversity of the economic and political strategies that Huanoquiteños elaborated in their production and exchange patterns after the reform. It is nonetheless possible to discern certain clusters and patterns in the association of variables that permitted some households to achieve a higher standard of living, as well as a higher status within the district. These patterned production and exchange strategies depended upon the specific relationships between household land base and other variables such as age, political status, credit, migration patterns, and participation in the market. The patterns I discerned were based upon an analysis of interviews I held with 30 heads of households from the community of Maska and the cooperative of Inkaq Tiyanan de Tihuicte.[12] Most important, these data demonstrated that, although it was not a unidirectional determinant, peasants had to have at least a certain amount of land in order to improve their political and economic standing.[13]

Land-wealthy households had greater access to credit, engaged in more complementary economic activities, grew more different kinds of crops, held more corporate land, and, with the exception of sharecropping contracts, also held more land in other kinds of tenure arrangements. They also owned more livestock, migrated less, and were less likely to turn to religious faiths other than Catholicism.

Despite a reliance of all households upon some corporate holdings, as some households succeeded in gaining access to more of the economic and cultural resources mentioned above, they were able to increased their landholdings, thus encouraging a dramatic process of economic differentiation.

In order to make the most of their economic opportunities and relax some of the constraints they were experiencing, all households, land-poor or not, established multiple strategies, which differed markedly from one another. For example, land-poor households improved their opportunities by channeling their energies into controlling commercial crops on irrigated land and by migrating outside the district. In addition, peasants turned to new kinds of noneconomic activities that indirectly had a significant impact upon their economic and political standing within the district. Poorer farmers were most likely to turn to Evangelicism, which gave them an ethical rationale for improving their farming, staved off demoralization, and tempered generational conflicts. Huanoquiteños also began to reevaluate participation in the existing civil-religious hierarchy as the chief way of earning respect in the district.

The Civil-Religious Hierarchy

Huanoquite's formal political structure was intertwined with its fiesta hierarchy, the *cargo* system. The sponsorship of fiestas was a colonial introduction that Huanoquiteños had embraced and transformed, coordinating their devotion to saints with their agricultural-ritual calendar. They mingled the personality traits of saints with indigenous deities and built churches upon indigenous sacred sites.[14] Ascendance through the colonially imposed political hierarchy, itself a superimposition upon indigenous authority structures, had been synchronized with ascendance through the religious hierarchy. Many scholars (see, for example, Earls 1973; Fuenzalida 1976:260; Isbell 1978) have pointed to the persistence of the intertwined civil-religious hierarchy, in which inhabitants, as they grew older, alternately ascended the ladder rungs of political office and fiesta sponsorship in postcolonial rural society.

José María Arguedas (1964:268–69) has observed that inhabitants garnered prestige from assuming fiesta sponsorship. John Earls (1973: 401) has argued that the hierarchy of cargos, or burden of sponsorship, corresponded to age grades, and that as one ascended the hierarchy, one acquired greater spiritual power. César Fonseca (1977:72–75), in contrast, sees the cargo system primarily as a politico-economic

mechanism in which the power and prestige of already-wealthy peasants were validated, since although surplus was redistributed on
fiesta occasions, even more was extracted from poorer peasants.
Frank Cancian (1965) has taken a similar position, arguing that the
civil-religious hierarchy in Mesoamerica did not act as a leveling
mechanism.

Finally, Roger Rasnake (1988) has observed that since they had to
interact increasingly with state bureaucracies, Bolivian Indian communities deliberately unraveled the intertwined civil-religious hierarchy, dividing functions permanently between ritual specialists
who served as repositories of sacred knowledge and individuals who
served as civil servants. In so doing, he argues, communities have
been better able to protect their ethnic autonomy.

Although occupying political office and assuming sponsorship of
fiestas continued to be important means for Huanoquiteños to acquire power at the local level, a number of other ways to accumulate
power appeared after the reform. Chapter 8 examines Huanoquiteños' engagement in politics at the regional and national levels. The
focus here is narrower and considers only peasant participation in the
civil-religious hierarchy and its significance for coordinating collective action within communities, cooperatives, and the district as a
whole. Local, regional, and national spheres of power necessarily
interacted with one another—peasants who accrued local economic
and political power played roles in district and regional politics, and
in both spheres, the personal accumulation of power did not necessarily coincide with the legitimate exercise of authority.

Prior to the 1969 reform, the majority of political positions, particularly at the district and prefectural levels, had been occupied
mainly by members of the landed elite, who frequently remained in
them for more than a decade. By 1940, positions at the prefectural
level had occasionally been occupied by peasants. Peasants also
sometimes held lower-level district council office, but only in 1980
did a peasant come to hold the position of district mayor.

Within communities and ayllus, peasants had always held positions of authority, and that authority had derived from their ascribed
and achieved status. They were not elected to office. Once communities achieved formal recognition as a result of the 1969 reform
legislation, they were required to elect their officers. The same was
true of workers on landed estates following their formation into
cooperatives. The proliferation of formal political positions within
communities and cooperatives provided Huanoquiteños with the
means to exert greater control over local politics. At the same time,

the sheer number of offices often succeeded in diffusing political power and inciting factionalism, while creating a semblance of democracy actively at work. The state's efforts to appease local demands for more power took the form of providing positions for many minor officeholders, who were often at odds with one another. Nevertheless, the very existence of these offices created a forum, for through them inhabitants could discuss issues important to them, experiment with new ways of reaching consensus among a large number of people, and attempt to obtain services and monies for their communities from the government.

Women did not hold political office and were deeply and openly ambivalent about their husbands' occupying such positions. If elected to office, they worried, their husbands might not fulfill their household obligations. As more men tended to migrate and assume political office, women had to take on more agricultural and domestic labor responsibilities.

The amount of land male heads of household held directly correlated with the number of political offices they occupied. Those who controlled more land came to occupy a wider range and number of political offices. Two contradictory trends affected election to political office. Individuals occupying more political positions and holding more land tended to be older. But another trend was becoming apparent. Education was beginning to supersede age in determining who would hold political office. The most recent set of officeholders were far younger and better educated than previous authorities. A reciprocal relationship thus existed between high economic and political status, with the one encouraging the other.

Individuals who held political office had far less time to devote to their own agricultural activities. They unanimously complained that the members of their collectivities did not assist them sufficiently in their personal household labor obligations. Community and cooperative members alike expressed reluctance to volunteer their labor to their elected officials, however, since they felt the latter were unable to reciprocate much. Although they spent inordinate amounts of time and money struggling with the bureaucracy in Cusco, officeholders more often than not returned empty-handed.

The officeholders complained in turn that if they embarked upon improvements on their own houses or in their agriculture, they were accused of embezzling funds or stealing supplies that had been set aside for community or cooperative projects. In fact, their constituents had good reason to be wary of such improvements to their personal property, since after the reform, corruption and individual aggrandizement at every level of local government had become a major problem. The constant gossip and criticism that circulated about officeholders and their behavior thus partly served as informal safeguards to prevent these probabilities from becoming reality.

One domain in which local elected officials could exert control was in scheduling collective labor projects for sowing, harvesting, and cleaning irrigation systems. Failure to schedule these properly could result in a poor harvest and loss of respect and support from their constituents. Conforming to the agricultural calendar and predicting climatic changes remained essential for ensuring the legitimacy of officeholders. The ability to bring together a sufficient labor force for community or cooperative projects was also a sign of the legitimacy of authority and rested, not only upon persuasion, but also upon age and skill in rallying allies to call upon all heads of household for labor corveés.

In postreform Huanoquite, inhabitants no longer alternately ascended the rungs of the civil and religious hierarchy.[15] Although fiestas inspired devotion and encouraged a sense of collective affiliation and interaction, they had become less important as a mechanism for asserting, exercising, and accumulating economic and political power.

Conversations with people revealed that the shift away from acquiring and expressing political status through participation in the civil-religious hierarchy was the result of numerous factors. Younger men confided that they no longer believed that "ancient" religious rites actually fulfilled the function of assuring agricultural productivity or warding off natural disaster. Nevertheless, they acknowledged that they often participated in the system in a nominal fashion because of pressure from older inhabitants who believed that these rites were essential to their agricultural providence. They were less willing, however, to devote the kind of energy and capital elders had invested in their festival sponsorships.

Vecinos, comuneros, and socios alike agreed that the cargo system had declined in importance. Prior to the reform, landlords had overseen the production of festivals and had demanded that peasants sponsor them for the benefit of the landed elite. Landlords required that peasants carry the saint images, provide much of the food and drink, and participate in festival activities *en masse* in order to show that they were fulfilling their moral obligation of Christianizing the pagan population. In addition, sponsorship of fiestas had been an important revenue-earning source for the district government.[16] After the reform, the remaining members of the landed elite in Huanoquite had a far more difficult time legitimately imposing their demands upon local inhabitants. Huanoquiteños were less likely to invest the money, time, energy, and anxiety in fulfilling a cargo properly.[17] Furthermore, the rapidly rising cost of living and the interest inhabitants had in educating their children dissuaded them from investing as much as they had done in the past in fiesta sponsorship.

Many peasants had begun to focus their aspirations for power upon other kinds of activities. Holding political office, for example, was considered a better way to attain higher status than submission to the cargo system. The widening political opportunities and the narrowing of the authority of the landed elite together contributed to the growing disjuncture between the civil and religious hierarchies.

Peasants often used fiestas as a vehicle for expressing political rhetoric. The performance of and threats to religious devotion and ritual sometimes served to create the conditions for political mobilization. The interrelatedness of religious devotion and political mobilization became apparent in 1984 during the festivities for Huanoquite's patron saint, the Virgin of the Assumption. The priest was supposed to bless the image of the Virgin upon her emergence from the church and her return to it at the end of the fiesta. That year, because of a bitter conflict between the priest and inhabitants over the use of church lands for a nursery school, the priest did not make his traditional appearance.

The anger and concern of people reached a high pitch. A huge crowd gathered in front of the church. Drink had also loosened people's tongues. Men and women alike made a series of impassioned speeches, denouncing the church, the landed elite, the civil guard, and the government. The content of these spontaneous speeches emphasized the moral irresponsibility and hypocrisy of bureaucrats and other individuals who so often expressed concern about the well-being of Huanoquiteños and encouraged self-sacrifice, made numerous promises to them, and then failed to uphold their commitments. Once the civil guard appeared, the crowd began to dissolve and the threat of riot and rebellion diminished. It was nevertheless a rare, significant moment in which Huanoquiteños collectively made explicit their dissatisfaction and anger about issues of importance to all of them.

The religious and the secular thus remained interwoven domains, but as participation in national political and economic life afforded peasants greater opportunities to attain status and prestige and to mobilize politically, the fiesta system began to lose much of its appeal for them. The fiestas still expressed social boundaries between insiders and outsiders and positions of class and status; they remained the focus for economic exchanges; for some, they were central to their ideas about religious devotion, ethnic identity, and living well; and they signaled points in the agricultural calendar. However, peasants no longer had to participate in the fiesta system in order to achieve political power and prestige. Furthermore, many Huanoquiteños strongly felt that local political and economic power for themselves and for their communities rested more upon their understanding of modern agricultural technology and production factors, access to credit, participation in the cash economy, knowledge of changing market dynamics, and participation in regional agrarian leagues and federations.

Evangelicism

Households and individuals emphasized individual achievement as they vied for political influence and competed in the market economy. As the fiesta system became less important to inhabitants, they discovered other means of building suprahousehold linkages. The most notable innovation during this period was the embracing of Evangelical Protestantism by many Huanoquiteños. Their turn to Evangelicism was a complex phenomenon, which played a role in building suprahousehold linkages and in diminishing the importance of the civil-religious hierarchy. The number of Evangelical converts in the district had increased after the reform, but did so dramatically in the 1980's. In 1984, approximately 20 percent of the residents in the district capital (165 people) had been baptized or were sympathizers. By 1991, 45 more had converted.

Unlike the process of conversion described by David Stoll (1991) for other parts of Latin America, where representatives of particular sects directly engaged in proselytizing, Evangelicism in Huanoquite appeared to be taking shape as a grassroots movement spearheaded by charismatic leaders. Interested people attended meetings in different members' houses every week, which focused on reading the Bible. Converts did not define themselves as members of a particular Evangelical sect. The "father" of the movement, Cirilo Mora, was a relatively prosperous private landowner who belonged to neither a cooperative nor a community. Nevertheless, he was originally from Huanoquite and participated actively in local politics, especially at the district level.

For some Huanoquiteños, Evangelical Protestantism was a means of gaining respect from the national society by embracing values of which the dominant classes approved—hard work, abstinence from alcohol, responsible fatherhood, and thriftiness. For many others, Evangelicism was, rather, an alternative means of national incorporation, adopted because they believed it would empower and unite them sufficiently to enable them simultaneously to assert their autonomy and distinguish themselves from the prevailing mestizo image of peasants as lazy, illiterate, wife-beating drunks (a view peasants themselves had absorbed to a degree).

Young men often found it difficult to gain access to needed labor for their fields, and since the first commitment of all Evangelical Protestants was to assist fellow believers, a growing number of labor parties were composed only of "brothers." This was a bone of contention between "the brothers" and non-Evangelicals, creating serious conflicts between them. At the same time, it forged a sense of community among the "brothers" that was difficult to establish in postreform Huanoquite. Women welcomed the new belief system, because they had suffered physical abuse by their husbands, particularly when the latter were drunk.

Evangelicism captured the imagination of many villagers, especially younger and poorer men and women, because they saw in it the possibility of creating a new kind of collectivity, in which a leader and his flock were bound to one another through the teachings of the Bible. These nontraditional practices permitted converts to opt out altogether from Catholic rites and the cargo system. The Evangelical movement provided members with an important means of building a new sense of corporateness, coping with social marginalization, and avoiding intergenerational conflicts.[18]

Evangelicism stressed individual achievement and material rewards, both goals of the agrarian reform, but it also replicated structures of domination and subordination that had existed under the landed elite. The "father" of the local Evangelical sect in Huanoquite, Cirilo Mora, watched carefully over his followers to ensure that they did not go astray or suffer, saying: "I give land to other Evangelicals who need it, in accordance with the word of God. I changed after coming to know Him. When my work succeeds, I teach them [other converts]. I give them advice so that they won't suffer."

An isomorphism thus appeared between the religious values espoused by Huanoquiteños who had converted to Evangelicism and the state's economic policies. The values of Evangelicism dovetailed nicely with the state's growing emphasis upon increasing production and participation in the market economy. At the same time, the notions of brotherhood and mutual aid as basic tenets of the faith (achieved through rigid discipline rather than the flow of alcohol) moderated the impersonal character of social relations typically found in a market economy. The ties among the brothers, and between the brothers, the "father" of the sect, and God resembled the paternalistic relationships that had existed between hacendados and their peons. Paradoxically, Evangelicism incorporated innovative means of succeeding in the market economy and carving out a space of relative autonomy from the state. In the words of two young Evangelicals:

Jesus Christ has changed my life. I have turned away from alcohol. The ideas that I have? To work hard, be a good father to my family, acquire a few things that my household lacks. [Ricardo Antitupa Quispe, co-op member]

Before knowing Jesus Christ, I never thought about working or about my fields or even about my children. Now I don't get drunk. I don't go to fiestas. I work in my fields. [Juan Roque, community member]

Finally, the dramatic surge in the popularity of Evangelicism in Huanoquite was in part a result of the scandalous and abusive behavior of the resident Catholic priest, particularly his implication in the theft of valuable paintings and objects from the church, his sexual escapades with local women, his inexplicable refusal to distribute food donated by the Catholic relief organization Caritas to Huanoquiteños, and his adamant lack of support for any local development projects proposed by Huanoquiteños.[19] In 1991, Huanoquiteños had still not resolved the problems they had with the priest. The district authorities had declared they could no longer rely upon legal channels to prevent the priest's abuse of his power. They themselves had been threatened with fines and imprisonment for their protests against the priest. They had decided, therefore, that the only solution was to organize collectively and set up a blockade to prevent the priest from entering the community, a proposal they planned to raise before the next general assembly.

Conclusion

This chapter has looked at some of the most significant mechanisms that fostered and reinforced differentiation among households as well as between communities and cooperatives after the reform. The uneven implementation of reform legislation, state economic policies, and the dynamics of the market markedly increased economic differentiation within the district. Agricultural production across all households required a degree of cooperation. Yet the individualization of household production and exchange and the tensions between communities and cooperatives impeded cooperation. In particular, the process of differentiation affected existing political hierarchies, weakened local authority structures, and brought about the proliferation of networks. And there was a limit to the labor peasants could invest in these organizations without overextending themselves. As a result of the growing differentiation among households and corporate entities, Huanoquiteños also found it difficult to forge consensus among themselves.

As the epigraph to this chapter from Alessandro Portelli makes clear, when class differentiation begins to establish itself, individuals are both allowed and expected to create their own identities. While the Peruvian state was promoting national integration and economic equality for all, Peruvians were confronting new, and sometimes insurmountable, boundaries and obstacles to equality among themselves. Although their efforts to overcome economic and political conflicts often failed, Huanoquiteños did not simply acquiesce to the way their economic and political space was being carved up, as a consequence first of differentiation and differential treatment by the state and then of the calculated violence Sendero perpetrated against the Tihuicte cooperative.

All of the tensions that emerged explicitly after the reform—between communities and cooperatives, between households of widely ranging economic and political standing, between peasants of different religious faiths, and between diverse formal political organizations and bureaucratic entities—would eventually become paramount in the degree of success that members of Sendero achieved in establishing themselves in the rural highlands. Ideas peasants had of work, the constitution of legitimate authority and high status, and the moral implications of the capitalist dictum that everything has its price would also shape peasant responses to Sendero and the state. In the next chapter, through the biographies of two men who were considered excellent farmers and political leaders in Huanoquite, we shall see how Huanquiteños attempted to build a sense of community under these conditions.

– 7 –

Two Lives Coming into Power

Indian materialism challenges the epic elements of history, since the memory of the defeated, which is the memory of the body trampled by "Logos," must first come to terms with unredeemed pain, humiliation, scorn, the surge of all suffering buried in the soul, or the blows of life, as Vallejo would have said. Hence this memory can be nothing other than reminiscence about what is near, of the detail: daily life.

Silvia Rivera Cusicanqui,
"Indigenous Women and Community Resistance"

The life of the countryside, so much pain, so much love.
Demetrio Pantoja Bejar, May 3, 1984[1]

This chapter offers the reconstructed biographies of two farmers, Demetrio Pantoja Bejar and Cirilo Rocca Quispe. Demetrio belonged to the community of Maska; Cirilo to the cooperative of Tihuicte. Both men had established themselves as highly successful farmers. They also commanded the respect and collaboration of other Huanoquiteños across the cooperative and community in working toward goals that could create unity rather than divisiveness among them.[2] Their lives, recounted in brief here, are meant to demonstrate the interesting ways in which particular individuals were able to make "new articulations between systems of meaning" (Kaplan 1990:14) and, I would add, material conditions, after the reform, that were neither relentlessly traditional nor wholly identified with state reform and indigenous assimilation or acculturation. In fact, both Demetrio Pantoja and Cirilo Rocca are, as Jeremy Beckett observes about one Austrialian aborigine in a similar position,

improvisers—bricoleurs—... whose personalities, positions in the world and experiences of it give them an idiosyncratic perspective.... The significance of most such individuals is not so much that they change anything, as that they explore the possibilities, the margins, of their cultural environment. [Beckett 1993:677]

Their lives also give us an idea of a path not riven by violence or nihilism—one that was taken by many peasants with varying degrees of success after the reform.

Demetrio Pantoja Bejar

Demetrio Pantoja Bejar was of lanky build and striding walk. He was 37 years old when I met him, and I lived with him and his family for a year. His eyes were intense and his hands were almost always busy. He was very soft-spoken. His dress betrayed a scarcely hidden preoccupation with his public image. He liked European-style clothes; wore boots; and always kept his several hats well brushed. Even though he had completed only three years of primary education, he spoke an unusually sophisticated and poetic Spanish.

Demetrio's house, which he had built himself, overlooked the plaza. It had two stories, several windows and two verandas. In addition, he had built a kitchen, a small room where his tall and dignified aging mother lived, and another small room occupied by his widowed sister. The whitewashed compound was solidly built of adobes. In contrast, his small patio was a jumble of manure piled up to be used as fertilizer, mud, chickens, roosters, pigs, cattle, horses, dogs, cats, and children. Demetrio and his wife, Victoria Zanabria Rado, had also begun building another house just off the plaza, which had a large vegetable garden and a small field attached to it. While I was there, they were using the house for storage but planned to move to it permanently once they had finished building it.

Demetrio had not lived in Huanoquite all his life. He had spent thirteen years in Lima working in construction for a private company. There he had honed his skills to such an extent that he was hired to build chalets for the very wealthy. He was a carpenter, mason, farmer, and jack-of-all-trades. His well-organized tools hung on the walls and lay on his shelves. They were in great demand among other farmers. He made most of his farming implements himself, including leather ropes, and often spent hours sculpting yokes out of very hard wood for his plow animals. He was a perfectionist.

Demetrio's manual dexterity, his ease in speaking Spanish, and his well-connected family and kin had assisted him in gaining high status in the eyes of Huanoquiteños. His close relatives included members of several families of the landed elite—the Bejars, Galdoses, and Bejar-Pazs (see figure on facing page for kinship ties between Demetrio Pantoja, his wife, and members of the landed elite). His own mother was a Bejar; his father, now deceased, had worked as a peon on the haciendas.

Demetrio was the oldest son. He had once lived for a long period of time in the high puna. One of his brothers, Crisóstomo, still lived

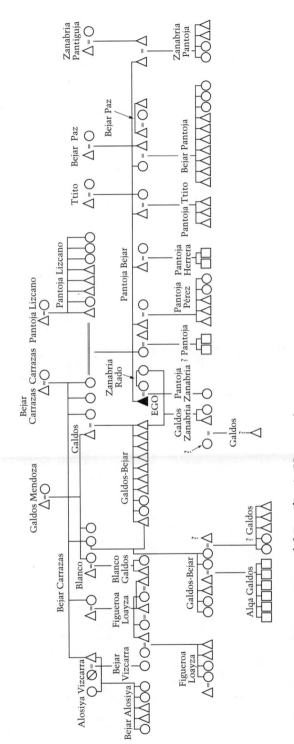

Intermarriage Between Powerful Families in Huanoquite

there and spoke proudly of his rejection of the "urban" way of life in the district capital. Crisóstomo was an uncompromising traditionalist, and he and Demetrio sometimes came to blows because Demetrio believed that the future lay in his ability to knit together the disparate worlds that he straddled rather than in rejecting one or the other world as Crisóstomo had chosen to do.

Another brother, Fortunato, had married into the household of Rafael Tito Lezama, who had given him a large tract of private land to work. Yet another brother, Victor, lived in Cusco, where he worked on civil construction projects. Demetrio's sister Ricardina had married and moved to Ayacucho. His widowed sister Elvira had married the overseer of Mallma, the Paz estate.

Both Demetrio and Victoria counted Braulio Galdos, a member of the Galdos branch of hacendados, among their extended kin. Braulio had been orphaned at an early age. His father had been shot and killed by the mayor in a conflict at the Tihuicte estate (see Chapter 5), and his mother, Victoria's sister, subsequently died of an illness. Braulio formed part of a powerful association of Galdos relatives, all of whom were his uncles. They owned one of the trucks that provided service to and from Cusco, where they worked in the San Pedro central market selling manufactured clothing that they had purchased in Lima. Braulio's wild temperament and his problems with drinking had made him a burden to Demetrio and Victoria, but they acted as his surrogate parents, and he in turn transported their agricultural products, bought consumer goods in Cusco for them, and helped them to make contacts with wholesalers and bureaucrats in Cusco.

Victoria came from a family with nine children. Her great-grandfather had accumulated land in Huanoquite, some say because of his prestige as a soldier in the War of the Pacific. Much of the land had been divided among offspring, sold off, or usurped by different hacendados. Victoria's mother was a renowned curer and midwife in the region, and Victoria had inherited much of her mother's wisdom about medicinal herbs and remedies.

Victoria had also lived outside of Huanoquite. After her father died, she had run away from home and gone to Lima, where she worked as a domestic servant. Demetrio and Victoria had met in Lima, and he had married her after she became pregnant. The combined affinal ties between Demetrio and Victoria and the power and privilege of their kin spread across a wide range.

The greatest curse upon Demetrio and Victoria had been their lack of sons. They had been blessed with only one daughter, Silvia. Victoria had miscarried seven times, and her inability to carry a son to full term had made her the object of some scorn and gossip within the village. She was convinced she was the victim of witchcraft. To compensate for their lack of sons, they had taken in Lucio, an abused child from a distant village, who had stayed with them for years as a substitute son and servant, not unlike the yanakunas of the past. Lucio was reaching adulthood and seeking to gain his own independence. Concerned about a male heir and, in Demetrio's words, his need for a "male companion," Demetrio and Victoria had adopted a small baby, Erlán, from Demetrio's brother, Crisóstomo, who already had a family of five to feed.

Demetrio had returned to Huanoquite from Lima after a debilitating illness. While he was sick, he had thought often of suicide:

I was working in the construction business when the pain began in my hand. It spread to my shoulder, then my other hand and arm, and down to my knees and feet. I tried different remedies but they failed. I worked until I could no longer bend my fingers. I went to the doctor at social security and then from doctor to doctor, spending money. The doctor told me it was psychological, that I was just lazy. I could only do easy tasks at work. My fellow workers accused me of being a coward. I returned to Huanoquite to die. They had to carry me everywhere. I could no longer walk. I decided to commit suicide by swallowing insecticide. Moises Ilarez tried to give me hope. He said I was still a young man and had to try to get better, whereas he was dying and could do nothing about it. Moises told me about a healer in Cusco, Gregoria, a large, fat woman. I went to see her. She told me to collect all sorts of herbs. People had to go out and get them for me. Gregoria carried me into the sun totally naked and for three days she gave me herbal baths and rubbed my body with nettles. I screamed with pain and wanted her to stop, but she was wise and did not. My joints still sometimes swell up, but I've been cured and I don't think of suicide anymore.

Demetrio's migration to and from Lima was the turning point in his life. While he was in Lima, his fields had been worked partly by his kin, partly by sharecroppers. When he returned periodically, he bought livestock with his savings, which he then turned over to his brother in the puna to raise while he was away. When he came back to die in Huanoquite, he was penniless save for the livestock he had accumulated and his land base, which was relatively small.

His brushes with death and poverty became incentives for him to work harder than most other Huanoquiteños. His profound understanding of what the lack of financial resources and political power, aggravated by racial discrimination, had meant in a metropolis like Lima compelled him to assert as much control as possible over his life and the direction it would take.

Cirilo Rocca Quispe

Cirilo Rocca Quispe's family was from the lower valley community of Chifia and the higher puna hamlet of Chanca. He was far less urbanized in his dress than Demetrio. He wore rough pants and shirts, rubber sandals, and a beaten up old hat. Although he was far more comfortable speaking Quechua, he had mastered Spanish as well. One of his brothers, Nicolás, was a member of Maska and had been a cattle dealer for many years. Cirilo participated in that business for three years, selling cattle from Chumbivilcas to people in Huanoquite and Cusco. His wife, Alejandrina Pantoja Calanche, a distant relative of Demetrio's family, and his three sons assisted him with his farming. Two of his brothers lived in Lima and worked as masons. One of his sisters was a vendor in Lima.

At 45, Cirilo was well-known for his leadership in the cooperative of Tihuicte. He, like Demetrio, lived in the district capital. He had engaged in regional politics for many years, participating regularly in demonstrations and serving as a representative from the cooperative to the Pachacutec Agrarian League.

Building a Reputation

Demetrio and Cirilo had developed practices and skills that depended upon their economic standing and their elaboration and use of knowledge they had acquired from within and outside Huanoquite. Their kin networks had initially provided them with human capital. Nevertheless, they could only activate these networks by meeting their reciprocal obligations, and both men were skilled at doing so. They provided their relatives with special services in return for labor and land. Demetrio often provided his services as a carpenter and house builder in exchange for land and labor. Cirilo did likewise as an economic broker and cattle dealer.

In Cirilo's description of his activities as an economic broker, he was acutely aware that peasant agricultural production was fundamental to the smooth functioning of the urban economy, but that the terms of exchange were highly unequal: "I have worked as a wholesaler and a retailer, providing food not only for my *paisanos* in Huanoquite but for all the pueblos of Cusco. I don't just trade with Huanoquiteños. My products are for [sale to] everyone. But it is difficult. Transport and food. If we raise the price, others lower it." In a general assembly, Cirilo expressed even more forcefully the need for inhabitants to assert greater control over economic policies that kept the prices of agricultural products low: "We do all the work for the *mistis*, who get rich from it, filling their stomachs with our food. Now it is time for the campesinos to be rich men and reap the benefits of our production."

Both men had reputations as innovative farmers and had relations of *compadrazgo* (fictive kin ties) that extended beyond the confines of Huanoquite. Cirilo was known throughout the region for his knowledge of seeds, especially potato seed, with which he experimented, in a process called *tamburuqotu*, to produce hybrid varieties better adapted to local climatic conditions and soils and more resistant to disease. Many farmers came to Cirilo for advice about seeds, which he willingly shared with them.

Demetrio had worked as a day laborer for SIPA for three years and had learned about fertilizer, insecticide, and new varieties of wheat, barley, and potatoes, but he had gone far beyond this initial knowledge. He conversed extensively with the two formally trained agronomists and livestock experts in the village, one of whom was his *compadre*; he tried out new strains of eucalyptus; he had become a beekeeper; and he was attempting to grow fodder in his house garden and oats in the puna.

He was also skilled in the arts of scheduling, which all farmers considered important, but few could do well. Scheduling depended upon knowledge of environmental conditions and animal behavior, calculation of time in relationship to labor needs, and the ability to forecast market conditions. Women played a crucial role in scheduling. They knew more about the availability of labor from different households, and their agreement to labor parties was essential, since they prepared the necessary food and drink. Demetrio's wife, Victoria, showed great skill in keeping abreast of the activities of other households, and with the help of her sisters, she always prepared abundant food and drink for labor parties. Demetrio attributed his success in organization and scheduling to his experience as a SIPA day laborer, the knowledge he had acquired from his father, and the complexity of his life and work in Lima.

Beyond their kin networks and their available economic capital (both had received credit from the Banco Agrario), Cirilo and Demetrio provided invaluable services to the cooperative and community. Each had played leadership roles in assisting peasants in obtaining additional lands for the cooperative and community and in articulating publicly what many inhabitants privately thought. They relied upon their kin networks, their knowledge of the ways in which institutions outside of Huanoquite worked, and their keen sensitivity to what Huanoquiteños regarded as the moral dimensions of proper ethical conduct. Cirilo had worked for SIPA but turned against it after SIPA agents abused women in the village. In his words,

I worked three years with SIPA. I myself went into Cusco to complain to the reform agents. Here, the SIPA managers had almost beaten me. Abusive technicians. They abused the young girls, the women. They always forced me to drink. I went to René Galdos. He was the justice of the peace. I was beaten up by three SIPA agents. I went to Cusco. I met Anibal Acurio, the journalist. He published what had happened in *El Sol* on January 7. I held a talk with Radio Tawantinsuyu [a popular peasant-oriented radio station]. I went to the Ministry of Agriculture to start the process to expropriate Tihuicte. When I was coming back to Huanoquite, I was scared. I left the documents I had brought with me with my relatives in Chifia. Then I went to Tihuicte. That was when I was beaten up by the agents. One had a gun. He demanded that I give him two bulls. I had learned how to answer questions from Acurio. I knew how not to give them the information they wanted. I was proclaimed a leader. Acurio's article was published. We threw out the SIPA agents. We expropriated Tihuicte.

Cirilo's courage in personally contacting a journalist, radio station, and reform agents in order to expose the behavior of SIPA personnel and facilitate the expropriation of Tihuicte earned him recognition as a leader.[3]

Demetrio, because of his experience in Lima, his facility in Spanish, and the support he received from powerful families in Huanoquite, was elected treasurer of the community. During that time, in conjunction with Tomás Chaparro, the community's president he pursued the litigation against Tito and Inkakuna Ayllu Chifia (see Chapter 5). His contacts in Cusco and Lima eventually played a key role in permitting the community to gain access to half of Tito's land. Both Cirilo and Demetrio had been able to assume leadership roles because they knowledgeably manipulated legal institutions outside Huanoquite, took advantage of their contacts, used the mass media to their advantage, and focused upon issues that were fundamental to people's well-being in Huanoquite.

Cirilo and Demetrio received recognition from Huanoquiteños as legitimate authorities within the cooperative and community, but they refused to operate solely within these formally structured arenas. Instead, they crossed these boundaries on a regular basis, particularly in their labor and marketing arrangements. They had also held multiple positions in the community, cooperative, and district political hierarchies, and had been elected sponsors of the most important fiestas in the district.

In comparison to many other peasants, Demetrio and Cirilo had reached the conclusion that, while certain tried-and-true practices and beliefs were important to their economic and political well-being—reciprocity, economic exchange networks, humility, respect for the land, hard work, gratefulness to kin and ritual benefactors—they needed to interweave these with innovative approaches and values in confronting new economic policies and forms of political organization. They began with sufficient well-distributed land to take the risk of experimentation, but they also developed distinct personal philosophies that structured the kinds of experimentation in which they engaged. They cultivated power for a purpose.

Demetrio had abandoned many rituals that he felt did not contribute to agricultural success, but he was also a devout Catholic who paid his respects to the saints and served as the major cargo holder for Huanoquite's most important fiesta, the feast of the Virgin of the Assumption on August 15. He was cynical about the benefits of many urban services, especially medical services, and relied upon indigenous curers. Despite his own lack of education, he was convinced of the value of education. Nevertheless, he recognized that education was not just something that occurred when one sent one's children to school. He harshly criticized the teachers to their face when one of them beat his daughter. In explaining his philosophy of education, he said, "You must recognize the innocence and wisdom of children. You must answer all their questions, and they will never stop asking questions. Some children know more than others because of their upbringing and the opportunities they have had. But all children are wise, and it is the responsibility of adults to tap their wisdom without discriminating against their age or standing in society." Demetrio had also taken a stance against exploitative and lazy hacendados despite his close ties to the Galdos and Bejar families. His primary concern was community solidarity, and he had gone to jail for participating in land seizures.

Cirilo had also developed a personal philosophy of life, influenced by his membership in the cooperative and his participation in regional politics. In his words, "I have always thought about how to work as a campesino. Everyone wants to eat. I want to work so that everyone, not only I, will be able to wear clothes and eat." Cirilo saw himself as representing the campesinos of Peru, whom he regarded as the mainstay of all Peruvians' well-being.

Conclusion

The personalities of Demetrio Pantoja and Cirilo Rocca were essential to their success. A number of other peasants in the district had as much land as Demetrio and Cirilo, but they were little respected by other villagers and unremarkable as political leaders. "He is rich but he is not a vecino," one man said in seeking to distinguish Demetrio from other farmers of similar standing.

The purpose of the preceding two chapters has been to illuminate the fluidity and contradictions of economic and political life in Huanoquite after the 1969 reform. New approaches to working, learning, engaging in politics, and expressing religious devotion resulted from the intersection of national policies with peasant interpretations of these policies. They also hinged upon the ways in which Huanoquiteños responded to one another in the course of revising their economic and political practices. "The multiplicity of individual experiences" (Zunz 1985:58) among Huanoquiteños cannot be reduced to a single model predictive of their farming decisions or political alternatives.

In painting Peru's dependency and the peripheral position of Andean highland society in broad brush strokes, scholars too often overlook the forms dependency takes and the fact that the efforts and effects of different individuals to establish a measure of autonomy and cooperation within these structural constraints are not monolithic. By filling in the details of the canvas, we may sacrifice the neat categories that make cross-national or macrolevel comparisons possible, but as Marc Edelman observes,

Microlevel analyses do not only "fill in gaps" in the studies of economists, sociologists, and political scientists. . . . Rather, on-the-ground research . . . permits incorporating into explanation real historical subjects whose activities, understandings, expectations and motivations may resemble only partially or not at all those attributed to them by analysts operating at higher levels of abstraction. [Edelman 1990:736–37]

In the midst of economic differentiation, Huanoquiteños' different approaches to farming and politics interacted with the structural forces and policies that gave rise to dependency, subordination, and competition. The nexus of this interaction shaped their lives after the reform, but also created the conditions for them to resist these structural constraints. As the next chapter shows, they sometimes actively and publicly fought against practices and policies they considered unjust in order to strengthen the autonomy of the district. In doing so, they often took terrible risks.

— 8 —

Power Struggles and Paths to Development

> Risk is the certain companion of uncertain freedom.
> Vivienne Shue, *The Reach of the State*

This chapter addresses how peasants in Huanoquite have attempted to carve out a space of partial autonomy from the state and set the terms of their engagement with it since the reform. It also offers a historical framework in which to place the next chapter, which explains why Sendero Luminoso, a guerrilla movement noted for its authoritarian and violent orientation, was able to establish a foothold in rural highland communities like Huanoquite.

Of special importance in understanding political struggles in Huanoquite after the reform are the ways in which peasants contributed to transforming authority structures at the local level so that they would better represent their interests. In addition to using existing political structures for new purposes, they also took advantage of the numerous intermediaries who came to perform functions of mutual interest to rural and urban inhabitants after the reform. Finally, they turned to formal and informal forums such as general assemblies and peasant federations, where they found, perhaps, the most congenial environment in which to recognize and act upon common interests.

One of the first lessons that those who wish to dominate learn is to speak the same language as those whom they wish to control. Thus, behaviors and discourse contributing to the coherence of community institutions and to political mobilization among peasants have also been crucial to the capacity of dominant regimes and classes to penetrate and manipulate these relationships, thereby creating *both* inequalities and cleavages within peasant communities *and* a degree of continuity in the terms of debate.

The 1969 agrarian reform in Peru did not produce extensive "leveling" among households. In addition, because the policies of the Velasco regime were not party-based, but rather corporatist in nature, the regime's ideology was not reproduced at every level of society, and

the state did not entirely restructure relations of production or re-
press class conflicts. Nevertheless, far more than ever before, the
state extended its reach to the local level in the countryside economically, administratively, and ideologically. It undermined the legitimacy of the landed oligarchy; it sent in technocratic agents to manage
peasant cooperatives; it reformed the educational system by nationalizing it and making education available to far greater numbers
of rural communities; and it established SINAMOS and government-
sponsored agrarian leagues as "substitutes" for a party.

Despite the state presence in rural districts, ayllus, peasant
groups, and communities remained paramount to the capacity of
peasants to organize their labor and land-tenure regimes, take political action, and confront contingencies. Disparities between the rich
and powerful and the poor and marginalized nevertheless moderated
the corporate nature of these units. The growing influence of individuals who belonged to no corporate unit, and the capacity of the rich
and powerful to exercise multiple options in order to fulfill their
obligations to the community, the cooperative, or the district as a
whole weakened the ability of different corporate units to act in a
united fashion.

Just as the Velasco regime was constrained in implementing radical agrarian policy by the legacy of interethnic, class, and bureaucratic conflicts within society and its own organizations, peasants
were entrapped by communal ideology, embedded in their communities. This ideology is very much a part of what has made community possible in the Andes, and it has continued to affect the course of
political struggle in highland agrarian society.

Florencia Mallon calls attention to the tendency among scholars
to see the survival of community institutions as a sign of resistance
to capitalism. Yet in the central region of the Andean highlands, she
remarks,

"community" has served as a weapon both of class struggle *and* class transformation. Indeed, as in other parts of Peru with a communal tradition,
communal ideology and relations of reciprocity have been a double-edged
sword since the colonial period. On the one hand, the rich have used them to
get access to labor and political power, which they could then manipulate for
private profit. On the other hand, the poor have called on communal ideology
and reciprocity to guarantee subsistence and remind the rich of their re-
distributive responsibility to the village as a whole. [Mallon 1983:341]

In Huanoquite, while some peasants have used communal ideology to organize themselves collectively,[1] other peasants, as well as
the remaining landed elite, state functionaries, and entrepreneurs,

have taken advantage of this ideology to obtain greater power for themselves and fracture collective interests and actions.

Before the 1969 reform, the principal mediators between the state and peasant communities had been landlords who acted as patrons to numerous peasant clients in a vertical fashion.[2] The functions these mediators performed were critical to their clients; the number of mediator statuses was limited; and the landed elite maintained "near exclusivity" in performing their mediating functions. Landlords "protected" peasants; offered them goods and services, including loans, in exchange for their labor; and the daughters of peasants sometimes gained entrée into urban society by providing domestic services and sexual favors to the landlord's immediate family or kin in Cusco or Lima.

Few supracommunity linkages were strong enough to counterbalance the more immediate patron-client ties between landlord and peasant. The same was true of the state, which, more often than not, was unable to counterbalance the power of local fiefdoms and preferred, therefore, to work in conjunction with them. While the policies of the landed elite and state frequently coincided, when they did not, it was nearly impossible for the state to impose itself upon the staggering number of differentiated communities throughout the Andes. Thus, the landed elite generally controlled the political options of peasants and limited the maneuverability of the state with respect to initiating changes in agrarian policy that might favor peasants in particular.

Following the reform, the exodus of most of the landed elite from highland communities created a space in which peasants were able to forge a variety of sociopolitical and economic relationships that could not be defined as solely vertical or class-bound. A number of new kinds of individuals came to play crucial roles in subsequent political struggles between peasants and the state. These individuals performed multiple functions and, unlike the landed elite, did not belong to a single socioeconomic stratum.

In the pages that follow, I refer to these individuals as intermediaries. Although they did not *always* mediate between peasants and the state, many of them functioned as economic, political, or cultural brokers. They assisted peasants in marketing their products; they used their education and contacts with bureaucrats and politicians at the regional level in order to leverage the state into providing services, money, and infrastructure to peasant districts; they assisted peasants in advancing their claims to land; and they sought to translate the state's new educational and development policies into practice in the countryside. Many of them had been active in politics at the departmental or district level.

The relationships Huanoquiteños forged with these brokers sometimes succeeded in strengthening socioeconomic and political links between Huanoquite and organizations outside the district, such as other peasant communities and the departmental bureaucracy. At the same time, no single locally based institution of political authority emerged in Huanoquite after the reform. This fact, together with the widening of space for new power relations to develop and the cleavages within peasant communities, was paramount to the ease with which outside forces, including members of Sendero Luminoso, intervened in village life and were able to seize control of the local political arena.

Paradoxically, the diverse relationships that peasants forged with government agents, and the multiple bases upon which power and political authority became founded locally, meant that the regime faced an almost unsurmountable obstacle to achieving its vision of national integration. Furthermore, as peasants gained a greater understanding of the workings of state-local power relations, they grew to distrust state behavior as never before.

After the reform, peasants became far more preoccupied with their relationship to the state and market than with their relationship to the remaining members of the landed elite. Cooperative and community members frequently debated the advantages and disadvantages of closer ties to the state versus greater partial autonomy. These preoccupations were not new; they became more salient, however, as peasants occupied the "busy crossroads" (Rosaldo 1989:20, 45, 196–217) between rural and urban paths, learning from and experimenting with other organizational arrangements that had become important since the reform. These "arrangements" included agrarian leagues, peasant federations, political parties, educational institutions, and informational channels such as newspapers and radio programs.

Peasants were assessing "the extent to which public institutions themselves could be used as an adjunct of local relationships" (Moore 1986:302). Using several case studies from Africa, Sara Berry (1988) has shown that a reliance upon numerous networks exacts an economic toll from peasants that has to be weighed against the benefits of participating in these networks. Despite the rhetoric of the state, at the local level, peasants were more often than not left to fend for themselves. For peasants in Huanoquite, activating multiple networks required a great investment of labor and time, and there were limitations to the effectiveness of their investments. Not only were their economic resources spread more and more thinly; as their options increased, the possibilities of establishing permanent, stable communities of membership decreased. In turn, this presented obstacles both to peasants and to the state. It presented obstacles to a regime interested in nation-building, and it hindered peasants from achieving stable control over economic and political resources. These dynamic tensions were reflected in the political struggles within Huanoquite and between Huanoquite and the state after the reform.

At the same time, Huanoquiteños have behaved, not as mere pawns, but as actors attuned to their social history and the contingency of events. Particular moments have periodically created the conditions for a sense of community to surface and given peasants the impetus to mobilize collectively, overcoming the conflict and dissent among themselves. Although moments of successful mobilization are rare and often only partially achieve the goals that peasants really desire, these moments become memories that peasants can then activate in the future. There is a sense among many of them that, while history may have gone awry, they still have the power to change it in the future. Only in this way can hope be kept alive.

A great sense of risk and excitement initially accompanied their participation in change. It is hardly surprising that their responses to greater state intervention in their lives were not uniform, and that their initiatives to restructure authority structures within the district to serve their own interests were often unsuccessful. As they reassessed their ideas of legitimate political authority and sought to put them into practice, Huanoquiteños discovered that they agreed neither on the underlying qualities they most wanted their representatives to exhibit nor on the goals they wanted them to achieve. They realized that preference and practice were rarely consonant. As Vivienne Shue remarks, based on her research in China,

True peasants . . . are hardly ever "true believers." Not so tightly bound as we by the exclusionary logic of Western science and secular modern rationalism, peasants all over the globe tend to be unembarrassed eclectics in the terms they use to understand the natural world, and the most ecumenical syncretists in their absorption of various moral systems and traditions. [Shue 1988:64]

Furthermore, given that Huanoquiteños wanted particular outcomes to take place, they often put their personal preferences to one side, because they knew that sociopolitical constraints would make it impossible to achieve them. F. G. Bailey elaborates upon this dynamic:

The outcome of a challenge against someone's definition of the situation depends upon three variables: the existing level of primal consensus, the resources that each party can deploy to make its definition prevail, and the openness with which the confrontation is made.

Other things being equal, the more open the challenge, the less easily is it ignored, the lower the chance of a negotiated settlement and the greater the likelihood of outright conflict. [Bailey 1991:52]

In short, Huanoquiteños behaved as astute political agents, despite their longing for another kind of world, another medium and morality in which ideal social relations might unfold. These sentiments accompanied their pragmatism and their rational choices. Although never completely hidden, and serving to orient Huanoquiteños' political behavior and capacity for collective mobilization, the question "What if . . . ?" remained largely offstage.

James C. Scott has introduced the key concept of a "hidden transcript" to describe the power of this offstage questioning in motivating political action. He argues that one principal kind of resistance among subordinate groups is characterized by interactive dialectical relationships between the exercise of public power and discourse and the development of "hidden transcripts" and discourses:

It is . . . in the . . . realm of relative discursive freedom, outside the earshot of powerholders, where the hidden transcript is to be sought. The disparity between what we find here and what is said in the presence of power is a rough measure of what has been suppressed from power-laden political communication. The hidden transcript is, for this reason, the privileged site for non-hegemonic, contrapuntal, dissident, subversive discourse . . . —gesture, speech, practices—that is ordinarily excluded from the public transcript of subordinates by the exercise of power.

He adds that where sufficient power exists,

to suppress dissent among subordinates, it becomes possible to speak of a hidden transcript within the hidden transcript. Subordinates may be too intimidated by the exercise of domination within the group to say or do anything at odds with what is required. Notice also that when such a situation develops, powerholders among subordinates may well come to have something of a vested interest in the overall pattern of domination that is a precondition of their own power. [Scott 1990:25, 27]

These power dynamics well characterize the position of peasants in postreform Huanoquite and help to explain why many peasant communities, after a seemingly prolonged period of quiescence, challenge the exercise of power by dominant elites. At the same time, they explain the kinds of obstacles to resistance presented to Huanoquiteños by individuals within their communities whose power derived from their clientelist relationships with merchants, usurers, cattle dealers, government agents, teachers, and landlords.

It is important to recognize that these sentiments and even programmatic scenarios are not a return to some utopian and idealized past in which a pristine morality reigned. On the basis of their experiences, Huanoquiteños continue to revise and refine their ideas of better living conditions, community, and national citizenship. Prevailing economic and political constraints usually prohibit them from acting upon these agendas overtly. Fears of reprisal by the dominant classes or the state, as well as their pragmatic concerns about economic survival, weigh heavily in their decisions not to oppose existing authority structures. Yet, as we shall see below, at key moments in the course of their daily lives, Huanoquiteños have acted together to try to bring about change or guide the direction it takes. They have fought for peasant representation in the district council; they have used informal gatherings, general assemblies, and supracommunity parties, federations, and leagues in very interesting ways to articulate, through seemingly innocuous dialogue, their principal concerns and possible courses of action; they have attempted to control the process of economic development in the district; and they have made a sustained effort to define the kind and quality of formal education their children receive.

The District Council

The most immediate locus of political struggle between Huanoquiteños and the state is the district council.[3] The "official" nature of the district as a political field offers less permeability for Huanoquiteños to exercise alternative actions or to develop alternative rhetoric than the political fields of communities. Within communities, more space exists for greater daily interaction among individuals, based on shared kin and social ties, labor activities, and terrritory. At the district level, the distance between dispersed communities and the differential advantages communities, as legal entities, obtain indirectly from the state through the district constrain their capacity to affect the actions of district authorities. On the other hand, relationships between the district and state are crucial to understanding how state policies interact with local authority structures, and, in turn, affect relationships between different corporate entities and their constituencies.

Political struggles at the district level reveal the distinct, and often conflictual, ideas, rhetoric, and practices of multiple peasant communities, as well as those of state officials and agents. In addition, the written documentation available provides a guide to the kinds of debates that have preoccupied peasants, whereas this historical depth is difficult to obtain from interviews and oral histories alone.

To come upon local archival records is always exciting, simply because one hears the voices of individuals and groups that are almost always suppressed, silenced, or categorized into larger generalized categories such as "peasants" or "hacendados" or "the military." In Huanoquite, I was lucky enough to be shown some of these records. They were discontinuous chronologically, with the bulk of correspondence and documentation falling between 1880 and 1930 and between 1970 and 1991. My understanding of the workings of the district council is thus biased by the documents I had available.

What leaps out in the early years is the scarcity of individual references to native inhabitants.[4] Powerful members of the landed elite ruled the district council, using it to further their personal objectives. When they took actions that were threatening or intimidating to the landed elite, Huanoquite's peasants were mentioned, not by name, but as *indios*. They also appear when members of the landed elite were pitted against one another and activated their clienteles of peasants, or when the need for local and state revenues (surplus extraction) led the elite to debate the kinds and quantity of taxes they could exact from peasants. Occasionally, peasants brought conflicts with hacendados, particularly those concerning the usurpation of communal lands, before the council. Peasants also appear in the records during center-periphery conflicts when local officeholders struggled with the enduring issue of Huanoquite's physical isolation from Paruro and Cusco. District officials sought to diminish Huanoquite's isolation by drawing upon the resident labor force to build regional infrastructure. Peasants, in turn, protested the levies by failing to appear for work.[5] Despite their concern with obtaining resources from the state in order to modernize Huanoquite, district council authorities made few advances and were repeatedly accused by other members of the resident elite of corruption and embezzlement of district council funds.

Changing national policies and the personalities of the members of the landed elite who occupied district council offices made an impact upon the workings of the council itself, although the record is scant in this respect. In the early 1900's, the official philosophy of *indigenísmo* was especially important in the way it influenced political action at the local level. While directed at the welfare of Quechua people, the movement was primarily promoted by intellectuals and, then, rhetorically, by the state during President Leguía's regime from 1919 to 1930 (see Rénique 1991; Tamayo 1980; Valcárcel 1981). Indigenísmo romanticized Quechua Indian lifeways and reified contemporary Indians. In 1920, the Constitution legalized indigenous communities. Indigenísmo structured interethnic relations, delimiting what a "good" Indian should be and differentiating it from the identities of "non-Indians." Indigenísmo was also an important means for Cusqueño intellectuals and aspirants to political power to foster the region's decentralization from coastal Lima by emphasizing Cusco's unique "Indian" identity. At the same time, the opening of the media to Quechua songs and dances, the emphasis upon stylized Quechua culture and festivals, and the promotion of "the Indian community" fed the visions of peasants, who saw in these ideas and rhetoric yet another way to advance their struggles for partial autonomy. In reality, few proponents of indigenísmo believed that respect for contemporary Indians included equal access to political power. In José Luis Rénique's words, "In Cusco, to speak of Indians was to speak of the structure of authority, of hierarchies that defined daily order" (1991:59).

Huanoquite's mayor during this period of time, Daniél Galdos, was deeply influenced by the current of indigenísmo sweeping the country. He was unusual in the lengths to which he went to defend indigenous rights and prevent abuses of indigenous labor. The actual policy decisions he made during his many terms as mayor of Huanoquite and the correspondence he left give us an idea of his views of the place of Indians in the future of the nation. Although he clearly did not believe in giving peasants equal political representation, he regarded himself as their protector. As a supporter of indigenísmo, Galdos believed that the traditions of Indians and the rights of native communities should be respected, and that Quechua Indians should receive recognition as Peruvian citizens. This did not preclude him, however, from also believing that Indians, once recognized and treated as citizens, could easily be integrated into national society, and that their traditions would no longer present obstacles to the success of modernization. In turn, the success of modernization in part depended upon harnessing Indian labor for purposes of economic growth and expansion. A fundamental contradiction, the category "Indian," thus had to be maintained in order to be done away with.

Neither the governor nor the provincial mayor approved of Galdos's policies or his respect for the new laws protecting native representatives passed by the Leguía regime. For example, Galdos informed the new governor that he knew he was "forcing native authorities [*envarados*, also known in Quechua as *varayuqkuna*] to work without paying them and making them pay for land titles." Galdos threatened to "tell the prefect" unless the governor "rectified his errors."[6] The varayuqkuna were traditional community authorities who were recognizable by the beautifully ornamented silver and wood staffs (*varas*) of office they carried. They were not officially recognized as authorities by the modern-day state, but commanded respect from members of communities or ayllus under their jurisdiction, often performing functions that the kurakas of the past had undertaken. They served important native religious functions, were sometimes guardians of communal land titles, and often called cohorts of Indians to collective labor projects. Thus, officials sought to use them as intermediaries in order to harness the labor of Indians without paying them and falsely pressured them for revenues in exchange for the right to retain communal lands.

During this period of time, Huanoquiteños, as was true of peasants throughout the highlands, felt fewer qualms about making complaints about landowners directly to district council authorities. Petitions from different indigenous communities demanding that their land and labor rights be guaranteed proliferated, and uprisings and land seizures surged. For example, Galdos reported to the prefect of Cusco that

the *indios comuneros* of Huanca Huanca have filed a complaint with me against Francisco Gamarra who lives in Cusco. Gamarra has prevented them from turning over the earth for their potatoes in their communal lands of Qqenqonay and other places. He won't allow them to use firewood or pasture for their cattle. He wants to make these private lands and tries to charge them a pasturing fee. The indigenous people have colonial titles to the land, and I therefore ask you to guarantee their rights.[7]

Galdos nevertheless found it difficult to enforce measures to protect the native population or extract local revenues in the form of fees and licenses from the landed elite. In a letter to the governor, he expressed his frustration:

I am trying to make improvements, but the notable *vecinos* are irritating and abusing my dignity, even though I am trying to do things for them that will serve as an example for posterity. My principles have always been to protect the defenseless race, work, and respect the laws and comply with them.[8]

In the 1930's, repression shut the window of opportunity that had been opened to Huanoquite's peasants by the philosophy of indigenísmo and the relatively sympathetic stances of mayors like Daniél Galdos. Once again, local political power reverted primarily to the landed elite.

The Changing of the Guard

In 1968, however, Huanoquite's district mayors, heavily pressured by peasants, began to change their tactics. News of the struggles in Huanoquite reached the national media, and the voices of Huanoquite's peasants were recorded in the district council and community archives, as well as in Cusco's major newspaper, *El Sol*.[9] In response to Velasco's attention to rural areas, mayors began lobbying in Cusco for roads and health posts; they demanded that the district be formally recognized as an archaeological zone with resources that were a valuable part of Peru's patrimony; and they formed a United Defense Front with other mayors from Paruro to send commissions to Lima requesting regional markets, educational centers, and roads. They also met with the provincial mayor to ask that he call an open forum to discuss the problems of each district.

Independently of their official representatives, Huanoquite's peasants also began to make demands upon the state. Together with peasants from other provinces in Cusco, they sent a delegation to the Ministry of Agriculture, requesting that "the new director of the Cusco Agrarian Reform zone be from Cusco," and, above all, that "he know Quechua so that he would not have to use interpreters in his contacts with peasants." They also participated in a department-wide demonstration in Cusco in 1970. Denouncing the "myths of support from the present government," they demanded that "bad functionaries be ousted" and "a process of moralization of government authorities take place."

One can trace a significant continuity in the themes of protest among peasants, despite changes in national regimes. For example, in yet another demonstration in 1984, peasants focused upon the "immorality of the Belaúnde government" and "the long history of exploitation by *mistis* and *gamonales* [the landed elite]." They demanded that "Ministry of Agriculture personnel speak Quechua and Aymara."

The events leading up to the visible and audible presence of peasants in local governance and regional politics stemmed directly from reform legislation that formally endorsed peasant electoral politics at the district level. District representatives began to organize politically to make demands on the state because they envisioned an epoch of modernization and development and a way to preserve their power in the face of an unpredictable regime that genuinely appeared to favor the peasantry.

Peasants, on the other hand, became eager to make demands upon the state now that they had legal recourse to fight for their lands and their rights as citizens. The district council constituted the principal political entity that could channel the demands of multiple peasant collectivities to the state. Most of these collectivities also now had their own elected representatives.

In the 1970's, Huanoquite's peasants began to seek control of the district council. A typical conflict over the office of district mayor ensued, pitting two members of the landed elite (they were actually relatives) against each other. Mario Romero, an intimidating absentee landlord who had served multiple terms over the years as mayor of the district, represented the old-style landed oligarchy. Jorge Gamboa, the opposition candidate, represented the younger generation that had emerged during the reform. A schoolteacher looking to accumulate power for himself through the new bureaucratic channels, Gamboa was an activist in SINAMOS and the Pachacutec Agrarian League, which represented Huanoquite's peasantry. He stressed the need to incorporate peasants into the processes of modernization and development. Most of the land belonging to Gamboa's family had been expropriated by the state, so he could no longer depend upon it for his livelihood, but his political resources and social ties with peasants permitted him to occupy a prestigious position in the district.

In an action possibly encouraged by Gamboa as a sympathizer of SINAMOS, peasants took to the streets in Huanoquite in 1974 and burned effigies of the local landed elite. Romero refers to that moment as "the inception of class war." Peasants applauded Gamboa for "supporting the revolution and the peasant masses."[10]

In 1977, Romero was once again "elected" mayor, taking office from Gamboa, who had been mayor from 1973 to 1977. The conflict between Gamboa and Romero turned violent. Gamboa accused Romero of "victimizing peasants who did not support him" and of "not performing his duties as mayor because he was an absentee landlord." Romero, in turn, instigated a suit against Gamboa for "having embezzled district council funds for himself." In addition, Gamboa was accused by Romero of "turning against the landed elite" and "inciting peasants to engage in subversive behavior." In a general assembly, Romero censured Gamboa, condemning his behavior in office:

In his period he only sought to improve his own well-being by means of the Sub-Agrarian League without having accomplished any projects that would benefit the pueblo. He has dedicated himself to creating problems among the *vecinos*, without calling general assemblies or participating in collective works. He has created divisions and discontent, with Chifia, with the Agrarian Production Cooperative Tupac Amaru of Llaspay. . . . He has engaged in sabotage and destroyed the district council. . . . All the teachers of Huanoquite should be replaced because of the great damage they have done to Huanoquite.[11]

The opposing faction, led by Gamboa, several other teachers, and a few peasants, aired their grievances over Radio Cusco and Radio Salcantay Sur, two popular stations that broadcast in Quechua. Romero angrily denounced them: "Without any motive whatsoever, they have done this in the name of SUTEP [the teachers' union, Sindicato Unido de Trabajadores de la Educación Peruana]. I will put an end to the abuses these evil professors commit in the name of this institution."[12]

At this juncture, Huanoquite's peasants played a notable role in deciding control of the district council. In an extraordinary assembly held in July 1978, attended by peasant representatives from the entire district as well as provincial authorities from Paruro, peasants raised their voices and pressured Romero to resign. For the first time, they openly proposed that the position of mayor be filled by a peasant.

In Saturnina Herrera's words, "To eliminate fights and enmity, the mayor should be replaced, even if it is by a campesino." And Ramón Eguilúz remarked with a certain degree of annoyance, "So long as these mayors are in office, no one can work in peace." Eguilúz refused to be persuaded by Gamboa's sympathies for peasants. "Furthermore, we condemn the teachers for holding festive lunches on school days," he added. "We would like them to understand that the National Educational Center that has been established is not for stars but for the pueblo of Huanoquite."[13]

Peasant support for the landed elite had eroded, and Eguilúz's statements suggest that some peasants already distrusted the "sincerity" of the teachers in assisting them in their efforts to control the district council. Although the vote went in favor of Romero remaining in office, he resigned the next year, and Enrique Bejar, also a member of the landed elite, became mayor. Bejar lacked the confidence of the population, however, and found it impossible to achieve anything in office.

Two years later, in 1980, Huanoquite's entire district council resigned, stating, "this council does not have the necessary support from the provincial authorities and from the pueblo. They have derailed the district's march toward its own development."[14] On June 18, 1980, Juan Bautista Quispe Antitupa, running on the United Left Front slate, became the first peasant ever elected to the office of district council mayor in Huanoquite.

I recount this history because it signaled qualitative changes in peasant relationships to the state and dominant ideologies and elites. The incident reflects the growing impotence of the old landed elite in the face of the reform law and a rupture in the subservient behavior of Huanoquiteños toward mestizos. It also revolved about three key processes that were intimately related to one another in the eyes of peasants and have been the focus of debate and political struggle in the district ever since: education, progress, and peasant unity. Huanoquiteños saw both education and progress as the bases for their integration into national society and as the means by which their children could achieve upward mobility. How to get resources for the purposes of education and progress, of what education and progress should consist, and who would control these developments were crucial issues for Huanoquiteños.

Once the district council was in their hands, Huanoquiteños began to feel highly optimistic about their march toward development. There was much to do. The truck road between Cusco and Huanoquite had been described as "a road of death. . . . Traveling to that zone was a veritable odyssey."[15] A doctor sent from Cusco to man the medical post in Huanoquite had abandoned his duties, calling it "an almost deserted . . . barbaric pueblo that deserves no attention from the Department of Health."[16]

Peasants from Huanoquite's communities and cooperatives now made concerted efforts to transform these conditions. They sent representatives to the Pachacutec Agrarian League; they elected "peasant students" to participate in SINAMOS training courses in Cusco. They demanded schools that functioned in their interest, especially an agronomy school, improvements to the medical post, the renovation of their plaza, a Sunday regional market, trucks and truck drivers who would follow enforced rules of scheduling, new roads, tractors, credit, electricity, and enterprises that would take advantage of their existing natural resources. They formed subcommittees and relied heavily upon the new local powers that had appeared in Huanoquite to press their demands with the state. They sent numerous letters and petitions to Cusco, Lima, and the various offices of the agrarian reform.[17]

Almost a decade later, few of their aspirations had been realized.

Not until 1986 did the state even begin to respond to peasant demands in Huanoquite, and by then, Sendero had been active in the region for at least four years. What happened? The notable failure of the state to support Huanoquite's desire for development until 1986 requires an explanation.

Several processes conspired to undermine the incipient unity peasants had begun to forge by taking initiatives against the landed elite and seeking to control local politics. They did not emanate from a single locus. At the national level, the reversals of the reform, ushered in by a conservative military coup in 1975, were compounded by a severe and generalized economic and fiscal crisis that began in 1980. The nation was wracked by inflation and debt. Urban migration was increasing rather than decreasing, exacerbated by a severe drought in the highlands. There was no sign that industrial or agricultural growth were likely in the near future. Just as important were the bitter land conflicts between communities and cooperatives and growing class differentiation at the local level that the reform law had catalyzed. At the same time, the reform had given peasants a capacity to participate in popular grassroots politics that intruded upon traditional paths to power.

Unintentionally, the proliferation of subcommittees created an image at the level of the regional bureaucracy of a lack of coordination within the district, and, indeed, rather than being able to mobilize around single demands, peasant efforts (and their labor) became diffused.[18] They were therefore less effective than they desired in achieving their objectives. Finally, and in part because of the obstacles peasants encountered in organizing in a unified manner, the new "progressive" intermediaries crucially intervened in village political life.

Grounds for Mediation: National Policies and Rural Politics

> And like bats chattering high up in the belfries of this structure, today's political struggles and bargains bear a haunting resemblance to ghostly ancestors long buried below.
> Vivienne Shue, *The Reach of the State*

The disappearance of the formal stratum of large landholders left a political vacuum in many peasant districts. This vacuum became an arena in which peasants vied for control over the channels the landed elite had dominated. After the reform, the individuals who came to occupy positions of power sought to satisfy the demands of local polities, although in order to do so, they often compromised local autonomy. They also took advantage of their power to further their own opportunities. Their structural position resembled that of the local ethnic lords (kurakas) of colonial Peru, but with an important difference. Compromise had always been essential to the capacity of Quechua highland communities to resist total cultural, political, and economic domination, but it also meant the sacrifice of ethnic autonomy for them. After the reform, peasants far more frequently had to weigh the value of "resistant adaptation" (Stern 1987:11), given that not one, not several, but many intermediaries presented their alternative faces of compromise and opportunism to them.

Control over land, literacy, marketing connections, and the capacity to manipulate ties to the regional and national bureaucracies became ever more important to villagers as ways to achieve recognition as powerful, authoritative, and necessary to the well-being of the district. Those who were most successful at balancing these demands were the well-to-do, who were at once able to be both more modern and more traditional than their less-fortunate relatives (Moore 1986:30). An irresolvable tension thus grew up between the idioms and consequences of constructive hierarchy, on the one hand, and destructive competition, on the other.

Huanoquite's peasants found themselves questioning the viability of their existing political structures and social relationships in protecting local autonomy and a sense of corporate identity. The legacy within Andean society of relying upon structures and processes that had encouraged compromise and mediation in order to provide a space to resist total incorporation into a nation that was not of their making was also the embryo that gave birth to the growing weakness of Andean communities.[19] The district itself, because it constituted the intermediary unit between the state and peasant communities, was where these struggles unfolded most explicitly.

The new stratum of intermediaries took advantage of existing cleavages within Huanoquite to enhance their own opportunities. They also brought with them ideas and ideologies that then became the focus of new kinds of struggles in Huanoquite over the meaning of national integration, the exercise of legitimate authority, and the kinds of objectives that communities could strive to meet through their local political organizations. As individuals from *outside* these entities involved themselves in trying to control the local political arena and competed with elected officials, the debates taking place *within* communities, cooperatives, and the district itself over the kinds of officeholders who could best represent local interests became more complex.

These intermediaries were not a homogeneous category, but the functions they performed with respect to the state and to the peasantry were similar.[20] As teachers, bureaucrats, extension agents, and entrepreneurs, they occupied key "directive, organizational and educational functions," mediating between the state and peasants (Feierman 1990:5). Many political struggles were fought out among Huanoquiteños at the nexus where peasant interpretations of state policies collided with those of intermediaries. Steven Feierman suggests that such individuals are able to make a substantial impact upon "the discourse of peasant resistance" because they

were men who had some primary education, who in many cases had worked as government functionaries at a very low level, and who had returned to peasant farming. They were peasants who had participated in the world of clerks. Because of their low level of education, and because they were not active in the world of government employment, they had greater autonomy than the chiefs or the better-educated bureaucrats. [Feierman 1990:23]

In Huanoquite, teachers most closely approximated Feierman's characterization and became central to peasant political struggles after the reform. Many of them no longer farmed the land, even though they hailed from Huanoquite. Regardless of their class background, most of them had lived in proximity to peasants for long periods of time and had been disturbed by the abuses peasants suffered and the impoverished conditions in which they lived. These individuals became the regional interface between the state and peasant communities.

The sentiments of concern teachers expressed for peasant welfare had another side to them, however. Many of their parents had lost land through the reform, and they themselves had neither the additional economic revenues from their parents' estates nor the social standing that ownership of an estate and the exploitation of peasant labor had once assured. They also knew well the practical hardships resulting from the centralization of powers and services in Lima, reflected in the lack of infrastructure in rural regions and the limited resources that reached the departmental capital, Cusco. Finally, many of them could be characterized as petty bourgeois and were extremely ambivalent about their own roots, whether they sprang from the Quechua peasantry or the landed elite. They had struggled to construct an alternative social identity and economic niche for themselves by becoming extremely skillful at mediating between peasants and the state. Most of them had supported the reform, and some of them had used their knowledge and connections to facilitate peasant demands for land and modernization projects. They would periodically take messages or letters from Huanoquite to bureaucrats in Cusco and would volunteer to buy luxury items there for the district council or for individuals. Moreover, they purchased Huanoquiteños' agricultural produce, reported on national political events, and circulated gossip, hardly an unimportant function.

Shue elaborates upon the importance of similar individuals in China who "inhabited the middle ground, reading the signals from both cultural complexes," and crucially linked "a no longer feudal base . . . to a not fully elaborated centralized bureaucracy" (1988:89).

The class backgrounds of these intermediaries differed. The parents of many bureaucrats and extension agents were owners of landed estates, and most of them were not from Huanoquite. The backgrounds of teachers and entrepreneurs were more varied. Many were the children of wealthier peasants from Huanoquite who had obtained an education and migrated to Cusco. Others were the sons and daughters of Huanoquite's landed elite. The most powerful entrepreneurs, the truck owners, were members of Huanoquite's landed elite who had either lost their land in the reform or chosen trucking as an occupation that could provide them with substantial economic returns. Regardless of their backgrounds, most of them had initially been convinced that the problems of peasants (and of Peru) would be resolved once land was redistributed to them. They also perceived legal protection, literacy, and economic opportunities to be essential to "the moralization of peasants," which, in turn, would encourage the dominant classes to recognize peasants as national citizens.

Elsa Ramírez, for example, was a young, thin, sallow-complexioned woman whose aunt lived in Huanoquite. She had studied criminal law in Cusco, but then returned to Huanoquite to run a store with the assistance of her aunt. In addition, she bought agricultural products wholesale from peasants and then sold them in Cusco. She displayed a real disdain for peasants, for life in the countryside, and for political parties. In her words:

I am always for the poor people. But the parties are opportunists. They claim to support the poor, but go where the money is. Most of the peasants here are ignorant and envious, drunks and lazy. The people from [parties] are untrained, incapable, make too many promises and spend too much time drinking. These people leave because they are bored. There are no comforts, no electricity. [interview, 1984]

Jorge Gamboa, whom we have already met, was the son of the owners of a large estate in Huanoquite called Pacco. After Pacco was expropriated, he became an active supporter of the Velasco regime, working in SINAMOS, running for mayor, and teaching in the local elementary school. A tall, calm, handsome man, still in his early thirties, and with some talent as an orator, he retained the bearing of a son of the landed gentry, but nonetheless had fairly good relations with many peasants, especially since he too bought their produce. The peasants also liked his support of agrarian reform. In addition, he had multiple ties with bureaucrats in Cusco and members of the declining landed elite in Huanoquite.

Alfredo Quispe, also a teacher, served the role of cultural broker, interpreting national policy, especially as regards education, to Huanoquiteños. Ultimately, he did not succeed in fulfilling his functions well. A man in his late twenties, with notable Indian features, he was not from the area, but came from a rural background; his parents had been campesinos in Apurimac. He spoke Quechua fluently and had received his training as a teacher in Cusco. Angry and disgruntled with peasants and the government alike, he spent most of his time making speeches about the ignorance of peasants and the worthlessness of the Peruvian government. Parents held him in low regard, because he had a reputation for using corporal punishment with students.

Felix Quispe, the district council secretary of Huanoquite and a native of the area, had few skills as a farmer. Yet he was a tremendous center of power because of his knowledge of paperwork—different forms, different seals, different signatures that were needed, the fees required, and the channels through which papers should be sent. Of course, he received substantial fees in exchange for his knowledge, and he spent most of his day in his wife's store presiding over what seemed to be a never-ending stream of people seeking stamps, signatures, and advice.

A number of minor brokers also wandered in and out of Huanoquite, especially those who were leaders of different political parties on the left and those seeking to purchase agricultural products or livestock as wholesalers.

Even as Huanoquite's peasants "worked" the district council, they were confronted with the machinations of these intermediaries. Although peasants initially welcomed their intervention, disillusionment gradually set in. Despite the different values they espoused, the behavior of these brokers often differed little from that of the old landed elite. The efforts of Huanoquiteños to revise existing relations of authority by coopting or attempting to appropriate the discourse of the national regime thus frequently met with failure. In the course of taking advantage of new state policies and laws in order to resolve struggles over existing hierarchical tensions, inhabitants contributed to the formation of new inegalitarian economic and political hierarchies. The changes that occurred, while they provided Huanoquiteños with opportunities for consolidating local politial power, also encouraged the emergence of authorities whose functions and powers created new obstacles to Huanoquiteños' efforts to resist domination.

In the case of the teachers, Huanoquiteños saw education as key to the benefits development could bring them as individuals and communities, as did the state. The Velasco regime had decreed literacy and education to be essential to modernization and national integration. In addition, concerns of a more material nature influenced peasant interest in education. Huanoquite's limited land base, combined with demographic growth, the number of peasants excluded from the reform who resided in communities, and the state's failure to provide necessary inputs that could lead to increased agricultural productivity, made education a valuable asset for peasants seeking upward mobility.[21] As one peasant in Huanoquite succinctly put it: "In our country we badly need education. With agriculture alone we are poor."[22] Another explained, "Too many of us have been trained by our ignorance alone."[23]

Minister of Agriculture Jorge Barandiarán had commented in 1969 on the future role education should play in Peruvian society: "It would be difficult to speak of anyone with more social emotion than students. They should apply the excess of their emotions in favor of the Agrarian Reform in order to provide assistance to their peasant communities."[24] A year later, he added, "The new system of national education will be implemented next year. . . . Peasant schools will be established, staffed by professionals, who will [thus] repay society for their education."[25] In March 1971, Velasco announced a new educational reform:

The educational reform of the revolution aspires to construct an educational system that will satisfy the needs of the entire nation, that will reach the great masses of peasants, always exploited and always deliberately maintained in ignorance, that will create a new consciousness in all Peruvians of the fundamental problems of our country, and that will contribute to, and forge, a new type of man within a new social morality that will emphasize the values of solidarity, work, creativity, authentic liberty, and social justice as a demand, responsibility, and right of each and every man and woman of Peru.[26]

The executive decrees passed by the Velasco regime threatened many Peruvians who harbored little ethnic identification with Quechua-speaking peasants and already found their class position jeopardized by the reform. Although the education Huanoquiteños received rarely served their interests and was provided to them by often-unqualified teachers who were ambivalent about their own identities as Peruvians, Huanoquiteños continued to consider education to be crucial to the future well-being of their children.

By 1978, however, many of them began to turn against the teachers and voiced their complaints about the teachers' disrespect for their children. Throughout 1980, in meetings or extraordinary assemblies, inhabitants periodically reiterated their complaints about the teachers—their long absences, their failure to distribute donated food to the children, and their use of corporal punishment.[27] In 1981, Huanoquiteños passionately demanded the transfer of all the teachers who "have accused the children of peasants of being useless and filthy."[28] That year, they succeeded in throwing the teachers out temporarily.

The form and content of education children in Huanoquite received did not coincide with their expectations. Local teachers denigrated students with racial slurs and presented them with a formal rendition of Peruvian history and knowledge that held little meaning for them. They refused to allow the students to speak Quechua. They encouraged individual competition, an idea foreign to the value that Huanoquiteños placed upon cooperation. They were not loathe to use corporal punishment. And, ignoring the demands of agricultural labor cycles, they severely sanctioned students for absences, while they themselves were frequently absent without notice. The district council, headed by Mayor Quispe, supported the Huanoquiteños' condemnation of the teachers, denouncing them in *El Sol* and on Radio Tawantinsuyu.[29]

The teachers returned in 1982, but their relationships to peasants and their attitudes had changed little. In one general assembly in 1984, peasants openly leveled a number of criticisms against the teachers, similar to the ones above, but this time they directed them to two educational supervisors from Cusco who were present at the meeting.[30] They also announced that they planned to send their verbal complaints to the Ministry of Education in writing. The response of one teacher was to expound on the problem of drinking among peasants: "Alcohol impedes the mental development of children. It affects the fetus and is manipulative. Because of the effects of alcohol, children don't go to school." One of the supervisors also responded, saying, "It isn't worth your time and money to send a letter to Cusco, because the ways schools are organized now is a Peruvian law, and no matter what you do, you won't be able to change it." Later, the supervisor confided to me that "all of Huano-quite's problems are due to the criollo race, which does everything with cunning and as little investment of personal labor as possible. They are the reason so many families are sending their children to school in Cusco, thus bringing about the downfall of rural educa-tion." The other supervisor expressed a slightly different point of view: "The teachers are politicized. They are communists, Trotsky-ists, and they attribute the problems of rural areas to external rela-tions of dependency rather than to internal relations of dependency." In 1986, Huanoquiteños protested once again against the teachers, demanding "a transfer of all educational personnel,"[31] but were un-successful in having their demand met.

Inferior rural education was not the only problem that beset Huanoquiteños. Despite their efforts to enter into national politics, they also continued to experience obstacles and rejection from state bureaucrats and party officials, who, notwithstanding their rhetoric proclaiming equal rights for all of Peru's citizens, discriminated against "the low ways of peasants," as one bureaucrat put it. These perceptions filtered down to peasants, who then struggled anew with whether or not simply to accept their own inadequacy as national citizens or depend upon "alternative interlocutors" to make their demands heard. Peasants were willing to spend enormous amounts of money and time in pursuing solutions to problems through inter-mediaries who might have more success influencing bureaucrats.

The Land Judge Prudencio Carcausto commented to me that one of the tragic outcomes of the reform had been that, despite the legal measures taken by the state to proclaim peasants national citizens, Peruvian society continued to denigrate and devalue agricultural labor. Consequently, peasants themselves often sought to enhance their standing in the eyes of the state by pursuing their objectives through intermediary figures who were either held in much higher esteem by the national society or gave the appearance of occupying a higher status. In his words,

Peruvians should value agricultural labor more. Because they do not, peas-ants believe that having and knowing teachers, lawyers, judges and the court system is better than agricultural labor, a matter of value and personal pride. In fact, agricultural labor is worth much more. The peasants are harvesting dreams. [interview, 1984]

Of course, once again, it was not that simple. Peasants were aware of the potentially exploitative and time-consuming nature of their efforts to deal with community problems through those figures of authority whom they themselves believed were "valued" by Peruvian society. The comments of different peasants in Huanoquite in this respect are revealing. Their statements were clear about what was at stake for them in placing their faith in the state, partisan politics, or intermediaries. They were increasingly aware that, in the process of being used by these intermediaries *and* the state, what they had to say and their values were being compromised. Take, for example, the following statements made by Huanoquiteños:

The director of the school is a wolf bitch, disguised as kindness and generosity. [Clemente Castañeda, 1980]

He [a teacher and merchant] seeks to gain the friendship of our pueblo with an eye toward advancing to a position in the district council. [unidentified, field notes, 1984]

When the vice president of Peru, Javier Alva Orlandini, came to Cusco, he offered to talk to the president on our behalf and donate a new tractor to Huanoquite. This was what he said, but to this day, he has not complied with his promise. [Santiago Cruz, interview, 1989]

At first, peasants enthusiastically welcomed the resources and skills of those able to channel their demands—for better education, for machinery, for good market prices—to the state. Gradually, however, they became far more circumspect, questioning altruistic rhetoric and promises. They listened harder and observed more carefully. In recognizing that false promises, personal opportunism, and outright racism were the order of the day, they also had to grapple with the diminishing alternatives for seeking political representation and economic leverage within the national society.

General Assemblies and Meetings

Although Huanoquiteños found it almost impossible to dissociate themselves in any permanent fashion from these uncomfortable alliances with intermediaries such as teachers and merchants, they did search for alternatives, leading to extreme tension in the district. These alternatives, few though they were, were extremely important channels through which peasants could directly voice their demands.

Among the most important were formal and informal meetings. They used these meetings to criticize individuals, air their grievances, and prolong debates that did not have easy resolutions. My first impression of these assemblies was that they were ineffectual decision-making bodies, since little was actually accomplished in terms of resolving problems or achieving concrete goals. The gatherings would last up to eight or ten hours; there was clearly an agenda; but nothing ever seemed to reach a conclusive decision. Often, even when a decision was reached, it was not subsequently enforced. Nevertheless, I grew to realize that the discourse that took place in these meetings was crucial to their success. The exchanges themselves continuously tested shifting political alignments, and the patterned course of the debates represented a form of due process or, if you will, parliamentary procedure.

Laura Graham points to the significance of similar kinds of meetings among the Xavante. The Western assumption is that "the individual is the locus of political activity in a democracy." Instead, Graham notes, at such meetings,

the locus of political activity lies . . . in the relationships between individuals . . . a collective production of multiple voices . . . accountability does not reside with any particular speaker but is distributed throughout the polity. The discursive practices . . . blur the boundaries between individuals to promote social cohesiveness and counteract the factionalism that constantly threatens to tear the community apart. [Graham 1993:717, 718]

The meetings I attended in Huanoquite were the most public indicators of the kinds of "hidden transcripts" villagers were elaborating. They often took place far from the village center, in the fields where people were working, by irrigation canals, or among members of work parties. They also took place on a larger and more formal scale as general assemblies in the schoolhouse or plaza. These meetings, despite all the conflictual dialogue that transpired, sometimes provided the flexible medium in which an ideology of corporateness could be composed and activated.[32] In the course of airing their grievances publicly, villagers discovered significant points of commonality among them that could then serve as the basis for collective policy-making and action.

Supracommunity Organizations: Peasant Federations and Agrarian Leagues

Peasants also tempered factionalism and the tension between national incorporation and local autonomy by participating in supracommunity organizations. Among the most important of these organizations were the Cusco Departmental Federation of Peasants (FDCC), the Revolutionary Agrarian Federation "Tupac Amaru" (FARTAC), and the United Left Front (IU). Through these organizations, they exchanged information with other peasants, discovered that they were encountering the same kinds of problems, and engaged in grassroots mobilization. They took advantage of government-sponsored agrarian leagues, but also worked with other groups that were often less compromising and more radical.

The following statements were made by a wide range of Huano-quiteños in formal interviews I held with them in 1984. I asked them what their most important memories were of political organizing. These are some of their answers.

I joined FARTAC. I learned who abuses us, why the harvest isn't good. We met with annexes in Paruro. I went to Cusco with a flag for the *hatun mitin* [great assembly]. We made them look at us, the orphans. We said that the cost of things was too high. The orphans need more land. We asked for a tractor from the government. We are orphans.

Here, Alejandro Farfán Quispe, a member of the newly founded cooperative of Tihuicte, used two key symbols, the flag and the idea of the orphan, to make his points. For him, the flag symbolized a demand for incorporation of the peasants into the nation on their own terms. Farfán calls attention to how peasants had always been treated as orphans, rejected as not being citizens of the nation. At the "great meeting" in Cusco, peasants spoke with one voice, holding high the Peruvian flag and demanding that they no longer be prevented from having their most basic needs met by "the family of the nation."

Silvestre Alvarez of Maska felt that the advice and support community members of Maska received, not directly from the state but from the agrarian league, allowed them to recuperate lands:

I was president of the community when I joined the Pachacutec Agrarian League. We were demanding that lands be transferred to the community. They helped us. For that reason, we regained our lands.

Hermógenes Chaparro, deeply traditional in his commitment to community and highly knowledgeable about the world of politics, recounted his memories of political mobilization against Romero, almost as a kind of pilgrimage in which uniting with other communities through a federation was crucial to their success:

I belonged to FARTAC, one of the leaders. We walked with the people, holding meetings, assemblies. We organized with the people in Cotahuana, Chanca, against Romero in Miskapata, to expropriate the estates.

Leonardo Herrera, also a member of Tihuicte, turned to the most traditional and radical of peasant organizations, the Peasant Federation of Peru (CCP), which had been established in 1947, to find out how to moderate the kinds of conflicts that characterized relationships between the cooperative and community:

I work with the Departmental Federation of Peasants so that I can learn in what ways we can prosper and how we can change existing sentiments.

Tomás Chaparro, younger brother to Hermógenes and president of Maska, shared a similar love for his community and explictly recognized the dangers of opportunism among many of the brokers in Huanoquite and his own fears about the consequences of economic differentiation in the district:

I do not work for love of money or power. I work for those who love my pueblo.

Finally, Huanoquite's first peasant mayor, Juan Bautista Quispe Antitupa, simultaneously expressed his excitement about the power of being organized into a political party that could represent the interests of all peasants, while rejecting the kind of factionalism and clientelism that party politics involved:

Political parties really don't play an important role for us. In reality, as people of the fields, we are one party, the party that defends ourselves.

While acknowledging that their participation in such organizations represented enormous sacrifices of time and money, Huanoquiteños had fond memories of these occasions. Their memories made explicit the concerns they considered central to political mobilization: land, labor, exploitation, unequal terms of exchange; the immorality of officeholders and of government in general.

Huanoquiteños also participated in high numbers in national strikes, sacrifice marches, and demonstrations against the Ministry of Agriculture, protesting the reversals of agrarian reform policy. In one demonstration in Cusco, on March 19, 1984, attended by at least 4,000 peasants from communities and cooperatives in the department of Cusco, Leonardo Herrera spoke publicly, forcefully expressing the reasons why he was there:

We in Huanoquite have always experienced isolation. Until now, we have suffered in our hearts all the injustices perpetrated by governments of misery and hunger. Now, we have come to Cusco to fight against these injustices. Death to the reactionaries. Let us find a new way of life.

Conclusion

The effects of "social conflict, exploitation and rural protest" place in relief "the material basis of intraclass and interclass struggle" that state agrarian policies themselves shaped (Isaacman 1993: 209). They also reveal how educational and bureaucratic institutions and the conflicts among agents working within them affected the course of these struggles. Finally, these local political struggles inadvertently incorporated struggles over representations that different members of Peruvian society held of one another.

In the postreform years, Huanoquiteños have searched for sources of political power and representation other than state institutions and organizations that would better satisfy their ideas of justice and morality, protect their local rights to resources, defend their national rights to citizenship, and moderate the economic and political divisiveness that uneven local development has accelerated. They have been fully engaged in experimenting with ways in which they can make claims upon the state and pressure local agents of the state. They have struggled to determine the paths that will give them greater representation at the regional and national levels; and they have faced the challenge of ascertaining the qualities of leadership that will best serve them, given the changing sociopolitical and economic conditions engendered by the reform and the subsequent policy reversals they have endured.

General assemblies and informal meetings have been crucial in shaping their debates about alternative channels of political representation, about the best way to implement local development plans, and about tactics they might adopt to control the behavior of alternative interlocutors to the state.

Supracommunity organizations have most adequately reflected many of their concerns, but peasant participation in these organizations has had unexpected consequences. While different national regimes have been more or less tolerant of peasant participation in federations, unions, and leagues, in general, they have regarded them as threatening to their legitimacy. The Velasco regime, in particular, viewed them as representative of a competitive alternative to its agenda of reform. Over the years, using legal and extralegal measures, the state has established a tradition of imprisoning federation and union leaders and violently repressing demonstrations and land invasions that these organizations have undertaken.

These reactive measures have shut off the majority of legitimate public channels that peasants can take advantage of to retaliate against "the immorality" of the state or of other individuals who play important roles in their lives. There are few alternative pacific means by which they can make known to the government their views of its policies, and they have little opportunity to build a sense of community whose ties extend beyond the territorial confines of differentiated households and corporate entities.

Despite its coercive power and reach into peasant communities through communist cadres, the Chinese state under Mao did not eradicate and, in some instances actually strengthened, the localism of agrarian society, Shue notes (1988:30–71). She points specifically to how the networks within the state bureaucracy reproduced the segmentation and peripheralization of rural society politically and administratively; state policies of self-sufficiency presented obstacles to economic development and national integration; and the intermediate position of cadres as local leaders situated between the demands of the central state and of their villages and work teams often led them to implement policies that prevented further penetration of the state and actually preserved village values and ideals that ran against the current of official state ideology.

There are important differences between the Chinese and Peruvian cases. Nevertheless, they have in common the paradox of a state seeking to achieve modernization and national integration but instead, through its own policies, encouraging involution, alienation, and, ultimately, a level of extreme violence that it did not predict.

21. (*right*) Demetrio Pantoja making a yoke
22. (*below*) Cirilo Rocca in front of his house

23. Fiesta celebrating the birthday of Mayor Juan Bautista Quispe
Antitupa (in front row wearing black leather jacket)

24. (*above*) Fortunato Eguilúz, mayor of
Huanoquite and a member of Tihuicte
25. (*right*) Fernando Loayza, storekeeper

26. (*below*) An informal political gathering
by a Maska work party, addressed by
Tomás Chaparro, their president

27. A portable altar (*retablo*) made by the folk artist Nicario Jiménez illustrating the violence perpetrated by the *pishtaco*, a creature that takes the form of an outsider and sucks the fat from Indians after killing them in order to manufacture different things. On the top level of the retablo, a colonial priest uses grease to make church bells, while the condor, an indigenous deity considered to be the Messenger of the Sun, looks on. On the middle level, foreigners use Indian fat to make airplanes; and on the bottom level, soldiers use Indian fat to make weapons (photo taken by Blenda Femenias)

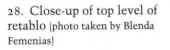
28. Close-up of top level of retablo (photo taken by Blenda Femenias)

29. Close-up of middle level of retablo (photo taken by Blenda Femenias)

30. Discussion among members of the entire district who have helped to clear one of Huanoquite's principal irrigation canals (photo taken by Stephen G. Bunker)

31. Work team putting the roof on a house

32. Huanoquiteños help-
ing to log and drag trunks
for electric posts

33. District labor to construct a water-powered
mill

Participation of Huanoquite's
operative members in a demon-
ation in Cusco

35. Demonstration of peasants in Cusco's Plaza de Armas protesting Peru's agrarian policies, March 19–22, 1984

36. Peasant demonstration in Cusco. The banner reads: "The Peasants United Will Win"

- 9 -

Questioning State Reform:
Sendero Luminoso

Ideology can be at once compelling, contradictory, and per-
nicious. . . . Just as no ideology is as coherent as it tries to
appear, no single voice remains without its inconsistencies
and contradictions.

Renato Rosaldo, *Culture and Truth*

After my initial year-long stay there in 1984, I returned to
Huanoquite for several months in 1989 and 1991. On my last
visit in July 1991, I went to the truck stop at Belén Pampa in
Cusco as usual at about 3 A.M. It was early enough for me to get a seat
in the cab. The dry season had begun and it was bitterly cold. I
greeted people, and we talked quietly. A few of them commented to
me how happy my compadre Demetrio would be to see me. They also
asked where my husband was. It was a hard trip for me. I had been
married in 1989. Now I was not. This too I would have to explain to
my compadre.

It was yet another eventful trip. There were many police and even
soldiers at the truck stop and at checkpoints on the road out of
Cusco. We didn't have to worry so much about robbery, but the
silence in the truck now signaled passengers' fears rather than their
discomfort. The truck driver, a dark-skinned man the Huanoquiteños had jokingly nicknamed Q'ara Chunchu (Jungle Skin), cheerfully
confided to me that the brakes were not working very well. In fact, on
the last hairpin curve before the village, the brakes almost failed. We
went sliding backward toward a precipice, stopped perhaps by luck,
perhaps by some skill.

It was early morning when we arrived, and I was excited and
nervous. I was not prepared, however, for what greeted me. Staggering down the street in front of the truck came Demetrio with two of
his friends. It was only 8 A.M., but he was obviously drunk. He looked
at me but did not see me. Then he fell into the dirt. Someone told him
I had arrived. He pulled himself up and came toward me as I got off
the truck. We embraced unsteadily. As I walked with him to the

house, a policeman and then a soldier stopped us to ask me for identification papers.

Demetrio, Victoria, and their family were now living in their new house. It had much more room than the old one, and windows through which the light poured. The potato harvest had been a good one, and the storage room was filled. The vegetable garden was flourishing. Demetrio even had a new horse in the patio. But Victoria looked worried even as she welcomed me.

During the time I was in Huanoquite, Demetrio alternated between drinking copious amounts of alcohol at all hours of the day and night, sometimes refusing to get out of bed in the morning, occasionally working very hard, and often weeping uncontrollably. Late at night, groups of men would visit the house to see Demetrio, and, whispering, they would all go off somewhere together.

It took me a long time to figure out the reasons for this remarkable and distressing change in Demetrio. That year, the district was preparing for municipal elections. They needed a new mayor. Yet since Sendero Luminoso had specifically targeted mayors in highland communities for assassination, very few aspired to the office. Those who did want to run were not necessarily held in high regard by other people. Both Izquierda Unida (the United Left Front) and Acción Popular (the conservative Popular Action party), which had large constituencies in the district, were asking Demetrio to run for office as mayor. A man as responsible and dedicated to community and family as he was could only feel tortured. His own description of life in the countryside, "so much love, so much grief," had come back to haunt him. He feared for his life. I have not returned to Huanoquite since that time. I have written letters but received no response. I do not know whether or not Demetrio ran for office.

Sendero's Guiding Lights

> Poverty is the propulsive force of revolution. Poor people are the most revolutionary, poverty is the most beautiful song; . . . poverty is not an insult, it is an honor, our highlanders together with the masses are the fountain of our revolution who, guided by the Communist Party, will construct a new world; the guide: ideology; the motor: armed struggle; the management: the Communist Party.
>
> Luis Arce Borja, *Guerra popular en el Perú*

On May 17, 1980, just before Huanoquiteños had elected their first peasant mayor to the district council, Sendero had begun its national campaign of armed struggle in the central highlands of Ayacucho. One of its first actions was to desecrate Velasco's tomb. Its public documents (see Arce Borja 1989) indicate that its intellectual leadership considered the failed reform as a signal for them to prepare their struggle against the state in rural areas. From their point of view, the reform had at least partially set the stage for revolution by eliminating feudal relationships in the countryside and nationalizing foreign industry. In a later official document, they explained the need to exacerbate the social polarization already evident in Peruvian society:

> In these times, the official left in Peru has not simply erred by having chosen the electoral path, but has deliberately put itself at the service of the democratic bourgeoisie with confusing proposals of reform within a system that was already attempted once by the military government of General Juan Velasco Alvarado and dismantled by the most reactionary sector of the armed forces, headed by General Francisco Morales Bermúdez: "The Stubborn Reformist Leads the Way to the Murderer." [Mercado 1986:62]

The women and men who became Senderistas comprised perhaps 5,000 active participants in all, with a network of sympathizers and passive supporters in both rural and urban regions of Peru. Sendero had begun organizing underground in the mid 1950's. Its direction had become more clear in the 1960's after the Communist Party of Peru (PCP) split into pro-Soviet and pro-Chinese factions. The future leader of Sendero, Abimael Guzmán Reynoso, belonged to the pro-Chinese faction, Bandera Roja, which did not believe in a "peaceful path to socialism" (Burt and Panfichi 1992:22). In the late 1960's, Guzmán split from Bandera Roja and formed yet another party, the "Communist Party of Peru on the Shining Path of José Carlos Mariátegui."[1] Subsequently, it focused its energies upon gaining peasant support in order to develop its Maoist-based revolutionary warfare.[2]

Sendero had its roots in a fundamentalist reading of José Carlos Mariátegui, founder of the Communist Party of Peru and author of *Seven Interpretive Essays of Peruvian Reality*, a classic read by almost all Peruvian school children. Mariátegui firmly believed that European socialism had to be adapted to the cultural realities of Quechua people in Peru's countryside, and that the Party's primary objective should be to destroy semifeudal rural relationships. Finally, these strands were woven together into a unique ideology by the charismatic Guzmán, better known by his nom de guerre, Presidente Gonzalo.

The Senderistas thought that by imposing the will of their minds together with strategic military skills on Peru's peasants and workers, they could engineer a great revolution. They believed they could convert science into a religion, and that it was necessary to use violence to do so, since, in their words, "Except for power, all is illusion."[3] They believed that Peru's semifeudal history, beginning with the Spanish conquest, had been fundamentally characterized by violence, and that the nation could therefore be radically transformed only with violence.

At a Crossroads

In 1982, Sendero Luminoso attacked Huanoquite for the first time. A squad of three men and three women blew up the Tihuicte cooperative's tractor, which was essential to the cultivation of its 800 hectares of relatively flat land. Before disappearing, they painted the walls of the colonial church with slogans proclaiming the glory of the coming revolution, identifying themselves by the now-familiar hammer and sickle. The destruction of Tihuicte's tractor brought the cooperative closer to the brink of bankruptcy. The Senderistas were caught as they fled to Cusco by way of the Inca road. Shortly thereafter, the *sinchis*, a special police shock force similar to the Green Berets, occupied Huanoquite. The special force remained for almost a year.

Tensions between the cooperative and the community of Maska intensified after the attack. Maska's comuneros, who had received little from the reform, repeatedly sought to invade cooperative lands. Taking advantage of this growing animosity, Sendero tried to win Maska's support, and Tihuicte's socios in turn began to perceive community members as allies of the Senderistas.

Direct Dialogue

Only in January 1986 did Engineer Edgar Hurtado, a representative of President Alán García's government (1985–90) and head of the Paruro microregional development scheme, journey to Huanoquite. Hurtado offered the district loans, doctors, funds toward an electricity project, a high school, a tractor, and an agrarian security force to protect Huanoquiteños, since an "Andean police force" did not exist in Peru.[4] He returned in June 1986 to encourage Huanoquiteños to attend the *rimanakuy* or "direct dialogue" in Quechua between President García and peasants in Cusco.

These overtures can best be characterized as belated, albeit innovative, efforts on the part of the state to alter peasant perceptions of it as an ineffectual, hypocritical (albeit powerful) entity that had reneged on most of its rhetorical commitments to them. They occurred in the wake of the increasing destabilization of the state by Sendero's activities in the highlands and human rights abuses against peasants by military and paramilitary forces (Guillén 1987).

On the other hand, the rimanakuy held great symbolic meaning for peasants, because it put them on an equal footing with the president. It also provides a fascinating example of peasants' efforts to arrive at a general consensus in their demands amid political chaos. I summarize below the concerns that peasants from the department of Cusco publicly expressed in the meeting.[5]

Their first concern was land tenure. They demanded that the state protect their collective land base; give them clear titles to land; and adjudicate more lands to their communities. They directed their requests specifically to the Ministry of Agriculture. Peasants also harshly criticized the corruption of ministry bureaucrats and land judges, citing the obstacles they had placed in the way of adjudication proceedings; their unjust return of lands to the landed elite; and the slow speed at which land disputes were resolved. They pleaded for "the authentic moralization of public organizations" and "immediate prohibitions against returning lands to the landed elite," and asked that "justices of the peace not intervene in land disputes, or that they submit them to communal decisions."

Their second set of demands concerned internal problems they were encountering owing to their limited land base and the unequal distribution of lands. In order to assure better distribution, control, and management of resources, they requested that only children residing in rural communities be permitted to inherit land, and that the sale, rental, and sharecropping of lands be prohibited. In short, they demanded "the recognition of the autonomy and power of the community in all community affairs." They also stated that they were not proposing a new distribution of lands—that is, a communal agrarian reform. Rather, they wanted tenure of existing communal lands to be revised to offset the unequal possession of resources.

Their third set of demands revolved about the presence of the state in communities and the issue of authority. They wanted the state to show greater respect for peasant communities and for community, district, and regional authorities. After their many years of dealing with the presence of state agents in their communities, they realized that these agents were going to remain key actors in their communities. They therefore asked that the state provide state employees working in rural areas and their families with basic services, and that, in return, these agents, in particular, teachers, be highly qualified and perform their functions properly.

Their fourth set of demands focused on the terms of exchange and the market: the market should not be permitted to be an obstacle to community development, and peasants should receive guaranteed prices and subsidies. Realizing that without an increase in production, this would be impossible, they asked that the state provide them with technical assistance, credit, and support for development projects that exceeded the technical and economic capacity of communities: roads, bridges, irrigation, and so on.

Many of these proposals revealed contradictions. Conflicts between communities and cooperatives, the differentiation among households, and the ambivalence among peasants about the constitution of legitimate authority made it difficult for peasants to be united in their political agenda. Nevertheless, poised between their desires "to be left alone" and "to be empowered," peasants seized the moment and worked hard to reach consensus about their visions of general welfare during the rimanakuy.

Despite the ostensible renewed interest of the García government in Huanoquite, it never delivered on any of its promises. When I returned there in 1991, Sendero had gathered momentum in the region. Authorities confided to me that they were sleeping at night in other people's homes for fear that guerrillas would attack them. The civil guard had killed one teacher. Huanoquiteños had formed themselves into a civil defense patrol. The number of attacks defined as "banditry" had risen; and Huanoquiteños had little faith in the protection offered by the police and special antiterrorist (Dirección Nacional Contra el Terrorismo, or DINCOTE) units that had entered the district. It is hard to gauge the degree to which violence had actually increased, since the terror that violent attacks provoked had magnified perceptions of it, creating further conditions for violence.

In an extraordinary open general assembly attended by all district representatives, the president of one community announced, "the civil guard only commits abuses. There is no legal justice here."[6] In direct counterpoint, one of the civil guards told me (assuming a sympathetic ear, since I was a North American), "The real problem is the Indians. What Peru needs to do is get rid of them just like the United States did with its natives."

Teaching Cultural Identity

A key factor contributing to Sendero's presence in Huanoquite had been the state's failure to provide sufficient support for rural education. This had redounded negatively upon both peasants and teachers, many of whom had been unable to penetrate the barriers to social mobility. Some of the teachers, condemned by peasants for their lackadaisical and racist behavior, and ignored by the state in their demands for better working conditions, despite their formation into a powerful union (SUTEP), turned against the state altogether to become sympathizers with or activists in Sendero. Guzmán had, in fact, stressed the key role in Sendero of intellectuals, who, "as high school and university students and professionals, should work in the service of the proletariat and peasantry, specifying and guiding them toward a new scientific national culture, and making them conscious that the only way they will achieve it is through revolution" (Arce Borja 1989:386). In one Huanoquite teacher's strident speech to the assembled members of Llaspay (CAP Tupac Amaru II), he pointed to the "falseness of the Constitution," stating that "the government wants people to stay illiterate, and it is responsible for the poor education in rural areas."[7]

One of Sendero's most effective tactics during its early evolution was to infiltrate and gradually take over control of particular unions. SUTEP was among the most important unions that Sendero members penetrated. In doing so, however, they constructed their own rigid views of ideal Peruvian society. They became quintessential hybrids themselves. Unable to achieve assimilation into either Quechua rural society or the dominant urban mestizo society, they forged their own path. Their ideology assumed that peasants were unable to fend for themselves, that they could not accurately identify their enemies, and that "the party" would have to take on the burden of "guiding the peasants" into violent overthrow of the state (Partido Comunista del Perú 1988) in order to create another kind of state, based not on national *integration* but rather on *separatism*, and an exeedingly narrow definition of separatism at that.

In hundreds of pages of public documents and interviews issued by Sendero, not once do they make mention of Quechua cultural traditions or values except to condemn them harshly as an impediment to their own project.[8] At the same time, as is true of any number of aspirants to political power and the state itself, Sendero sometimes uses multivalent symbols of "Quechua culture"—traditional dress and weapons, songs, language, busts of Indian revolutionary leaders such as Tupac Amaru—as vehicles to gain the sympathy, support, and control of peasants. The presence of these symbols in political rhetoric does not imply, however, that Sendero will actively include peasants as national political representatives in a new order or that Sendero's design of national economic and political policies will substantively change in accordance with peasant demands. Thus, while Sendero uses messianic elements tactically (and must do so to gain popular support), it is not a nativistic movement that seeks to revitalize Quechua lifeways.

Vivienne Shue's observations on the behavior of the rural cadres in postrevolutionary China are instructive in understanding the position of members of Sendero, in particular, teachers. The latter, while they have not yet been able to institutionalize the Communist Party of Peru as the new national state, are attempting to do so, and are finding themselves in a similar predicament to rural communist cadres in China:

Many givens of Chinese politics were decisively overturned when the Communist Party came to power, but the abiding tension between state center and locality was not one of these . . . the party's network of rural cadres, though in many important respects they differed vastly from the old local gentry, pressed as they became by the structure and the expectations of the new administrative system to act at once as agents of the state and defenders of their regions, they frequently adopted a dual role not unlike that of certain segments of the old regime elites. As with the gentry, local party cadres have endured now blame by the center, now hostility from the people, for their perceived lapses of loyalty to one side or the other. [Shue 1988:79]

And in describing the *muchachos de confianza*, Indian guards trained by rubber companies in the Putumayo to divulge the dangerous activities of Indians to their bosses, Michael Taussig comes close to capturing the decidedly complex and potentially violent roles such intermediaries play in creating both terror and representations of terror:

What is at stake here is . . . the typical colonial ploy of using indigenous culture in order to exploit it. But, of course, things are never quite so simple. Even the manipulators have a culture and, moreover, culture is not so easily "used". . . . The *muchachos* embodied the salient differences of the class and caste system in the rubber boom. Cut off from their own kind whom they persecuted and betrayed and in whom they often inspired envy and hatred, and now classified as semicivilized and dependent on the whites for food, arms, and goods, the *muchachos* typified all that was savage in the colonial mythology of savagery—because they were in the perfect social and mythic space to do so. [Taussig 1987:122]

The fault lines that developed within rural districts such as Huanoquite were particularly useful to Sendero. Its members showed great skill at allying themselves with one faction and then eventually taking control of or destroying it. It is interesting, in this respect, to note the comments of one Huanoquite teacher, Manuel Vallejo Castaña, echoed by others. A Sendero sympathizer, Manuel was an active member of SUTEP; he had participated in the 1960's uprisings in the La Convención Valley, and later in Antapampa, and had worked with SINAMOS in setting up training courses for peasants. He was quick to denounce the landed elite and the factionalism within the district, characterized by patron-client relations, commenting "only when the elite is killed will life change in the countryside." At the same time, he also denounced Huanoquiteños, stating, "they are very indifferent. . . . They are not interested in education. They are conformists, alienated from the progress of their own community. As long as the community does not understand what education is, things will be difficult."[9]

Most remarkable was the immense gap between the expressed desires for education on the part of peasants and the teachers' repeated declarations that peasants had no interest in education at all. Clearly, the debate was not about education per se, but rather about the kind and quality of education peasants were demanding, the behavior of teachers with respect to peasants, and the goals the teachers had in pursuing educational channels as a means of asserting their own ideological and political position.

Between Reform and Revolution

The years following the reform have witnessed significant changes in Huanoquiteños' relationships to the state, their participation in national and local politics, and the means they have adopted to defend their communities' autonomy. Almost all local political positions are filled by peasants, a remarkable achievement. Yet their capacity to capture state resources for their communities and for the district as a whole is severely limited. The protracted economic and fiscal crisis in Peru has placed further burdens upon peasants. It has led to soaring urban unemployment and the erosion of buying power on the part of both rural and urban residents. Migration, as an alternative or complement to rural agriculture, is no longer economically viable for many peasants.

The growing weakness of the state, which, at the very least, previously gave community leaders access to goods and services for their constituents, now means that elected representatives, however legitimate their mandate, often no longer have the means to meet the minimal collective demands of their constituencies. They often therefore resort to dishonest practices in desperation. Although cor-

ruption may be the easiest way "to get things done," it is also indica-
tive of the discrimination against peasant society that persists within state institutions, and of how little protection the state can offer
local communities. It is in these circumstances that Sendero has
been able to gain sympathy and support from peasants.

The behavior of both wealthy Indians and the landed elite changed
noticeably after Sendero became an active political force in the district. One of the major problems that the district faced was amassing
the necessary labor for collective projects. Peasants confronted the
difficulties of balancing their individual labor tasks with their labor
obligations to the district council and cooperatives or communities.
In this no-win situation, wealthier peasants simply refused to comply
with collective labor obligations. Usually, the entity that suffered
most as a result was the district. The remaining landed elite, despite
receiving benefits from these projects, almost never contributed their
labor to them. In 1991, many of the resident landed elite had left
Huanoquite and sold their properties if they could find buyers. The
few who remained, as well as wealthier peasants, had begun to participate on a much more regular basis in collective work projects,
fearing reprisals if they did not by Sendero, from which some of them
had already received threats.

Although it appears that the majority of Huanoquite's peasants
have rejected the alternative of armed struggle, some see it as the
only means available to them to transform their subordinate position
within the nation-state. Younger, more educated peasants are among
those willing to take this path as supporters of the guerrilla movement. That local authorities can achieve little in the interests of
their own constituencies, given the weakness of the state, has led
these peasants to question the legitimacy of their representatives and
the criteria upon which their power is based.

The ideology and practices of Sendero do not, in most instances,
coincide with basic peasant interests and demands. Nevertheless, in
trying to understand why some peasants would support this movement, it is important to keep in mind that the organization of Sendero
gives cells or columns flexibility in interpreting its rigid Marxist-
Leninist-Maoist ideology on the ground. Secondly, the members of
Sendero in Huanoquite have been able to seize upon the frustration of
peasants and their antagonism to the state, making the latter their
target through public trials of, and extreme violence against, members of the "neocolonial bureaucratic structure" represented by "servants of the state."

Not surprisingly, Huanoquiteños are aware that the state exists in its most insidious form at the local level, where law enforcement agents and small clusters of the landed elite continue to act with impunity, eluding formal legal sanctions and informal disapproval on the part of communities. Tensions have grown between those Huanoquiteños who still believe that intermediaries are their only hope of legitimately gaining access to the state; those who believe that the presence of these intermediaries is wholly destructive of Huanoquite's partial autonomy from the state; and those who with good reason fear the escalation of violence that will occur if they take a public position.

In an interesting discussion of scholarship on the Mau Mau movement in Kenya, which bears important similarities to Sendero, Allen Isaacman makes it clear that people participated in Mau Mau for diverse reasons, and that the diversity of their motivations serves as a cautionary warning to scholars to "move beyond the one-dimensional notion that all-powerful nationalist movements spoke for and led the illiterate peasant masses or at least some subset who were particularly prone to revolutionary action" (Isaacman 1993:258). For example, Isaacman points to recent literature on Mau Mau that argues that peasants joined because of "fierce competition for land and labor." Other scholars argue that the "more privileged squatters, in combination with . . . relatively privileged petty traders, farm foremen, and diary clerks, were the driving force." Still others have demonstrated that a younger generation, separated from land as a channel for upward mobility, challenged the state. Finally, some have stressed that Mau Mau was a grassroots mass movement, spearheaded by peasants protesting the willingness of their own chiefs to compromise their autonomy in dealings with the state. Likewise, people joined Sendero for very different reasons, interpreting its tenets in terms of their own interests and dreams, not terribly different from those enumerated above.

At first, Sendero held public trials and killed "servants of the state" with at least the partial consensus of peasant collectivities. Its tactics have changed, however. It has abandoned the forum of public trials in favor of violent direct execution. Despite its objective of achieving a new kind of society that will represent peasants and workers, Sendero has created an authoritarian totalizing ideology that cannot, and does not want to, account for the differences among peasants, their value systems, their economic positions, and their aspirations.[10] In the course of attempting to mobilize peasants to participate in their movement, Senderistas have fallen prey to many of the same pitfalls as the state. They have a single political model of peasants as ideal revolutionaries. If reality does not conform to their model, then it is not the model that should be questioned or revised but rather the peasants themselves. In similar fashion, the state has repeatedly attempted to fashion Quechua peasants according to its model of the Peruvian citizen as one who, given the proper incentives, will respond enthusiastically to the capitalist dictum that everything has its price.

Neither Senderistas nor state officials, in their respective ideologies and approaches, have been willing to face the contradictions and conflicts in the political organization and economies of peasants, or even their heterogeneity. Nor have they risked trying to ascertain peasant self-perceptions. Finally, as Isaacman (1993:227) notes, an emphasis on interclass struggle tends to ignore the important roles that generational, gender, and religious differences play in struggles over scarce resources and power.

As Huanoquite's peasants have encountered increasing difficulty gaining state support in their efforts to resist Sendero, many of them have turned to more local forms of resistance: the formation of peasant civil defense groups; sustained efforts to achieve infrastructural projects using their own labor, materials, and kin networks; and greater community supervision over the selection and behavior of their own representatives.

Ironically, Sendero finds these differentiated forms of political mobilization most threatening to its own objectives. One of its principal tactical goals is to polarize Peruvian society by leaving peasants with increasingly fewer options to choose among in organizing politically without turning either to the state or to Sendero.

The history of political struggle in Huanoquite involves a continuing debate among Huanoquiteños about the nature of legitimate authority. Within the district, these debates have revolved about intergenerational conflicts, the unequal distribution of land, and the excessive demands made upon peasant labor. They have also reflected the uncomfortable dilemma of authorities themselves, whose primary skills lie in mediating between peasants and the state, and therefore, in compromise.

Underlying these debates is the more sustained struggle of Huanoquiteños to balance accommodation to these officeholders with their desires for national integration on their own terms. These terms are not set in stone and are often contradictory and unclear. Yet the same preoccupations tend to appear again and again, in the words of Huanoquiteños and the actions they take: a demand for recognition as diverse collectivities; greater local control over equi-

tably distributed collective resources—land, labor, water, and forests;
services from the state that will empower their communities and
permit them to participate on a more equal basis in the national
society—irrigation works, appropriate technology, roads, credit, better terms of exchange on the market, and an educational and judicial
system that works for them.

Although it cannot be singled out as the only reason for the
present state of violence in Peru, the 1969 reform substantially expanded the space that peasants could seek to dominate politically
and economically. It did so while attempting to retain firm control
over the direction that economic and political change would take.
Furthermore, it fostered the growth of an educated group of intermediaries, some of whom were children of peasants, others, of members of the landed elite. These intermediaries had placed great hope
in Velasco's agrarian reform initiative. Their disillusionment when it
failed to enhance their own economic and political mobility, and did
not lead to their notions of an ideal rural society, was correspond-
ingly great. Perhaps unwittingly, they had also absorbed many of the
landed elite's attitudes to peasants. In the upshot, as a man who had
defected from Sendero put it:

We created another social stratum within the same community; another
overseer; another owner, because we felt we had more power than other
peasants. We created another race, another social problem within the con-
glomerate of the same community. And thus, we also created those who
exploit and those who are exploited. Exploited, the peasants are illiterate,
and they let others run things who know a little more, who have a little more
culture, who have a little higher level of education. We were the ones who
began to govern and to exploit our own brothers, and thus we rose to become
new millionaires, new hacendados. We were too close to them [our own
brothers] to know ourselves as we really are. The peasants try to benefit from
those who have a little more experience, culture. We leave as millionaires
and abandon again the poor who are trying to recuperate their lands, trying to
improve themselves. We leave them totally abandoned and even annihilate
the community. [interview, 1991]

And a lawyer who had been a member of the Peruvian Communist
Party said:

Sendero Luminoso is, perhaps, an exaggeration of good faith. When I was
young, and also when I became a lawyer and before the agrarian reform, I was
absolutely certain that when land was given to the peasants, the Peruvian
problem would be resolved. I had the idea that every peasant worked, a little
lazy, a bit of a thief because he worked for someone else, the hacendado, but if
the land were his, he would work it with great eagerness. It was a lie. It hasn't

been that way. As a result all my faith in that epoch has crumbled, because reality is different. . . . A harsh hand is needed. The peasants are cold, they can't walk, they get drunk, man and woman, they lie sprawled out on the ground. How is a country going to develop? How is a community going to grow? We need, now we don't say a whip, because this is no longer the epoch of the whip, but something that will obligate them to work for themselves, something within each person, each community, a spiritual matter that will make them work for themselves. Perhaps it is this faith that belongs to Sendero, who have taken up arms because they want to improve things, but by a very bloody, drastic, and severe path. They are a violent reaction to so much abuse, so much immorality, which can be seen among all of Peru's politicians today. [interview, 1991]

In these complex statements, we can see how former members of Sendero and, no doubt, active members as well, struggle with the historical legacy of unequal economic and political relations and focal points of power in the countryside. Externally embedded in differentiated land and labor relationships, internalized to a degree by the habits of paternalism, backed by coercive power, these practices and attitudes cannot simply be eliminated through ill-designed reform policies emanating from a guiding state or party ideology; by good faith, moral fiber, and spirituality; or by violence grounded in "scientific" theory. Rather than leading to the elimination of corruption and greater equality as Sendero hoped, violent revolution seems to have had a remarkable capacity to destroy community, and even the idea of community, altogether.

Conclusion

Marginality is not simpy a linear consequence of economic impoverishment. Instead, Huanoquiteños' aspirations and their sense of political empowerment increased after the reform. At the same time, they encountered challenges and obstacles to their efforts to realize their aspirations. Some of the difficulties they faced were the direct consequence of state attempts to control the direction that peasant economic and political mobility should take. In the course of trying to meet these challenges, Huanoquiteños have struggled to arrive at new grounds for community solidarity, and they have argued over the usefulness of intermediaries in gaining access to the state and in providing a buffer from the unwanted intrusions of the state. I have tried above to replicate the debates surrounding these issues in order to demonstrate the complex dynamics that undergird peasant political action and bring into focus the significant commonalities that inform peasant relations both to the state and to Sendero in their communities.

Carol Smith has shown how the "promise of justice provided by a world ideology [that] had no concept or strategy for multicultural states . . . came up short against a particular local history" in Guatemala. The Guatemalan regime thereupon attempted to control the political and economic forces it had unleashed by adopting "greater infrastructural and despotic powers," but the Guatemalan state nonetheless "remains decidedly weak with respect to ideological (hegemonic) control. Since such states are inherently more vulnerable to and more likely to generate popular resistance, the possibility for violent revolutions remains high in Guatemala" (Smith 1990c: 280–82).

Peru also fits this model, although the state's weak ideological control over peasants is exacerbated by its lack of economic power. The blurred boundaries that characterize the social position of Sendero's members and the cleavages within peasant communities mean that the state has little ability to maintain control and surveillance in order to fight back against Sendero or gain the loyalty of peasant communities. At the same time, the diversity and divisions among peasant communities and cooperatives has prevented rural inhabitants from forming a united front against either the state or Sendero. This weakness has also been a source of strength for the peasants, however, since no centralized party or power has ever found a single cultural source or symbol with which to destroy or assimilate Quechua peasants.[11]

It remains to be seen whether or not Huanoquiteños will succeed in challenging the more direct and violent inroads that both the state and Sendero Luminoso are making in their communities by refusing to accommodate to any kind of cultural, economic, or political diversity that falls outside their own totalizing ideologies.[12] Though their ultimate objectives may differ, both Sendero and the state have placed inordinate emphasis upon the power of education and ideology to transform "bad Indians" into "good Indians." They also share in common a desire to rob peasants of their identities in order to shore up their own identities and political power.

As Huanoquiteños encounter these challenges to the survival of their communities, they continue to farm their land, market their produce, engage in general assemblies and collective work projects, participate in Catholic religious festivals and Evangelical Protestant celebrations, and go through legal channels to resolve land disputes.

Still, although they rarely voice their concerns openly, the fragility of their communities is uppermost in their minds. One evening, while drinking with Demetrio Pantoja, his wife, Victoria Zanabria, and Crisóstomo Castañeda, a district authority, I asked them what they thought about Huanoquite's future. After a long silence, Demetrio replied, "We, the peasants of Peru, all of our pueblos, are bathed in blood, tears, sweat and sacrifice. And we are bathed in the violence of the hacendados, of the elite, and of the military. There are always new masters in Peru. These are national problems that we confront locally. We need to decentralize the state, expropriate more lands, and organize ourselves into popular organizations to defend ourselves."

Huanoquiteños have sustained a long struggle to defend themselves through their own organizations despite the obstacles they confront—an inefficient, centralized, incompetent, poor, and violent state; an authoritarian and equally violent guerrilla movement; their own internal divisions; institutionalized racism; and the persistent efforts of the dominant classes to reify ethnicity. If anything, the processes set in motion by the agrarian reform have shaken the foundations of Peruvian society and catalyzed the struggles of Peruvians to transform relationships between the state and agrarian communities. Most Huanoquiteños have not yet embraced the overthrow of the state. However unsuccessful they may thus far have been in constructing relationships with the state that better serve their needs, they remain deeply involved in attempting to meet this challenge, albeit under exceedingly disadvantageous conditions.

Conclusion

> It is most important that we begin our work from the con-
> scious knowledge that our overall analytic task is one of ad-
> dressing not a mechanism, not a system, but *a process*. . . . To
> regard ourselves as students of process will mean paying at-
> tention to history . . . and . . . individuals—to the effects, that
> is, of particular choices and unique events that might have
> happened otherwise. But the kind of process I have in mind is
> more than tracing mere sequence or searching for some sign of
> evolution *through time*. It is more than a narrative history
> of "shocks to" or "cumulative effects upon" the polity, where
> the polity is still portrayed as a more or less solid object. A
> politics-as-process orientation . . . would . . . lead us to explore
> for patterns of flux and flow among those *internal* elements,
> arrayed in tension, that constitute and animate the polity
> itself. In particular, such a process approach would press us
> into recognition of all those mutually conditioning interac-
> tions that occur among elements of the polity that we are
> accustomed to think of as rather distinct and, often, therefore
> as rather static.
>
> Vivienne Shue, *The Reach of the State*

The effects of the current civil war upon Huanoquite have been
"light" in comparison to those experienced in the central highlands or the squatter settlements of Lima. Walking into the
district capital at mid-morning, one would almost surely encounter a
deep quietness. Most of the men would be far away, working in their
fields. A few stragglers might have become entrapped in tippling in a
store down some side street. Women would be gossiping in their
kitchens while they cooked and tended their infants. Some might be
herding or washing clothes. Most of the children would be at school
if the teachers had arrived that day. The truck to Cusco would have
gone down the day before, and the only sound rupturing the peace of
the morning would have been the rumbling of the truck arriving
from Cusco.

This image is a partial, although not entirely false, one, possibly
giving the impression of an idyllic highland hamlet, a more or less
"solid" and "static" polity. Through this book I have tried to spec-

ify the kinds of mechanisms that contributed to the "patterns of flux and flow" in highland communities after General Velasco's reforms. In complex ways, these patterns transformed the relationships among all rural inhabitants, as well as between peasants and the government agents operating at different levels of society, designing, representing, interpreting, implementing, and responding to state agrarian policies and ideology.

In an essay on Islamic, Indic, and Malaysian law, Clifford Geertz (1983:167–234) proposes that it is possible for us to produce a "thick description" of the legal ideas central to a culture and that distinguish its notions of law from those of any other culture. I concur rather with Sally Moore (1989:278), however, that this kind of "thick description" does not "take one very far in understanding what people do on the ground or why they do it at particular times and places." As she puts it so well, these ideas, elegantly presented though they may be, if they lack context, ultimately become ahistorical and object-oriented. They become "statements without speakers, ideas without their occasions, concepts outside history" (Moore 1989:278).

Huanoquiteños, landlords and peasants alike, did not interpret the agrarian reform law in a uniform fashion. And attorneys and land judges were instrumental in shaping their respective interpretations of the law. While all Huanoquiteños sought to use the reform legislation on their own behalf, their defenses differed from one another as they attempted to act as agents, re-forming legal "facts" and the various kinds of knowledge that had entered into their worlds, influencing and structuring their claims. The "traditional categories" Huanoquiteños deployed in their legal struggles were not rigid. They showed a fluidity that was at one and the same time the product of the dramatic changes they were apprehending and assessing and of the history of the socioeconomic relations that had systematically emerged from their experiences. These categories were also a product of their creative use of improvisation, invention, construction, and choice (Rosaldo 1989:91–108).

In 1969, when Velasco passed his agrarian reform law, peasants responded to the powerful call to national incorporation that the regime had set in motion. They took diverse paths and often clashed with one another in defending their rights to land and labor. As we have seen, different sectors of Huanoquite's peasantry envisioned alternative land and labor regimes in terms of prior principles and practices. Even when they had been repressed, these principles and practices remained alive as important memories, and sometimes they were engraved in documents. Most important, despite the different kinds of accommodations that peasants had made to the loss of their land and exploitation of their labor, they still considered control over territory to be fundamental to the construction of their identities. Although it abstractly espoused the equal right of all peasants to regain control over their lands, the reform in reality did not, and could not, give equal weight to all Quechua peasants who believed they had valid claims.

Peasants also had to reevaluate their ideas about legitimate political authority. Those peasants and landlords who moved astutely within the bureaucracy and knew best how to reach their objectives through persuasion, manipulation, and corruption gained the attention of peasant communities and cooperatives alike. The presence of such individuals might be desirable and advantageous if they could serve as allies in the courtroom, succeed in untangling bureaucratic snags, and facilitate access to state resources. The success of these individuals depended greatly upon their skill and capacity to draw upon multiple sources of capital, translating economic and symbolic capital into political power. These same individuals frequently acted opportunistically and often divided communities against themselves.

Participation in grassroots organizations, federations, and government-sponsored agrarian leagues played a central role in tempering conflict and fostering collective action and discourse among peasants. Although the rhetoric of the reform, and even the legislation itself, did not make explicit the government's attitude to racism or to how interethnic relations should unfold in Peru, the regime's assertions that peasants were important national actors, and its recognition of at least some of their rights to land, fueled peasant efforts to seize greater political power for themselves. The regime's position also provoked peasants to resist state efforts to bring about homogeneity.

Peasant federations, in particular, began fighting for precisely the kinds of recognition the state and the dominant classes were unwilling to grant peasants. Within districts such as Huanoquite, the issues of being a campesino *and* a national citizen arose as communities and cooperatives with newly established administrative structures attempted to gain access to state services and money, and to reclaim their land and water rights. Conflicts between different levels of the state bureaucracy, federations, and peasant communities, as well as within peasant collectivities, over how to interpret state policies and the importance to be attached to ethnic identity and economic equity in the process of "nation-building" were exacerbated.

In attempting to control these struggles, the state became increasingly repressive, especially after the demise of the Velasco regime, ultimately restricting the capacity of peasants to make demands on it. At the same time, however, this repression created the conditions for either violent rejection of the state by peasants or their increasing dependence upon intermediaries and bureaucrats in addressing the higher levels of the bureaucracy.

More often than not, as we have seen, reliance upon intermediaries resulted in the formation of dispersed power centers that competed with the state. In turn, peasants found themselves enmeshed in a web of networks that sapped their economic resources. The new functional niches that intermediaries came to occupy in most highland communities after the reform allowed them to perform some valuable services for peasants. Nevertheless, their ideas about development, education, and the future of a Peruvian nation that would be represented by peasants and workers depended far more upon authoritarian and coercive mechanisms than upon the consensual mechanisms that peasants deployed.

Despite these difficult conditions, as a result of the reform, Peruvians have been forced to accept that peasants have a legal right to control their own means of production and participate in the market economy and local governance. In addition, the active struggles in which peasants have engaged to broaden the political space the reform made available to them have proceeded in part because of the reform policies themselves. Peasants have a greater land base than ever before; they are more able to assert control over their own labor; and their knowledge of bureaucracies and legal systems has deepened considerably. These changes have empowered peasants even as they have created divisiveness and instability.

Memory has played a central role in peasant political struggles. The social and political topography that colonialism engendered created memories of ideal sociopolitical and economic organization. It also created memories of the loss of authority and personal power. The agrarian reform became the basis of a new set of memories. The bleak economic and political prospects of peasants amid civil strife under a weak government have transformed peasants' mixed experiences of the reform into an overwhelmingly positive and fond memory of the Velasco regime, notwithstanding the conflicts that pitted peasant against peasant, and peasants against the state, and called into question the foundations of legitimate authority within peasant communities. On the other hand, many who are not peasants consider the reform to be a principal cause of all the problems that Peru now faces.

For the majority of Huanoquiteños, as for many Andean highland peasants, however, their very empowerment constitutes the central paradox of the reform. Velasco gave them yet another stake in comprehending and fighting against the experiences and structures of domination that were part of their lives. They did so by envisioning a different kind of world, taking the risk of articulating their imaginations by speaking their minds, laboriously translating their thoughts into cogent legal defenses, and strategically seeking to improve their livelihoods. They participated actively in shaping the history of the reform—its failures and successes. In sustaining their struggles to organize among themselves and to gain power from a highly unstable state that penetrated communities to a far greater extent than ever before during the reform, peasants have ensured that the terms of their incorporation into the Peruvian nation-state have yet to be wholly determined, either by those presently in power or by those who would like to eliminate the existing state altogether.

Epilogue

As this book goes to press, Peru's highland peasants have yet to experience substantially greater economic power or enhanced democratic freedom. Alberto K. Fujimori prepares for the 1995 general elections, having amended the Constitution in 1993 so that the incumbent president may run for office for a second term. The new Constitution, voted on in a referendum, passed by a bare majority, reflecting doubt among the general population about Fujimori's controversial economic policies and dictatorial measures. Fujimori's potential opposition includes Fernando Belaúnde Terry of the conservative Acción Popular party, who has been president twice before; Luis Cáceres Velásquez, former mayor of Arequipa and leader of the National Peasant and Workers Front (FNTC), who is running as the representative of the independent political movement Peru 2000; and the former United Nations secretary general Javier Pérez de Cuellar. Pérez de Cuellar has not yet confirmed whether or not he will run as the candidate of a broad opposition front.

Many of Sendero's leaders have been arrested, including Abimael Guzmán. In 1991, Fujimori passed a legislative decree authorizing peasant defense patrols to bear arms so long as they functioned under the control of the military. The decision to arm peasants so that they could protect their communities and, more important, assist police and special antiterrorist forces in fighting against Sendero has had mixed consequences. It demonstrated the weakness of the state in performing one of its principal functions—ensuring internal order. It also militarized the countryside, provided additional cover to the military in the case of abuses it committed, and heightened existing conflicts among different groups of peasants. By January 1992, over 300 peasants belonging to patrols had been killed (Burt and Panfichi 1992:32). At the same time, the patrols have played a crucial role in the government's initial success in defeating Sendero and in returning the nation to greater stability.

Although violence has subsided (half as many people were killed in the civil war in 1993 as in 1992) and Peru has once again attracted foreign investors, peace remains elusive. Many innocent civilians are behind bars without recourse to due process in the civil court system. In the civil courts, they are tried by "faceless" judges; that is, their identities remain anonymous. Army troops continue to strafe highland peasant communities and lowland Indian populations indiscriminately, supposedly searching to eradicate the last holdouts of Senderistas. Sendero also continues to fight back with equal violence in order to prevent Fujimori from fulfilling his promise to the Peruvian people—that he will eliminate Sendero by 1995.

In April 1994, Peru declared its agricultural sector to be in a state of emergency until December 31 because of damage by heavy rains and flooding. The International Potato Center predicts that more than 50 percent of Peru's staple potato crop will be destroyed by late blight, the same fungus that caused Ireland's nineteenth-century potato famine. Emergency funds are available to peasant households as compensation for the destruction of their lands, but they cannot be distributed unless the lands are titled. Inadvertently, the state of emergency has speeded the titling of lands since, according to the National Agriculture Organization (ONA), some 70 percent of Peruvian farmers do not have title to their land. In addition, while Peru has about 129 million hectares of potentially arable land, because of lack of financing, only 3.73 million hectares are under cultivation.

These dismal conditions provoke one to ask whether there is anything to be done. Even as a global economy, unfettered by national boundaries, emerges, perhaps the Peruvian government would be wise not to forsake the goal of domestic agricultural self-sufficiency, a goal that can only be realized with the full knowledge, cooperation, and participation of Peru's highland peasants. The civil war in Peru will not be won by weapons, money, or the enactment of laws alone.

It will require that Peruvians heed the plea with respect to Quechua peoples that José María Arguedas made to the "doctors of development" in "Huk docturkunaman qayay" almost three decades ago:

> Take a good look at me, recognize me . . .
> No, brother mine. Don't sharpen that blade against me; Come close.
> Let me know you. . . .

APPENDIXES

Appendix A

History of Huanoquite's Social Organization

TABLE A.I
Tributary Population and Social Organization

Unit (caciques)	Tribute payers	Widows	Children	Women	Total
Repartimiento de					
Guanuquito (2)	207	38	228	564	1,037
Repartimiento de Corcca (1)	74	17	100	276	467
Pueblo de Curimarca	20	3	22	36	81
Pueblo de Tantarcalla (1)	26	1	20	64	111
Repartimiento de Coror y					
Guancaguanca (1)	79	17	81	306	483
Pueblo de Chanca	47	8	54	103	212
Repartimiento de Arabito	62	18	74	186	340
Repartimiento de los					
Mascas (2)	263	53	223	675	1,214
Pueblos de Unchurco,					
Condorcalla, Rocoto	22	◄------65------►			87

Allocation of Indian labor grants (encomiendas) to Spaniards
Guan(u)quito: encomienda de d. Antonio Vaca de Castro
Corcca: encomienda de d. Pedro Arias de Avila
Curimarca: encomienda de d. Tristan de Silva
Tantarcalla: encomienda de d. Gomez Arias de Quiñones
Coror, Guancaquanca and Guacachaca: la Corona Real de Su Majestad
Chanca: encomiendas de d. Gomez de Tordoya, Pedro Vasquez de Vargas, doña Francisca de Robles, Juan Fernández y Valençuela
Arabito: encomienda de d. Gomez de Tordoya
Mascas: encomienda de d. Tristán de Silba
Unchurco, Condorcalla, Rocoto: encomiendas de d. Pedro Vásquez de Vargas, Gomez de Tordoya, Antonio Vello Gayoso

Source: Based on figures from Noble David Cook, Alejandro Malaga, and Therese Bouysse, eds., *Tasa de la visita general de Francisco de Toledo (1570–1575)* (Lima: Universidad Nacional Mayor de San Marcos, 1975).

TABLE A.2

Parish Structure and Social Organization (1689)
Parish of Guanoquite (pop. 740)

MOIETIES (2 main caciques)
Mascas
Inkakuna

PARCIALIDADES (2 caciques)
Tantarcalla
Chanca (located in an estancia belonging to d. Basco de Valverde)

HACIENDAS
Huancacrara (Monjas del Monasterio de Sta. Clara)
Tiuicti (Lic. d. Joseph de Carvajal)
Churopucyo (doña Isabel de Ambite)
Chipia (doña Beatris de Vidaire y Azagra)
Cantoc Uayco (doña Clara de Cardenaz)
Parpai (Alferes Nicolas de Morillas)
Sondor (comisario Santiago de la Villa)
Molle Molle (Alferes Phelipe del Castillo)
Llaspay (monsegñor Fernando Davila)
Matara y Cotaguara (Juan Feliz Davila)

ANNEXES
Corca (pop. 360; encomienda de d. Marcelo Osnaio de Orden de
Santiago)
    Haciendas
    Mallma (Juan de Ibarra)
    Corimarca (doña Ana de la Borda)
    Rumaray (caciques de San Francisco Borja)
    Cusibamba (d. Agustín Jara de la Cerda)
    Totora (doña Josepha Jara de la Cerda)
Guanca Guanca (pop. 384)
    Haciendas
    Miscca (Joseph Martines Palomino)
    Rocoto (Diego de Molina)
    Runcuguasi (Gonzalo Rodriguez)
San Juan de Coror (pop. 350)
    Haciendas
    Coror (Jacinto Luis Palomino)
    Paco (d. Basco de Valverde)
    Cochauana (Juan Francisco del Castillo)
    Aravito (doña Angela Salas y Valdes)
    Araypallpa (d. Basco de Valverde)

Source: Based on figures from Horacio Villanueva Urteaga, *Cusco 1689:*
Informes de los párrocos al obispo Mollinedo del Cuzco (Cusco: Centro de
Estudios Rurales Andinos "Bartolomé de Las Casas," 1982)

TABLE A.3
Population Figures and Land Tenure Structures
Repartimiento de Huanoquite

Unit	Native inhab. & "forasteros" with land			"Forasteros" without land		
	Women	Men	Absent	Women	Men	Absent
Ayllu Maska	82	111	9	7	10	4
Parc. Incacona	57	70	6	—	—	—
Ayllu Chanca	2	2	—	22	27	1
Parc. Chanca	—	—	—	45	53	7
Parc. Tantarcalla	24	23	3	14	19	6
Pueblo Huanca Huanca						
Parc. Collana	21	22	6	—	—	—
Parc. Urinsaya	20	21	3	—	—	—
Ayllu Urinsaya	—	—	—	1	3	—
Parc. ?	23	27	4	—	—	—
Parc. Yungas	2	3	—	—	—	—
Pueblo Coror						
Ayllu Collana	22	23	3	—	—	—
Ayllu Inga	29	38	4	—	—	—
Parc. Conde	20	29	3	—	—	—
Parc. Tiuicte	—	—	—	4	6	2
Parc. Chifia	—	—	—	34	57	13
Parc. Sondor	—	—	—	17	18	6
Parc. Aucabamba	—	—	—	15	17	3
Parc. Llaspay	—	—	—	8	10	—
Parc. Cotaguana	—	—	—	6	7	5
Parc. Molle Molle	—	—	—	28	49	10
Parc. ?	—	—	—	8	10	4
Hcda Chacapampa	2	1	—	3	4	—
Hcda Parpay	—	—	—	31	28	12
Hcda Mallma	—	—	—	13	15	3
Hcda Hunacacrara	—	—	—	11	13	1
TOTAL 1,405	304	370	41	267	346	77

Source: Based on figures from Archivo General de la Nación, Tributos. 1831. Leg. 6, cuerpo 182, fs. 192. "Matrícula de indígenas en el quinquenio de 1830, prov. de Paruro, hecha por el subprefecto d. Manuel Oblitas y d. Manuel Paz y Tapia, apoderado fiscal de revista por despacho del Gobierno Superior."

Note: It appears that, in most instances, *parcialidades* had split off from preexisting ayllus or had been ayllus that had become privatized but were smaller in scale than haciendas. The inspection data show 145 more men than women, and an almost equal number of native and non-native inhabitants with land (725) as non-native inhabitants without land (690), a difference of only 35. Approximately 9 percent of the entire population is documented as being "absent" at the time of the inspection.

TABLE A.4
Population Figures (1972)

	Population	Number of families	Kind of settlement
Dist. Huanoquite	3,314	781	
Aravito	263	63	Hacienda
Araypallpa	35	11	Hacienda
Araypallpa Pacos	13	5	Hacienda
Aucabamba	11	3	Hacienda
Aucahuasi	8	2	Hacienda
Chanca	143	39	Hacienda
Chifia	67	10	Hacienda
Huaillonca	8	1	Hacienda
Huallhuaqui	12	3	Hacienda
Huanccasa	5	2	Hacienda
Lllulluchani	22	5	Hacienda
Llaspay	77	15	Hacienda
Mallma	39	9	Hacienda
Mollebamba	207	46	Hacienda
Paco	120	27	Hacienda
Pacochoco	10	1	Hacienda
Paqques (Paccas?)	45	10	Hacienda
Parpay	72	21	Hacienda
Paucarpata	44	8	Hacienda
Qauqella	6	2	Hacienda
Qeñaparo	55	16	Hacienda
Qeshuacos	5	1	Hacienda
Qeshhuanaya	16	2	Hacienda
Qochabamba	17	4	Hacienda
Qotawana	43	7	Hacienda
Qusunaqra	5	1	Hacienda
Rocoto	9	3	Hacienda
Tihuicte	18	3	Hacienda
Uyllumpa	3	1	Hacienda
Amaru Pata	20	5	Fundo
Casa Blanca	52	15	Fundo
Huanccanccalle	4	1	Fundo
Inquil Pata	10	2	Fundo
Pichic	5	1	Fundo
Pulpera	7	1	Fundo
Qenqorqe	6	1	Fundo
Cedrony	27	6	Estancia
Ccashuas	4	1	Estancia
Molinos	5	1	Estancia
Mulampampa	5	1	Estancia
Toctohuaylla	4	1	Estancia
Cruz Pata	7	2	Caserio
Huanca Huanca	305	86	Anexo
Ccoror	149	38	Pueblo
Qeñapaco	70	21	Pueblo
Villcabamba	56	11	Pueblo
Huanoquite	700	164	Pueblo
Huancacrara	8	1	Parcialidad
Incacona	119	22	Parcialidad

TABLE A.4
Continued

	Population	Number of families	Kind of settlement
Qallpa Qallpa	33	6	Parcialidad
Qeñaparo	22	6	Parcialidad
Roccoto	47	11	Parcialidad
Toctohuaylla	209	44	Parcialidad
Tintimpunco	23	6	Parcialidad
Wiñaypoqo	44	6	Parcialidad

Source: Based on figures from Sistema Nacional de Apoyo a la Movilización Social, *Información censal: Población y vivienda, 1972: Dpto. del Cusco*, ser. 1, vol. 3 (Lima: SINAMOS, 1977).

TABLE A.5

Population Figures and Social Organization after the Reform (1975–87)

Unit	Heads of household (1987)	Pop. (1983)	Community recognition
COMMUNITIES			
Maska	99	397	Mar. 24, 1969
Tantarcalla	109	502	Dec. 10, 1926
Incacuna Ayllu Chifia	130	520	July 16, 1963
Molle Molle	62	245	July 4, 1984
Rocco	45	152	June 11, 1987
Toctohuaylla	62	310	July 25, 1966
Vilcabamba	43	138	February 13, 1987
Huanca Huanca	131	235	July 11, 1975
Koricancha Arabito and			
Araypallpa	99	350	January 22, 1987
COOPERATIVES (CAP)			
Llaspay	50	250	
Tihuicte	70	350	
Chanca	62	310	
HACIENDAS			
Mallma Alta			
Mallma Baja			
La Perla			
Chifia Chico			
Molle Molle Baja			
Quishuarcalla o Coror[a]			
Rocoto[a]		152	
Paco[a]		122	
Runcuhuasi and Cusimarca[a]			
Queñaparo[a]			
Pumabamba[a]			
Quinuara Grande			
Pumahuanca			

Sources: Figures based on interview data (1984); Huanoquite Medical Post (1983); Reforma Agraria, Archivo General, Proyecto Integral de Asentamiento Rural (PIAR), Zona Agraria XI (1975); Oficina de Comunidades Campesinas, Cusco, "Ministerio de Agricultura, Región XX, Subdirección de Comunidades Campesinas y Nativas" (1987). Population figures are approximate. Discrepancies exist in comparing all data bases.

[a] These estates had been partially expropriated and adjudicated to Peasant Groups (Grupos Campesinos), a category that was initially not recognized by the Velasco regime but was subsequently granted a legal status. Peasant Groups were usually composed of several conglomerates of peasants but were not considered formal communities.

Reform Statistics in Huanoquite District

TABLE B.I
Land Tenure Structure After the 1969 Reform

Unit	Families	Expropriated (hectares)	Transferred (hectares)	Remaining to Estates (hectares)
Cooperativas Agrarias de Producción (CAPs)				
Tihuicte	60	782	782	
Chanca	41	6,884	6,884	
Llaspay	45	1,535	1,535	
Poqquestaca	24	422	422	
Arabito	65	3,933	3,933	
TOTAL	235	13,556	13,556	
Comunidades campesinas (CC)				
IAC	80			
Parpay		2,268	2,268	
Chifia Grande		182	182	
Chifia Chico		200		200
La Perla		206		206
Maska	123			
Miscapata A		97	97	
Miscapata B		99	99	
Mallma Baja		209		209
Molle Molle B		563		563
Tantarcalla	104			
Huancacrara		266	266	
Mallma Alta		318		318
Huanca Huanca	66			
Quishuarcalla o Corror		1,031	655	376
Ccauqella		727	727	
Toctohuaylla	58			
Quinuara Grande		784		784
Pumahuanca		234		234
TOTAL	431	7,184	4,294	2,890
Grupos campesinos (GC)				
GC 1	47			
Casa Blanca		455	455	
Queñaparo		648	332	316
Pumabamba		574		574

TABLE B.1

Continued

Unit	Families	Expropriated (hectares)	Transferred (hectares)	Remaining to Estates (hectares)
GC 2	22			
Pacco		1,731	1,201	530
Pulpera		457	457	
Quishuares		619	619	
GC 3	32			
Rocotto		2,045	979	1,066
Runcuhuasi & Cusimarca		837	759	78
Molle Molle		268	268	
TOTAL	101	7,634	5,070	2,564
GRAND TOTAL	767	28,374	22,920	5,454

Sources: Figures based on data from the Archivo General de la Reforma Agraria, including the Proyecto Integral de Asentamiento Rural, Zona Agraria XI; Oficina de Comunidades Campesinas; and the Segundo Juzgado del Cusco.

TABLE B.2

Proportions of Land Controlled by Family and Unit

Units (families)	Amount of land	Hectares/ family	Distribution of land (postreform)	Pct. of land transferred
13 Hcdos.	5,454	420	19%	
235 CAPs	13,556	58	48	59%
431 CC	4,294	10	15	19
101 GC	5,070	50	18	22

Sources: See Table B.1.

Abbreviations: Hcdos., hacendados; CAPs, cooperativas agrarias de producción; CC, comunidades campesinas; GC, grupos campesinos.

REFERENCE MATTER

Notes

The following abbreviations are employed in the notes:

AGN   Archivo General de la Nación [General Archive of the Nation], Lima

AHC   Archivo Histórico Departamental del Cusco [Historical Archives of the Department of Cusco]

BN   Biblioteca Nacional del Perú [National Library of Peru], Lima

CC   Oficina de Comunidades Campesinas [Office of Peasant Communities, a division of the Ministry of Agriculture], Cusco

CD   Concejo Distrital [District Council], Huanoquite

IAC   Inkakuna Ayllu Chifia

RA, AG   Reforma Agraria, Archivo general [General Archives of the Agrarian Reform Office], Cusco

RP   Regístro Público de Propiedades Inmuebles de Cusco [Public Register of Real Estate, Cusco], Palacio de Justicia

SJ   Segundo Juzgado [Second Land Court], Cusco, Zona XI

Introduction

1. Velasco's speech announcing the reform is quoted in Pease and Verme 1974:93.

2. Throughout the rest of this book, I refer to the Shining Path guerrilla movement as "Sendero" or "Sendero Luminoso."

3. Surprisingly few analyses of Sendero have moved away from broad generalizations to pose the question of how peasants themselves relate to members of Sendero and its ideology or to the Peruvian state. Still fewer analyses illuminate how peasants have engaged in political action in the context of dramatically changing political and economic conditions. Exceptions are Berg 1986; Degregori 1989, 1990; Manrique 1989; and Starn 1991, which provide firsthand accounts of peasant relationships to Sendero Luminoso. Carlos Iván Degregori, who lived and taught in Huamanga, Ayacucho, for many years, gives excellent accounts (1989, 1990) of the social background of members of Sendero. Deborah Poole and Gerardo Rénique (1991,

1992) and Enrique Mayer (1991) have pointed out that some scholars have unduly emphasized a polarization between the urban and rural, traditional and modern, and core and periphery. In doing so, they have ignored the wide array of political organizations in which Peru's peasants have participated in order to strengthen their bargaining leverage with the state, the long history of peasant rural-urban ties through migration, and the historical depth of class and interethnic tensions throughout Peru. Other obstacles confront scholars attempting to make sense of Sendero. Numerous public documents issued by Sendero give us a clearer understanding of its ideology, but do not provide much insight into how, practically speaking, peasants have engaged with Sendero's ideas and actions, or how members of Sendero interact with peasants on a daily basis. The latter is increasingly more difficult to ascertain, given the dangers of working for sustained periods of time in the countryside, the clandestine nature of Sendero, and the fear that prevents many peasants from openly voicing their opinions of the behavior of either Sendero or the military and paramilitary.

4. Since Sendero Luminoso is, by definition, a clandestine movement, I cannot be sure of the degree of sympathy or active support for the movement among Huanoquiteños. I base my assertion upon numerous conversations with inhabitants and the fact that most Huanoquiteños continued to express a desire to lobby the state for various forms of infrastructural and economic support.

5. A substantial corpus of scholarly literature has been devoted to general analysis of Peru's 1969 agrarian reform. Land tenure before and after the reform is evaluated in Caballero 1980 and 1981. Lowenthal 1975; Matos Mar and Mejía 1980a and 1980b; and Albert 1983 discuss the reform process, policy measures, how they were implemented, and their general consequences. Using case studies from the southern Peruvian highlands, Guillet 1979 and Seligmann 1987 discuss similar issues. Quijano 1979 and Sánchez 1979 review peasant movements and land seizures that took place during the reform. McClintock 1981 examines how the reform changed attitudes and political behavior among peasants, primarily in coastal regions, and the impact of postreform policy reversals is evaluated in McClintock 1982 and McClintock and Lowenthal 1983. Cleaves and Scurrah 1980; Stepan 1978; North 1983; and North and Korovkin n.d. explain how the role and composition of the Peruvian state affected the reform process. Amat y León 1980 addresses economic and food policies promoted after the reform. Pásara 1978 and 1982 and Seligmann 1993a offer detailed studies of changes in the legal order during the reform.

6. Steve Stern (1993:55) elaborates upon Isaacman's point in encouraging scholars to pay attention to the "three motors" that shaped the paradoxes and anomalies of colonial economic life: the European world system, local strategies of resistance, and the linkages between mercantile and elite interests and those of the "center." Only by examining the interactions between these do we begin to move away from explanations that assume a unidirectional transformation of homogeneous labor regimes from feudalist to capitalist

ones as the capitalist world system has imposed itself. Instead, we discover heterogeneous labor regimes that present contemporary states, as they did colonial administrations, with real problems of economic, political, and cultural control.

Chapter 1

1. For further discussion of the dynamics of interethnic relations and labeling, see De la Cadena 1991; Di Leonardo 1984; Seligmann 1989, 1993b; Stoler 1989.

2. Agustín Gamarra seized the Peruvian presidency in a military coup and was subsequently elected on constitutional grounds to the presidency, serving a four-year term. Henry Dobyns and Paul Doughty point out that, along with Gutiérrez de la Fuente, a prefect of Arequipa, Gamarra "firmly established the pattern of generals leading coups d'état that would prevail as Peru's most decisive technique of transferring political power" (Dobyns and Doughty 1976:158).

3. See Zuidema 1964; AHC, leg. 25, cuad. 2, cuerpo 4, 1585.

4. See Poole 1984 and Zuidema 1964 for further information on the status and territorial location of these groups.

5. The *reducción* of Huanoquite was formed from twelve dispersed population centers (Cook et al., 1975:xxxvii). In the economic production and population statistics collected for the purpose of enacting the Toledan reforms between 1569 and 1575, numerous sociopolitical units are listed within what was subsequently known as the district of Huanoquite. The relative status of many of these units remains unclear.

6. *Obrajes* produced finished cloth, using a fulling mill and employed a larger labor force than the simpler *chorrillos*, whose main requisite was running water. Attaching a textile sweatshop to an already existing agricultural estate was a profitable undertaking. Moscoso 1965, (cited by Tamayo 1981:50) reports, for example, that San Juan de Taray, originally valued at 13,000 pesos, became worth 76,000 pesos once the textile workshop was added to it.

7. BN, Lima, D6804, 1888. "Expediente relativo al estado administrativo de la subprefectura de Paruro," por Rafael Serrano, fs. 18.

8. For further analyses of how these activities contributed to the Tupac Amaru rebellion and Wars of Independence, see Golte 1980; Mörner 1977; Bonilla et al. 1981.

9. For other examples of the changing nature of local authority during this time, see Hünefeldt 1982; Lockhart 1968; Mörner 1977; Stern 1982a.

10. For an analysis of how railroads affected agrarian societies in Mexico in a similar fashion, see Coatsworth 1981.

11. CD, Copilador de cuentas, 1909–14:77–79; ibid., 1910:152 (Huanoquite).

12. A telling commentary on Belaúnde's incoherent vision of development appeared in Cusco's local newspaper, *El Sol*, shortly after Velasco

became president: "As for the Civic Center [in Paruro], supported by [the] Popular Cooperation [agency], the work has been abandoned. The engineers drew up inconvenient maps that disregarded the routes of already-existing streets and ignored the recommendations of local authorities. Because it is a tax-funded agency of the central government, the engineers of Popular Cooperation did not listen to the remonstrations of the [local] authorities" (*El Sol,* January 7, 1969).

13. CD, Libro de oficios, 1927 (Huanoquite).

14. CD, Libro de actas, 8/22/81 (Huanoquite).

15. *El Sol,* May 5, 1970.

16. Klara Kelley (1976:221) has summarized the status of population centers in regions where economic and political power are highly concentrated rather than conforming to central-place theory, which assumes perfect competition and integration into the market economy: (1) a hierarchy of commercial centers lacking interstitial placement of levels and instead often showing descending levels with increasing distance from the highest-level center; (2) more low-level centers than predicted by the central-place model; (3) orientation of each lower-level center to only one center in the next level, rather than two or three, as in central-place models; (4) draining of hinterland population, income, or resources by the highest-level center; and (5) concentration of a political elite in a single high-level center, which is almost always the most important economic center.

17. In stories about the *hak'akllu* compiled by Efraín Morote Best (1988: 102–3), it is said to have the ability to bore holes in the rocks where it nests. Many believe that the Incas knew the herb used by the bird to dissolve rock, making it possible for them to build massive edifices out of huge blocks of stone. More recent narratives tell of imprisoned Indian leaders using this herb to break out of their cells and escape.

Chapter 2

1. Quoted in Pease and Verme 1974:93. Velasco also stressed that the law was intended to "end forever an unjust social order" and to achieve "the final destruction of ancient economic and social structures that have no validity in our epoch" (speech of June 24, 1969, quoted in Bonilla 1979:17–19).

2. Gonzalez and Díaz 1991, Dongo 1986, and Robles 1975 explain the philosophical and intellectual roots of Peruvian agrarian law.

3. Matos Mar and Mejía 1980a provides the most comprehensive description of the design and implementation process of the agrarian reform, as well as macroeconomic data on the impact of the new agrarian structure upon income redistribution, productivity, and the economic linkages between rural and urban sectors. While other authors have discussed the process of implementing the reform, they have been biased in focusing far more on the coast than on the highlands. Indeed, the coast was far more appropriate to the Velasco regime's visions of agroeconomies of scale. However, the

central and southern highlands became the heart of peasant unrest and social violence, and we therefore need to understand the reform process in these regions better.

4. The "vigilance" council acted as a watchdog, making sure that the administrative council performed its duties properly. It was also responsible for ensuring that peasants performed their public labor obligations (*faenas*) for the community.

5. Agrarian Reform Law, Executive Decree 17716, title XII, chapter II, articles 153–70 sets out in detail how the members of the Agrarian Tribunal were to be elected, the functions of the tribunal, and the obligations of the land judges. Also instructive in understanding the dynamic character of the reform are the annual speeches by the president of the Agrarian Tribunal between 1969 and 1973 (Figallo 1970, 1971, 1972, 1973).

6. Pásara (1978, 1982), Figallo (1985; personal interview, 1991), and González (1991) discuss the innovations in the reform of the judicial system that the Velasco regime put in place.

7. Matos Mar and Mejía 1980a:183. According to these authors, 15,826 agricultural units, consisting of 10,523,073 hectares, were targeted for expropriation between 1969 and 1979, and 7,789,811 hectares were allotted to 337,662 beneficiaries. Proportionally, cooperative enterprises constituted 45.2 percent of the beneficiaries and received 62.3 percent of the adjudicated lands. Peasant Groups and Communities totaled 43.5 percent of the beneficiaries but received only 29.9 percent of the adjudicated land. Although property was jurally considered to be corporate, land rights were primarily household-based within Peasant Groups and Peasant Communities (Ibid.: 178, 181).

8. Quoted in Pease and Verme 1974:248. The reaction of the U.S. government to the Velasco regime was severe, particularly since one of Velasco's first measures was to nationalize the International Petroleum Company (IPC), followed by the Peruvian subsidiaries of other U.S. multinational corporations. When the United States cut off aid to Peru, Velasco's government turned to eastern Europe for support, while disavowing any direct association with communist ideology. Provision of aid and weapons to Peru by the USSR further incited U.S. hostility.

9. The law stated that SINAMOS was responsible for "coordinating, stimulating, and channeling all initiatives related to citizen participation" (D.L. 18896).

10. Television broadcast, 1991. Fujimori said that the 1969 reform legislation had "fooled the peasants, offering them bills of 50,000 thousand intis and then bills of 5,000,000 million intis to buy the same quantity of things"; as a form of "centralism, a product of Limeñan racism toward peasants," it had offered only "false alternatives, including the 'zero credit' option, which had been responsible for producing the great crisis, translated into misery, migration from the countryside to the cities, and the encouragement of peasants to cultivate coca illegally."

Chapter 3

This chapter is a substantially revised version of Linda J. Seligmann, "The Burden of Visions Amidst Reform: Peasant Relations to Law in the Peruvian Andes," *American Ethnologist* 20, no. 1 (1993d): 25–51.

1. Many errors exist in all available data bases for Huanoquite. It is likely, for example, that the population figures given for Peasant Groups and communities that did not receive formal governmental recognition were greatly underestimated. This means that if these figures are broken down by household, each household received less land than the statistics indicate.

2. Instead of presenting the numerous pages of testimony, I have synthesized much of their content for the purposes of this book. The References section lists primary sources. I reviewed testimony from 23 lawsuits that took place in the course of expropriation and adjudication proceedings, found in the general archives of the Agrarian Reform Office in Cusco; 16 transferral proceedings from the Second Land Court of Cusco; and documents covering the process of formal recognition for five communities in the district, found in the Peasant Communities Office in Cusco. My residence in Huanoquite and conversations with people there helped me understand the context of these disputes and depositions.

3. Although it is almost impossible to prove, rumor was rife among members of Cusqueño society that land judges received payoffs from particular attorneys or members of the landed elite for ruling in their or their clients' favor. I never heard of a judge who was *not* corrupt from the vantage point of Cusqueños. Even attorneys like Marroquín and González acknowledged that the new court system, while it might have diminished the possibility of corruption and fraud, did not entirely do away with it.

4. SJ, Quishuares, case no. 40-75, Apr. 4, 1974.

5. RA, AG, 10-11-5, Exp. 410715, Aug. 27, 1970.

6. Ibid., May 20, 1975.

7. Ibid., Feb. 5, 1971.

8. In most cases the content and structure of the claims were also a product of the conflictual nature of disputes incited by the reform between similar, but different, peasant groups. For example, in the Llaspay case, as soon as the temporary workers made reference to their need for more lands because of population pressure, so did the permanent workers.

9. RA, AG, 10-6-5, Chanca, Oct. 10, 1973.

Chapter 4

1. RA, AG, 10-13-5, Casa Blanca, Exp. 405057, Oct. 12, 1973, Dec. 27, 1973, Jan. 10, 1974.

2. Ibid., May 27, 1974.

3. SJ, Pacco, case no. 190-75, Feb. 26, 1976.

4. RA, AG, 10-7-5, Sept. 30, 1973.

5. SJ, case no. 162-75, IAC, Sept. 22, 1975.
6. RA, AG, 10-21-5, Miska Pata A, Exp. 412411, Sept. 10, 1975.
7. Ibid., Oct. 13, 1975.
8. RA, AG, 10-12-5, Exp. 41-716, Dec. 27, 1974; ibid., n.d.
9. The Huancacrara case was typical of many in the highlands. Intense conflict arose between the overseers of Huancacrara, who were peasants demanding equal rights to land expropriated from the estate of Huancacrara. The other peasants wished to exclude the overseers, given the way they had been abused by them over the years. At the same time, community members of Tantarcalla who had occasionally worked on the estate were attempting to strike a deal with the owners. Both the community members and permanent workers invaded the property (RA, AG, 10-20-5, Huancacrara, Exp. 41676, Aug. 9, 1972, June 18, 1975, Sept. 12, 1975, Sept. 22 1975). The overseers eventually persuaded reform officials that they should be included in the allotment of land, and the estate was finally turned over to all the permanent laborers, including the overseers, in March 1976.
10. SJ, Qeñaparo, case no. 208-75, Mar. 8, 1976.
11. RA, AG, 10-8-5, Roccoto, Exp. 402176, Nov. 4, 1973.
12. SJ, IAC/Maska, Exp. 50-81, Feb. 12, 1981.
13. CC, Huanca Huanca, May 15, 1975.

Chapter 5

1. SJ, IAC/Maska, case no. 126-74, Exp. 50-81.
2. AHC, Colegio Nacional de Ciencias, 1585, 1648.
3. CC, IAC, Exp. 17732.
4. SJ, IAC/Maska, Exp. 50-81, Exp. archivado 136.
5. Ibid.   6. CC, IAC, Exp. 17732.
7. RP, v. 15, ff. 89, 1902.   8. SJ, case no. 126-74.
9. SJ, case no. 170-75.
10. In personal interviews with Nerio González, Noé Hanco, and Prudencio Carcausto, all of them referred to Cabrera y Lartaún's visita.
11. CC, IAC, Exp. 17732.
12. RA, AG, Llulluch'ayuq, 10-9-5, Aug. 27, 1973.
13. I do not know how many members of IAC were consulted before their president reached this agreement with Tito, but it is documented as having been approved at a general assembly of all the members.
14. RA, AG, Llulluch'ayuq, 10-9-5, Oct. 19, 1973; Sept. 8, 1975.
15. Ibid., n.d.
16. Archivo Reynaldo Alviz M., f. 2195, registro 44, 1981–82.
17. SJ, IAC/Maska, case no. 50-81; Archivo Reynaldo Alviz M.
18. RA, AG, 10-9-5, Llulluch'ayuq, Aug. 27 1975.
19. SJ, case no. 170-75, May 4, 1976.
20. SJ, IAC, case no. 170-75; SJ, case no. 0244, 1981, Instrucción 97-80.
21. SJ, IAC/Maska, case no. 50-81.

22. Archivo Reynaldo Alviz M., f. 2195, registro 44, 1981–82.
23. SJ, IAC/Maska, case no. 50-81.

Chapter 6

1. A dynamic tension has always existed between the workings of hierarchy and the ideology of collective identity in Andean highland societies as
a process rather than as a given concrete entity. Deere 1990, Fonseca and
Mayer 1988, Lehman 1982, Mallon 1983 and 1987, and Rasnake 1988 offer
detailed historical analyses of transformations in economic and political
hierarchies in Andean highland societies and their relationship to the formation of collective identity in ayllus and communities.

2. Established in the mid 1950's, the Peruvian Ministry of Agriculture's
Agrarian Research and Promotion Service (SIPA) represented an early effort
to "modernize" indigenous highland agriculture and was responsible for
introducing chemical fertilizer, pesticides, and hybrid seed varieties in many
places. For discussion of SIPA's influence on the central highland community
of Huayapampa, see Fuenzalida et al. 1982: 87–169.

3. Chapter 9 discusses further the identity of the members of the Sendero
cell responsible for blowing up the tractor. They were not members of the
community of Maska but rather schoolteachers. It is unclear, however,
whether or not they received intelligence of any kind from community
members. In the years that followed, Tihuicte's members often repeated that
they believed Maska had been instrumental in what had occurred.

4. From 1973 to 1975, the cooperative made a profit of S./355,170. In
1976, it made a profit of S./163,540, divided among 65 members. Starting in
1976, however, its financial difficulties increased, reflected in the sharp rise
in loans from the Banco Agrario that it was no longer able to pay back (1976:
S./3,000,000; 1977: S./5,000,000; 1978: S./7,000,000; 1979: S./17,000,000;
1982: S./24,400,000; 1983: S./35,500,000). Macroeconomic forces, particularly the dramatic surge in inflation and Peru's foreign debt, helped account
for the astronomical debt the co-op incurred (Libro de actas, Tihuicte 1984).
A drought in 1983–84 made Tihuicte's financial situation even more precarious.

5. The *topu* is a relative measure (see Rostworowski 1964:1–31). Its size
depends upon the technology used to sow the land (foot plow or yoke of
oxen), the quality of soil, cultigen, slope of the land, and labor force. It may
even depend upon amount of irrigation water needed. Standardized by bureaucrats and development agents to correspond to one-third of a hectare, the
measure is rarely equivalent to farmers' calculations, thus creating confusion, misinformation, and statistical problems in making comparisons.

6. The annual redistribution of community lands included the important task of resetting the boundaries of communal lands that belonged to
different communities. This practice had the critical function of reinforcing
communal land control and acknowledging individual usufruct rights. *Raymis de costumbre*, the sectors of puna community lands that were sown

collectively as well as in usufruct, were determined each year at the *co-lindasqa*, or boundary-setting ceremony, in March. Armed with consensus, community officers decided where and what members should sow, and which sector of community lands should be turned over and aerated for the following agricultural season. Raymis lasted several years, so changes in their location did not necessarily occur annually. However, because demographic pressure on the land had increased, the length of time that lands lay fallow had decreased from seven to sometimes only three years. The land-surveying ceremony also made explicit for everyone to whom rights of usufruct were granted. Enforcement of such rights was crucial, and members pointed out single furrows in the middle of nowhere to me, explaining that they represented physical claims to raymi lands that had been granted to them in usufruct. If one did not perform this physical act of taking possession, another member could claim and take over the visibly unused land. Within raymis, an annual rotation cycle operated, called *tiqray*. An ideal unirrigated cycle was potatoes the first year, barley the second, broad beans the third, barley again the fourth, and then a fallow period.

7. For the sake of convenience, I distinguish between *owner* and *share-cropper*, but the terms are imprecise, since the "owner" did not always own the land but rather had rights to it. It was not unusual for sharecropping contracts to occur on land held in usufruct.

8. A fascinating, but relatively unexplored, area of research is the employment that members of the landed elite pursued once their lands were expropriated. Instead of investing in urban industry, many of them became rural entrepreneurs. For example, the woman mentioned in the text had begun renting small, but highly productive, pieces of land in different parts of the southern sierra. As a new kind of absentee landowner, she was disparaged by both Huanoquite's peasants and the remaining members of the landed elite and was unable to establish a foothold in the web of socioeconomic and political ties that continued to operate between them.

9. Beasts of burden were a major production factor for Maska's comuneros, because the land they held in usufruct was often three to four hours' journey from the district capital. In contrast, the lands of Tihuicte's members were within walking distance of their residences. Tihuicte therefore borrowed horses from Maska for particular labor tasks rather than investing in their ownership. Maska's comuneros owned an average of two horses and a maximum of seven, whereas Tihuicte's members owned an average of one and a maximum of two horses.

10. Comunidad de Maska, Registrar de la Comunidad, 1984.

11. Libro de actas, Tihuicte, Mar. 21, 1983.

12. The detailed data gathered from these interviews are available in Seligmann 1987.

13. I conducted these interviews with male heads of households. While the interviews included specific questions about household organization of production, and women often contributed to the interviews, I did not gather sufficient data to make a comprehensive analysis of the labor contributions

of wives in the reproduction of the household itself. Although I use the term *household,* my focus is thus upon male heads of households, whose economic and political standing were indeed affected by the activities and position of their spouses and children. Collins 1988, Deere 1990, and Smith 1989 offer excellent data on the effects of family size, migration patterns, division of labor, and the structuring of gender relations upon changes in the composition and reproduction of production units, and economic differentiation among them.

14. Sponsorship of festivals also provided a means to establish a sense of collective solidarity and alliances in the process of expressing religious devotion and accumulating the resources necessary for the enactment of dances, the provision of food, drink, and music, and the adornment of saints' images with elaborate costumes. In other words, peasants used Catholic festivals to express their religious devotion and defend their identity as distinct from that of the landowning class that ordered them to perform the fiestas. The two sides of the festival system existed in tension, reproducing themselves over the years. It is interesting in this respect to note the comments in the early twentieth century of Mayor Galdos, who wrote to the provincial authorities expressing his alarm and concern that it was "still necessary to regulate these spectacles to avoid the scandals that the Indians commit at night at the foot of the altars" (CD, Copilador de cuentas, June 16, 1909).

15. In looking at the relationship between holding religious office, holding political office, age, and landholdings, I found that male heads of households continued to participate in the civil-religious hierarchy but did not do so systematically. In order to hold office and fiesta sponsorship positions, they usually had to control over five topus of land. Those who alternately ascended the civil-religious hierarchy were middle landholding households with from five to twenty topus. The poorest households had no religious cargos or political offices, and the wealthiest households had opted out altogether from the cargo system and held only high political office. In addition, amount of land was more determinant than seniority in inhabitants' ability to achieve high status, and they had begun to rely more upon participation in politics than upon the fiesta system to exercise and accumulate power.

16. Archival documents from the early 1900's meticulously record the taxes that the district council imposed on those who sponsored fiestas. Debate arose during that time between the district mayor and governor over the justice of collecting such taxes only from peasants. In 1909, the mayor wrote to the governor protesting angrily that private landowners refused to pay their fiesta licenses even when they sponsored dance groups, fireworks, or bullfights. He added that those who refused to pay defended themselves by saying that they "owned private properties and could do that which best suited them" (CD, Copilador de cuentas, June 16, 1909).

17. Some fiestas had become entirely unimportant to peasants, while others had increased in value. Festivals such as the feasts of Cruz Velakuy (the Day of the Cross), Natividad (Christmas), and Santa Rosa (the patron saint of the civil guard) that had largely been enacted by and for the landed

elite no longer inspired much enthusiasm from inhabitants. In contrast, fiestas for the patron saints of communities and cooperatives, and the regional pilgrimage to the Christ figure of Qoyllur Rit'i were considered of utmost importance to peasants. The latter fiestas included cargos held by comuneros or socios rather than vecinos.

18. David Stoll's general discussion of why peasants might convert to Evangelical Protestantism fits Huanoquiteños: "The appropriate question seems, not why many people convert, but why more do not. One of the most common effects of conversion is to put households on a more stable basis, by overcoming male addiction to alcohol, reining in male sexual license, and establishing church authorities, as a sort of appellate court for aggrieved women. . . . But born-again religion is not just a utilitarian exercise in which the disadvantaged adapt to capitalist development by organizing themselves into benefit societies. . . . By appealing to the deepest needs of people, evangelical churches help them redefine themselves, reorganize their lives, and move in dramatic new directions" (Stoll 1991:13).

19. Huanoquiteños had asked the priest to donate a small portion of church lands so they could establish a local nursery school. They had written to the archbishopric in Cusco requesting the land from the church. Their letters finally resulted in the calling of an unexpected early-morning general assembly by the priest and a representative of the archbishopric. The priest announced to the hastily assembled population that no need existed for a nursery school, since all he saw were pigs rather than children being herded on church lands. The representative of the archbishopric, ignoring Huano-quiteños' deeper concerns, scolded their authorities for having sent missives to his office on "dirty paper." He then praised the architecture of the colonial church and declared that funds would be made available to restore it and the paintings it contained. In short, he made it clear that displaying the wealth and power of the church was more important than educating Huanoquite's children.

Chapter 7

1. In Spanish Demetrio's comments are imbued with a lilting power, lost in the translation to English: "La vida del campo, tanto dolor, tanto amor."

2. In the interviews I conducted, I asked each person to name the five best farmers in Huanoquite. Demetrio Pantoja and Cirilo Rocca appeared repeatedly in the list. When I asked people for the criteria they considered in characterizing someone as a good farmer, they mentioned ownership of many livestock; ability to buy land from hacendados; a high level of agricultural production and sale of many products on the market; success in obtaining credit; long, hard work; and services to the community. People drew a clear distinction between "the character" (*su caracter*) of officeholders who only "thought about themselves" (*egoistas*) or were "self-centered" (*ingreido*) and those who thought about "the people" (*el pueblo*) or "everyone" (*todos*).

3. It was not accidental that the abuse of young women by SIPA agents in

Huanoquite incited villagers to take action against the agents. They also did so against the priest for the same reason. Although I cannot make a case as strongly as James Howe does for the Kuna, I would conjecture that in Huanoquite, too, there was, in Howe's words, "ethnic boundary-drawing [that] replicated domestic strategy: in both [domestic and political spheres] marriageable young women were protected on the inside, while men who wished to have those women were kept on the outside. The crucial difference, of course, is that in the domestic sphere select young men would eventually be let in, while in the political, exclusion was permanent" (Howe 1991:25). In the domestic sphere, although boundaries were by no means as clearly marked in Quechua society as in Kuna society, people made distinctions between insiders and outsiders. A number of outsiders, particularly those who were abusive in terms of economic exploitation of villagers, were also considered illicit contenders for the sexual favors of village women.

Chapter 8

1. The corporate nature of many Andean peasant communities persists to a degree because of the functions of communities with respect to their productive resources. Communities continue to act defensively as units in the face of encroachment upon their lands or exploitation of their labor; as a means to pressure the state for resources and services; and in order to manage important day-to-day productive activities, which include gaining access to and controlling land in different ecological zones and managing water rights and common grazing lands (Mayer and de la Cadena 1989). This is not, however, to suggest a functional model for the persistence of the corporate community. Many communities gradually privatize most of their lands; their system of water rights may cease to function effectively owing to fragmentation of communities along class or other lines; and internal conflicts may lead parts of a community to split off to form their own units. On the other hand, especially given the history of communal organization of economic production and the state's relationships to rural highland society, a basis exists for the continuous reconstitution of new ideas of "community."

2. I refer specifically to the postindependence period in Peru, not the colonial or Republican periods, when local ethnic lords (*kurakas* or *caciques*) organized extensive networks among themselves and were key mediators with the colonial regime and Crown bureaucrats (see Spalding 1984).

3. For analytical purposes, in most highland districts, three levels exist where relationships of political authority can be structured, revised, challenged, and affect people's lives in an ongoing fashion: relationships between the district as a whole and the state; relationships between different corporate entities within the district, represented by their respective officeholders; and relationships between officeholders and their constituencies within corporate entities. Obviously, there are a number of informal channels as well where activities and discussion take place that affect existing political structures.

4. CD, 1909–14, 1919–30, 1970–84, Huanoquite. District council records also document that particular mayors stole the minutes and financial records of the council. The efforts of subsequent mayors to retrieve them were unsuccessful. This explains the lack of records from 1930 to 1970.

5. Huanoquite's peasants did not accept these labor drafts pacifically. Throughout the archival record, there are references to the difficulties authorities encountered in harnessing local labor for their projects and their dependence upon the traditional community elders (*varayuqkuna*) for making peasants comply with corvée labor tasks.

6. CD, Copilador de cuentas, Huanoquite, 1909–14, Jan. 2, 1910.

7. CD, Libro de oficios, Apr. 15, 1920, Huanoquite.

8. CD, Copilador de cuentas, Mar. 26, 1909, Huanoquite.

9. References to the mobilization of Huanoquite's authorities and peasants appear periodically in *El Sol* from 1968 through 1980; and in district council, community, and cooperative records of general assemblies.

10. Comunidad de Maska, Libro de actas, Apr. 26, 1975.

11. CD, Libro de actas, Huanoquite, May 22, 1977; Sept. 23, 1977.

12. Ibid., Oct. 3, 1978.   13. Ibid., July 20, 1978.

14. Ibid., June 18, 1980.   15. *El Sol*, Jan. 13, 1977, 1.

16. Comunidad de Maska, Libro de actas, Feb. 12, 1978.

17. Numerous references to these undertakings are found in community, cooperative, and district council minutes. See for example, CD, Libro de actas, Huanoquite, Dec. 7, 1978; Jan. 22, 1979; Jan. 25, 1979; all entries, 1980.

18. The following is a partial list of subcommittees established only at the district level after the reform: the Pro-Educational Complexes Committee; Health Post Committee; Transport Committee; Telephone Committee; Electricity Committee; Pro-Food Donations Committee; Pro-Irrigation Committee; Committee in Defense of the Artistic and Religious Patrimony of the Church of the District; Mothers' Club; District Committee for the Regional Development of the South and East (ORDESO); Committee of Small Entrepreneurs; Committee for the Construction of the Civic Center; Committee Pro-Defense of Huanoquite; Civil Defense Patrol; National Agrarian Security Force; and Committee for the Military Draft. This list by no means includes community or cooperative organizations, or the numerous labor drafts in which peasants were expected to participate.

19. I do not mean to imply that Huanoquite was experiencing a gradual transformation from a closed corporate community to an open one (Wolf 1955, 1986). The district had been remarkably heterogeneous prior to the reform, although class differentiation among peasants was far less pronounced. Accommodation, adaptive resistence, violent upheaval, and creative instrumentality have always been part of the fabric of Huanoquiteños' political life. They participated in the Tupac Amaru uprising of the late eighteenth century, the Wars of Independence in the early nineteenth century, and the War of the Pacific in the late nineteenth century. They hanged a priest from the bell tower of the church, and in the twentieth century, they repeatedly

invaded landed estates. Over the years, as we have seen, they also elaborated and resorted to a wide array of tactics of daily sabotage to gain access to more resources and to confine the abuses of colonial officials and landlords.

20. The characterizations offered in these two chapters of intermediaries are drawn from formal interviews and conversations I had with such individuals; conversations about them with other Huanoquiteños; the proceedings of general assemblies and meetings; and the course of daily life. In reading of the organization and activities of Sendero, it becomes apparent that many of these brokers played key roles (although not as the intellectual vanguard) in the movement throughout the Andean highlands. Although, it is impossible to know with certainty if these brokers were members of Sendero, enough of them made veiled references to their sympathies with the movement that I am willing to take the risk of assuming that they were either sympathizers or activists. That Huanoquite has been targeted for Sendero actions makes it even more likely that they were participants in one fashion or another. Unless the individual was a public figure (a politician, for example), I have used pseudonyms.

21. Carlos Iván Degregori describes why peasants in Ayacucho fought for free education: "Peasant mobilization reached its maximum expression in the struggle for education and against local authorities and the state. If the low or zero profitability of the latifundios and their rapid abandonment explains the low profile of struggles over land in the region, this same 'extreme poverty of land' would explain the intensity of the struggle for free education, since education would thus appear as almost the only channel for social mobility, [n]ot only for the upper classes, but this time, also for the peasantry" (Degregori 1990:118).

22. Germán Cusimayta, interview, 1984.

23. Jesús Castillo, interview, 1984.

24. *El Sol*, June 28, 1969, 2.

25. *El Sol*, May 13, 1970, 2.

26. Velasco 1972:63. Velasco made this speech on February 8, 1971, at the inauguration of the second meeting of the Permanent Executive Commission on Education, Science, and Culture. In his anthology of speeches, the "theme" he gave to this speech was "the educational system as a mechanism for integrating the peasantry into the social order" (Sistema educativo integrador del campesino en el ordenamiento social).

27. CD, Libro de actas, Huanoquite, Sept. 18, 1980; Oct. 20, 1980.

28. Ibid., Jan. 15, 1981.

29. The director of Huanoquite's National Education Center admonished the district council for having brought Huanoquite's educational problems to the attention of a far wider public by taking advantage of the mass media. He claimed that had they discussed the problems with him personally, he would have resolved them. The council, having already attempted numerous times to resolve the problems informally, responded "we have no reason to hide the abuses of the teachers that are against the law" (CD, Libro de actas, 1980, Huanoquite). The conflicts within the district over the teach-

ers' attitudes and behavior persisted after their return and took up a great amount of time at district council and community meetings.

30. The statements on the part of the teachers and their supervisors were either made in the course of the District General Assembly in Huanoquite on April 5, 1984, or were comments made in informal discussion during the time the supervisors remained in Huanoquite (April 5–7, 1984), which I then wrote down in my field notes.

31. CD, Libro de actas, Mar. 1986, Huanoquite.

32. These meetings provided one arena in which villagers could manipulate or challenge dominant authority structures somewhat in the way John Lonsdale attributes to local groups in Africa saying, "Political structures are not only systems of constraints but also fields of opportunities; they work, generally speaking, but they are also there to be worked" (Lonsdale 1981:14). Gavin Smith observes that villagers may, post hoc, state that successful outcomes of political struggles have been due to collective solidarity, when in fact self-interested individuals may have been central to the outcome (1989:233–34). The kind of deindividualization that may take place in these settings is by no means unhierarchical, since age, gender, and education tend to determine who dominates the discussion (see also Graham 1994).

Chapter 9

1. See Burt and Panfichi 1992; and, Poole and Rénique 1992 for accurate and clear accounts of the history and philosophy of Sendero Luminoso.

2. Sendero calls itself the Communist Party of Peru, but a number of other parties vie for the same name—the Peruvian Communist Party–Unidad, the Communist Party of Peru–Patria Roja, and the Revolutionary Communist Party.

3. This is a favorite Sendero slogan, quoted in Degregori 1990–91:10.

4. CD, Libro de actas, Huanoquite, January 1986.

5. This summary is taken from a transcript made by Jesús Guillén Marroquín (1987) of the rimanakuy held in Cusco.

6. Clemente Castañeda, Maska, Libro de actas, Huanoquite, July 1991.

7. Field notes, Huanoquite, May 25, 1984.

8. See, e.g., *Guerra Popular en el Perú*, compiled and edited by Luis Arce Borja, 1989; numerous issues of Sendero's newspaper, *El Diario*, in particular, *El Diario*, July 5, 1989; *Entrevista al Presidente Gonzalo*, compiled by the Partido Comunista del Perú, Comité Central, 1988; *Desarrollar la guerra popular sirviendo a la revolución mundial*, n.d.; and Mercado 1986.

9. Manuel Vallejo Castaña, interview, Huanoquite, Apr. 7, 1984.

10. By contrast, the totalizing ideology of the Chinese Communist Party manifested itself mostly in economic policies. Rural cadres of the CCP often buffered peasants from the central government. In the process, the cadres accumulated a great deal of power for themselves, but as Shue 1988 and Siu 1989 point out, they also generated eclectic economic and political practices at the local level. In Cambodia, the attempt to erase all differences, eco-

nomic, political, and ethnic, was far more extreme (see Kiernan 1985), and Sendero's actions resemble those of the Khmer Rouge more than they do those of the CCP either under or after Mao.

11. This idea paraphrases Carol Smith's (1990b:282) observations on the state of civil war in Guatemala.

12. President Alberto Fujimori's most recent move to control Sendero was the dissolution of the Peruvian Constituent Assembly and judiciary, with the assistance of the military, on April 5, 1992. He justified this by claiming that these bodies were inept and corrupt. While he has obtained widespread approval for his actions, they make it far less likely than ever before that peasants will be able to make claims of any sort on the state. Furthermore, they also give the state and its military forces far greater leeway in penetrating rural communities with impunity. Unless Fujimori, through this strategy, is able (1) to eliminate Sendero; and (2) to build anew democratic representation at all levels of society, it is possible that support for Sendero will grow. While most analysts of Peru have been unable to assess the impact of Fujimori's policies, partly because of the popular support they enjoy, they generally agree that he is achieving a semblance of order within the country mainly because of his will to rule and the support of the armed forces (although they, too, remain divided).

References

Primary Sources

ARCHIVAL SOURCES

Archivo General de la Nación [cited as AGN], Lima

Tributos, 1831. Leg. 6, cuerpo 182, fs. 192. "Matrícula de indígenas en el quinquenio de 1830, prov. de Paruro hecha por el subprefecto d. Manuel Oblitas y d. Manuel Paz y Tapia, apoderado fiscal de revista por despacho del Gobierno Superior."

Archivo Histórico Departamental del Cusco [cited as AHC], Cusco

Colegio Nacional de Ciencias, 1585, Leg. 25, cuad. 2, cuerpo 4, fs. 14. "Títulos de la Hacienda de Parpay."
Colegio Nacional de Ciencias, 1648. Leg. 25, cuad. 2, cuerpo 3, fs. 2. "Mitimaes de Guanuquite."

Archivo Reynaldo Alviz M., Cusco

f. 2195 v., regístro 44, 1981–82

Biblioteca Nacional del Perú [cited as BN], Lima

D6804, 1888. "Expediente relativo al estado administrativo de la subprefectura de Paruro," por Rafael Serrano, fs. 18.

Comunidad de Maska, Huanoquite

Libro de Actas, 1970–89
Registrar de la Comunidad, 1984

Concejo Distrital, Huanoquite

Copilador de Cuentas, 1909–14
Libro de Oficios, 1919–30
Libro de Actas, 1970–89

Cooperative de Tihuicte, Huanoquite

Libro de Actas, 1973–89

Huanoquite Medical Post
Population figures and distances, 1983

Oficina de Comunidades Campesinas [cited as CC], Cusco
The date of formal recognition of the community is given in parentheses. However, these proceedings sometimes lasted several decades, and the documents include titles and records of prior lawsuits, many of which originated in the colonial period.

Huanca Huanca (July 11, 1975), May 15, 1975.
Inkakuna Ayllu Chifia, Exp. 17732 (July 16, 1963), case no. 36-34, Reinvindicación Comunidad Inkakuna Ayllu Chifia contra Donato Montañez Quispe, Sept. 24, 1974.
Maska, Exp. 45 (1968–69)
"Ministerio de Agricultura, Región Agraria XX, Cusco, Sub-dirección de Comunidades Campesinas y Nativas" (1987)
Tantarcalla (Dec. 10, 1926), Exp. 804, Jan. 5, 1927; Exp. 4727, 1941; Exp. 33213, Apr. 1965

Reforma Agraria, Archivo General, Zona Agraria XI [cited as RA, AG], Cusco

10-13-5, Exp. 405057, *Casa Blanca;* Oct. 12, 1973; Dec. 27, 1973; Jan. 10, 1974; May 27, 1974
10-6-5, *Chanca;* Oct. 10, 1973.
10-20-5, Exp. 41676, *Huancacrara,* Oct. 3, 1969; Sept. 29, 1972; July 11, 1973; Aug. 21, 1973; August 9, 1972; Sept. 12, 1975; Sept. 22, 1975; June 18, 1975
10-11-5, Exp. 410715, *Llaspay,* Aug. 27, 1970; May 20, 1975; Feb. 5, 1971
10-9-5, *Llulluch'ayoc,* Aug. 27, 1973; Oct. 19, 1973; Sept. 8, 1975; Aug. 27, 1975
10-21-5, Exp. 412411, *Miska Pata Alta,* Sept. 10, 1975, Oct. 13, 1975
10-25-5, Exp. 415474, *Miska Pata Baja,* Nov. 22, 1973
10-12-5, Exp. 410716, *Molle Molle,* Dec. 27, 1974
10-7-5, *Quishuares,* Sept. 30, 1973
10-8-5, Exp. 402176, *Roccoto,* Nov. 4, 1973
Proyecto Integral de Asentamiento Rural [cited as PIAR], Zona Agraria XI, 1975

Regístro Público de Propiedades Inmuebles de Cusco, Palacio de Justicia [cited as RP]
Incacona, v. 15, f. 89 (1902)

Segundo Juzgado, Cusco, Zona XI
Inkakuna Ayllu Chifia, Exp. 136, 1972; case no. 162-75, Sept. 22, 1975; case no. 01244, instruccion no. 97-80, 1980
Inkakuna Ayllu Chifia/Maska, Inkakuna Ayllu Chifia/Maska, case no. 126-74, Nov. 21, 1974; case no. 170-75, May 4, 1976; Exp. 50-81, Jan. 1, 1981, Feb. 12, 1981

Pacco, case no. 190-75, Feb. 26, 1976
Queñaparo, case no. 208-75, Mar. 25, 1971; Mar. 8, 1976
Quishuares, case no. 40-75, Apr. 4, 1974; Feb. 26, 1976

LAWS

Estatuto de comunidades campesinas, decreto supremo 37-70 A (1970)
Ley 002 (1980)
Ley 17716 de la reforma agraria (1969)
Nueva ley general de aguas y su modificatoria, DL 17752 (1970)
Ley 18896 (establishment of SINAMOS, 1971)

NEWSPAPERS

La Crónica: 1918
El Sol (Cusco), Jan. 7, 1969, June 28, 1969, May 5, 1970, May 13, 1970, Jan. 13, 1977

Secondary Sources

Abu-Lughod, Lila. 1991. "Writing Against Culture." In Richard G. Fox, ed., *Recapturing Anthropology: Working in the Present,* 138–62. Santa Fe: School of American Research Press.
Adams, Richard N. 1959. *A Community in the Andes: Problems and Progress in Muquiyauyo.* Seattle: University of Washington Press.
Adorno, Rolena. 1991. "Images of *indios ladinos* in Early Colonial Peru." In Kenneth J. Andrien and Rolena Adorno, eds., *Transatlantic Encounters: Europeans and Andeans in the Sixteenth Century,* 232–70. Berkeley and Los Angeles: University of California Press.
Albert, Tom. 1983. *Agrarian Reform and Rural Poverty.* Boulder, Colo.: Westview Press.
Alberti, Giorgio, and Enrique Mayer, eds. 1974. *Reciprocidad e intercambio en los Andes peruanos.* Lima: IEP.
Allen, Catherine. 1988. *The Hold Life Has: Coca and Cultural Identity in an Andean Community.* Washington, D.C.: Smithsonian Institution Press.
Amat y León, Carlos, ed. 1980. *Realidad del campo peruano después de la reforma agraria: 10 ensayos críticos.* Lima: CIC y Editora Ital Perú.
Amin, Samir. 1974. *Accumulation on a World Scale.* New York: Monthly Review Press.
Aparicio Vega, Manuel Jesús. 1967. "Instrucción para el establecimiento de la Intendencia del Cuzco." *Revista del Archivo histórico del Cuzco* 12: 268–302.
Appleby, Gordon. 1976. "The Role of Urban Food Needs in Regional Development, Puno, Peru." In Carol Smith, ed., *Regional Analysis,* 1:147–78. New York: Academic Press.
Arce Borja, Luis, ed. 1989. *Guerra popular en el Perú: El pensamiento Gonzalo.* Brussels: Luis Arce Borja.

Arguedas, José María. 1964. *Puquio: Una cultura en proceso de cambio*, vol. 5. Lima: Universidad Nacional Mayor de San Marcos.

——. [1966] 1983. "Huk doctorkunaman qayay." In Sybila A. de Arguedas, Antonio Cornejo Polar, Francisco Carrillo, and Humberto Damonte, eds., *José María Arguedas: Obras completas*, 5: 251–57. Lima: Editorial Horizonte.

Baca Tupayachi, Epifanio. 1983. *Cuzco: Sistemas viales, articulación y des arrollo regional*. Cusco: Centro de Estudios Rurales "Bartolomé de Las Casas."

Bailey, F. G. 1991. *The Prevalence of Deceit*. Ithaca, N.Y.: Cornell University Press.

Bastien, Joseph. 1978. *Mountain of the Condor: Metaphor and Ritual in an Andean Ayllu*. Saint Paul: West Publishing.

Beckett, Jeremy. 1993. "Walter Newton's History of the World—or Australia." *American Ethnologist* 20 (4): 675–95.

Berg, Ronald. 1986. "Sendero Luminoso and the Peasantry of Andahuaylas." *Journal of Interamerican Studies and World Affairs* 28 (4): 165–196.

Berry, Sara. 1988. "Property Rights and Rural Resource Management: The Case of Tree Crops in West Africa." *Cahiers des sciences humaines* 24 (1): 3–16.

Blanco Galdos, Hugo. 1972. *Tierra o muerte: Las luchas campesinas en Perú*. Mexico City: Siglo veintiuno.

Bonilla, F. 1979. *Reforma agraria peruano: Texto único concordado del D. L. número 17716, sus ampliatorias y conexos*. Lima: Editorial Mercurio.

Bonilla, Heraclio, et al. 1981 [Bonilla, H., P. Chaunu, T. Halperin, P. Vilar, K. Spalding, and E. J. Hobsbawm]. *La independencia en el Perú*. Lima: IEP.

Borah, W. W. 1983. *Justice by Insurance: The General Indian Court of Colonial Mexico and the Legal Aides of the Half-Real*. Berkeley and Los Angeles: University of California Press.

Bourdieu, Pierre. 1991. *Language and Symbolic Power*. Cambridge, Mass.: Harvard University Press.

——. 1977. *Outline of a Theory of Practice*. Trans. Richard Nice. London: Cambridge University Press.

Bourque, Susan, and Kay Warren. 1981. *Women of the Andes: Patriarchy and Social Change in Two Peruvian Towns*. Ann Arbor: University of Michigan Press.

Brisseau Loayza, Jeanine. 1975. *Le Cuzco dans sa region. Etude de l'aire d'influence d'une ville andine*. Ph.D. diss., Université de Bourdeaux.

Bueno, Cosme. 1951. *Geografía del Perú virreinal (siglo 18)*. Lima: Daniel Valcárcel.

Bunker, Stephen G. 1986. *Peasants Against the State: The Politics of Market Control in Bugisu, Uganda, 1900–1983*. Urbana: University of Illinois Press.

Burt, Jo-Marie, and Aldo Panfichi. 1992. *Peru: Caught in the Crossfire*. Jefferson City: Peru Peace Network–USA.

Caballero, José María. 1980. *Agricultura, reforma agraria y pobreza campesina.* Lima: IEP.

——. 1981. *Economía agraria de la sierra peruana antes de la reforma agraria de 1969.* Lima: IEP.

Cancian, Frank. 1965. *Economics and Prestige in a Maya Community.* Stanford: Stanford University Press.

Cardoso, Fernando, and Enzo Faletto. 1969. *Dependencia y desarrollo en América Latina.* Mexico: Siglo veintiuno.

Cleaves, Peter, and Martin J. Scurrah. 1980. *Agriculture, Bureaucracy and Military Government in Peru.* Ithaca, N.Y.: Cornell University Press.

Coatsworth, John H. 1981. *Growth Against Development: The Economic Impact of Railroads in Porfirian Mexico.* DeKalb, Ill.: Northern Illinois University Press.

Cobo, Bernabé. [1582–1657] 1979. *History of the Inca Empire.* Trans. and ed. Roland Hamilton. Austin: University of Texas Press.

Cohn, Bernard S. 1989. "Law and the Colonial State in India." In June Starr and Jane F. Collier, eds., *History and Power in the Study of Law,* 131–52. Ithaca, N.Y.: Cornell University Press.

Collier, George A. 1989. "The Impact of Second Republic Labor Reforms in Spain." In June Starr and Jane F. Collier, eds., *History and Power in the Study of Law,* 201–22. Ithaca, N.Y.: Cornell University Press.

Collins, Jane. 1988. *Unseasonal Migrations: The Effects of Rural Labor Scarcity in Peru.* Princeton: Princeton University Press.

Cook, Noble David, Alejandro Malaga, and Therese Bouysse. 1975. *Tasa de la visita general de Franciso de Toledo (1570–1575).* Lima: Universidad Nacional Mayor de San Marcos.

Cooper, Frederick, et al. 1993 [Cooper, Frederick, Florencia E. Mallon, Steve J. Stern, Allen F. Isaacman, and William Roseberry]. *Confronting Historical Paradigms: Peasants, Labor, and the Capitalist World System in Africa and Latin America.* Madison: University of Wisconsin Press.

Custred, Glynn. 1974. "Llameros y comercio interregional." In Giorgio Alberti and Enrique Mayer, eds., *Reciprocidad e intercambio en los andes peruanos,* 209–51. Lima: IEP.

Daubenmire, R. 1972. "Some Ecological Consequences of Converting Forest to Savanna in Northwestern Costa Rica." *Tropical Ecology* 13: 624–44.

Davies, Thomas M., Jr. 1970. *Indian Integration in Peru: A Half Century of Experience, 1900–1948.* Lincoln: University of Nebraska.

De la Bandera, Damian. [1557] 1965. "Relación general de la disposición y calidad de la provincia de Huamanga llamada San Joan de la Frontera y de la vivienda y costumbres de las naturales della." In Marco Jiménez de la Espada, ed., *Relaciones geográficas de Indias,* vol. 183. Madrid: Biblioteca de Autores Españoles.

De la Cadena, Marisol. 1991. "'Las mujeres son más indias': Etnicidad y género en una comunidad del Cusco." *Revista Andina* 9 (1): 7–29.

De Trazegnies Granda, Fernando. 1979. *La idea de derecho en el Perú republicano del siglo XIX.* Lima: Pontificia Universidad Católica del Perú.

Deere, Carmen Diana. 1990. *Household and Class Relations: Peasants and Landlords in Northern Peru.* Berkeley and Los Angeles: University of California Press.

Degregori, Carlos Iván. 1989. *Qué difícil es ser Dios: Ideología y violencia política en Sendero Luminoso.* Lima: Zorro de Abajo.

———. 1990. *El surgimiento de Sendero Luminoso: Ayacucho, 1969–1979.* Lima: IEP.

———. 1990–91. "A Dwarf Star." *Report on the Americas: Fatal Attraction, Peru's Shining Path* 24 (4): 10–19.

Di Leonardo, Micaela. 1984. *The Varieties of Ethnic Experience: Kinship, Class and Gender Among Italian-Americans.* Ithaca, N.Y.: Cornell University Press.

Dobyns, Henry. 1964. *The Social Matrix of Peruvian Indigenous Communities.* Cornell Peru Project Monograph. Ithaca, N.Y.: Cornell University

Dobyns, Henry, and Paul Doughty. 1976. *Peru: A Cultural History.* New York: Oxford University Press.

Dongo Denegri, Luis. 1986. *Derecho Agrario Peruano,* vols. 1, 2, and 3. Trujillo: Marsol Perú Editores.

Doughty, Paul. 1968. *Huaylas: An Andean District in Search of Progress.* Ithaca, N.Y.: Cornell University Press.

Earls, John. 1971. "The Structure of Modern Andean Social Categories." *Steward Anthropological Journal* (Urbana, Ill.) 3 (1): 69–105.

———. 1973. "La organización del poder en la mitología Quechua." In Juan Ossio, ed., *Ideología mesiánica del mundo andino,* 393–414. Lima: Ignacio Prado Pastor.

Edelman, Marc. 1990. "When They Took the 'Muni': Political Culture and Anti-Austerity Protest in Rural Northwestern Costa Rica." *American Ethnologist* 17 (4): 736–57.

———. 1993. *The Logic of the Latifundio: The Large Estates of Northwestern Costa Rica Since the Late Nineteenth Century.* Stanford: Stanford University Press.

———. 1994. "Landlords and the Devil: Class, Ethnic and Gender Dimensions of Central American Peasant Narratives." *Cultural Anthropology* 9 (1): 58–93.

Escobar, Gabriel. 1973. *Sicaya: Cambios culturales en una comunidad mestiza andina.* Lima: IEP.

Escobar, Mario. 1977. "Estudio comparativo de los valles del Urubamba y el Apurimac." Paper presented at the III Congreso Peruano del Hombre y la Cultura Andina, Cusco.

Evans, Peter, Dietrich Rueschemeyer, and Theda Skocpol, eds. 1985. *Bringing the State Back In.* Cambridge: Cambridge University Press.

Feierman, Steven. 1990. *Peasant Intellectuals: Anthropology and History in Tanzania.* Madison: University of Wisconsin Press.

Figallo Adrianzén, Guillermo. 1970. *Memoria del presidente del Tribunal Agrario.* Lima: Editoriales Unidas.

——. 1971. *Memoria del presidente del Tribunal Agario*. Lima: Editoriales Unidas.

——. 1972. *Memoria del presidente del Tribunal Agrario*. Lima: Editoriales Unidas.

——. 1973. *Memoria del presidente del Tribunal Agrario*. Lima: Editoriales Unidas.

——. 1985. *Política y derecho agrario*. Lima: Editores Empresores.

Figueroa, Adolfo. 1983. *La economía campesina de la sierra del Perú*. Lima: Pontificia Universidad Católica del Perú.

Flores Galindo, Alberto. 1978. "Apuntes sobre las ocupaciones de tierras y el sindicalismo." *Allpanchis Phuturinqa* (Cusco) 11/12: 175–85.

Fonseca, César. 1977. "Diferenciación campesina en los Andes peruanos." *Vicus Cuadernos* (Amsterdam) 1: 61–86.

Fonseca, César, and Enrique Mayer. 1988. *Comunidad y producción en la agricultura andina*. Lima: FOMCIENCIAS.

Frank, André Gunder. 1967. *Capitalism and Underdevelopment in Latin America*. New York: Monthly Review Press.

——. 1978. *World Accumulation, 1492–1789*. New York: Monthly Review Press.

Fuentes, Hildebrando. 1905. *El Cuzco y sus ruinas*. Lima: Imprenta La Industria.

Fuenzalida, Fernando. 1976. "Estructura de la comunidad de indígenas tradicional: Una hipótesis de trabajo." In José Matos Mar, ed., *Hacienda, comunidad y campesinado en el Perú*, 219–66. Lima: IEP.

Fuenzalida, Fernando, Teresa Valiente, et al. 1982 [Fuenzalida, F., T. Valiente, J. L. Villarán, J. Golte, C. I. Degregori, and J. Casaverde]. *El desafío de Huayopampa: Comuneros y empresarios*. Lima: IEP.

Geertz, Clifford. 1983. "Local Knowledge: Fact and Law in Comparative Perspective." In *Local Knowledge: Further Essays in Interpretive Anthropology*, 167–234. New York: Basic Books.

Golte, Jürgen. 1980. *Repartos y rebeliones*. Lima: IEP.

González Holguín, Diego de. [1608] 1952. *Vocabulario de la lengua general de todo el Perú llamada lengua Qquichua*. Lima: Instituto de Historia, Universidad Nacional Mayor de San Marcos.

Gonzalez Linares, Nerio. 1991. *Derecho procesal agrario, parte general*, vol. 1. Cusco: Editorial Mercantil.

Gonzalez Linares, Nerio, and Florencio Díaz Bedregal, eds. 1991. *Temas de derecho agrario contemporáneo*. Cusco: Instituto de Derecho Agrario y Ambiental.

Gould, Stephen Jay. 1989. *Wonderful Life: The Burgess Shale and the Nature of History*. New York: Norton.

Graham, Laura. 1993. "A Public Sphere in Amazonia? The Depersonalized Collaborative Construction of Discourse in Xavante." *American Ethnologist* 20 (4): 717–41.

Grindle, Merilee. 1977. *Bureaucrats, Politicians, and Peasants in Mexico: A*

Case Study in Public Policy. Berkeley and Los Angeles: University of California Press.

——. 1986. *State and Countryside: Development Politics and Agrarian Policies in Latin America.* Baltimore: Johns Hopkins University Press.

Guerrero, Andrés. 1990. *Curagas y tenientes políticos: La ley de la costumbre y la ley del estado (Otavalo 1830–1875).* Quito: Editorial El Conejo.

Guillén Marroquín, Jesús. 1987. "Rimanakuy Cusco." In *Rimanakuy '86: Hablan los campesinos del Perú,* 189–200. Cusco: Centro de Estudios Rurales Andinos Bartolomé de Las Casas.

Guillet, David. 1979. *Agrarian Reform and Peasant Economy in Southern Peru.* Columbia: University of Missouri Press.

Hanks, William. 1986. "Authenticity and Ambivalence in the Text: A Colonial Maya Text." *American Ethnolologist* 13 (4):721–44.

Hobsbawm, Eric, and Terence Ranger, eds. 1983. *The Invention of Tradition.* Cambridge: Cambridge University Press.

Howe, James. 1991. "An Ideological Triangle: The Struggle over San Blas Kuna Culture, 1915–1925." In Greg Urban and Joel Sherzer, eds., *Nation-States and Indians in Latin America,* 19–52. Austin: University of Texas Press.

Hünefeldt, Christine. 1982. *Lucha por la tierra y protesta indígena del Perú entre colonia y república, 1800–1830.* BAS 9. Bonn: Bonner Amerikanische Studien.

Huertas Vallejos, Lorenzo, and Nadia Carnero Alborran. 1983. *Diezmos del Cuzco, 1777–1853.* Lima: Universidad Nacional Mayor de San Marcos.

Isaacman, Allen. 1991. "Peasants, Work and the Labor Process: Forced Cotton Cultivation in Colonial Mozambique, 1938–1961." Paper presented at the Program in Agrarian Studies, Yale University, New Haven.

——. 1993. "Peasants and Rural Social Protest in Africa." In *Confronting Historical Paradigms: Peasants, Labor, and the Capitalist World System in Africa and Latin America,* 205–317. Madison: University of Wisconsin Press.

Isbell, Billie Jean. 1978. *To Defend Ourselves: Ecology and Ritual in an Andean Village.* Austin: University of Texas Press.

Jacobsen, Nils. 1983. "El caso de la economía ganadera en el surperuano, 1855–1920." *Allpanchis* (Cusco) 21: 89–146.

Kaerger, Karl. 1979. *Condiciones agrarias de la sierra sur peruana (1899).* Trans. Christine Hünefeldt. Lima: IEP.

Kaplan, Martha. 1990. "Meaning, Agency and Colonial History: Navosavakadua and the *Turka* Movement in Fiji." *American Ethnologist* 17: 3–22.

Kelley, Klara Bonsack. 1976. "Dendritic Central-Place Systems and the Regional Organization of Navajo Trading Posts." In Carol Smith, ed., *Regional Analysis,* 1:219–54. New York: Academic Press.

Kiernan, Ben. 1985. *How Pol Pot Came to Power: A History of Communism in Kampuchea, 1930–1975.* London: Verso.

Kriger, Norma. 1992. *Zimbabwe's Guerrilla War: Peasant Voices.* Cambridge: Cambridge University Press.

Lambert, Bernd. 1977. "Bilaterality in the Andes." In Ralph Bolton and Enrique Mayer, eds., *Andean Kinship and Marriage,* 1–27. Washington, D.C.: American Anthropological Association, Special Publication No. 7.

LeGrand, Catherine. 1986. *Frontier Expansion and Peasant Protest in Colombia, 1850–1936.* Albuquerque: University of New Mexico Press.

Lehman, David, ed. 1982. *Ecology and Exchange in the Andes.* Cambridge: Cambridge University Press.

Lira, Jorge A. 1982. *Diccionario Kkechuwa-Español.* Bogota: Secretaria Ejecutiva del Convenio "Andrés Bello," Instituto Internacional de Integración; Instituto Andino de Artes Populares.

Lockhart, James. 1968. *Spanish Peru, 1532–1560.* Madison: University of Wisconsin Press.

Lonsdale, John. 1981. "States and Social Processes in Africa: A Historiographical Survey." *African Studies Review* 24 (2–3): 139–225.

Lowenthal, Abraham F., ed. 1975. *The Peruvian Experiment: Continuity and Change under Military Rule.* Princeton: Princeton University Press.

McClintock, Cynthia. 1981. *Peasant Cooperatives and Political Change in Peru.* Princeton: Princeton University Press.

———. 1982. "Post-Revolutionary Agrarian Politics in Peru." In Stephen M. Gorman, ed., *Post-Revolutionary Peru: The Politics of Transformation,* 17–66. Boulder, Colo.: Westview Press.

McClintock, Cynthia, and Abraham F. Lowenthal, eds. 1983. *The Peruvian Experiment Reconsidered.* Princeton: Princeton University Press.

Mac-Lean y Esteñós, Roberto. 1965. *La reforma agraria en el Perú.* Mexico: Biblioteca de Ensayos Sociológicos, Instituto de Investigaciones Sociales, Universidad Nacional Autónoma de Mexico.

Mallon, Florencia. 1983. *The Defense of Community in Peru's Central Highlands: Peasant Struggle and Capitalist Transition, 1860–1940.* Princeton: Princeton University Press.

———. 1987. "Patriarchy in the Transition to Capitalism: Central Peru, 1830–1950." *Feminist Studies* 13 (2): 379–407.

Manrique, Nelson. 1989. "La década de la violencia." *Márgenes* 5–6: 137–82.

Martínez, Hector. 1980. "Las empresas asociativas agrícolas peruanas." In Carlos Amat y León, ed., *Realidad del campo peruano después de la reforma agraria,* 105–55. Lima: CIC Editora Ital Perú.

Matos Mar, José. 1976. *Yanaconaje y reforma agraria en el Perú.* Lima: IEP.

Matos Mar, José, and Fernando Fuenzalida. 1976b. "Proceso de la sociedad rural." In José Matos Mar, ed., *Hacienda, comunidad y campesinado en el Perú,* 15–52. Lima: IEP.

Matos Mar, José, and José Manuel Mejía. 1980a. *Reforma agraria: Logros y contradicciones, 1969–1979.* Lima: IEP.

———. 1980b. *La reforma agraria en el Perú.* Lima: IEP.

Mayer, Enrique. 1972. "Censos insensatos: Evaluación de los censos campesinos en la historia de Tangor." In John V. Murra, ed., *Visita de la provincia de León de Huánuco en 1562, Iñigo Ortíz de Zúñiga, visitador,* 339–66. Huánuco, Peru: Universidad Nacional Hermilio Valdizán.

———. 1985. "Production Zones." In Shozo Masuda, Izumi Shimada, and Craig Morris, eds., *Andean Ecology and Civilization: An Interdisciplinary Perspective on Andean Ecological Complementarity*, 45–84. Tokyo: University of Tokyo Press.

———. 1991. "Peru in Deep Trouble: Mario Vargas Llosa's 'Inquest in the Andes' Reexamined." *Cultural Anthropology* 6 (4): 466–504.

Mayer, Enrique, and Marisol de la Cadena. 1989. *Cooperacíon y conflicto en la comunidad andina: Zonas de producción y organización social.* Lima: IEP.

Mellafe, Rolando. 1969. "Frontera agrícola: El caso del virreinato Peruano en el siglo xvi." In Alvaro Jara, ed., *Tierras nuevas: Expansión territorial y ocupación del suelo en América (s. xvi–xix)*, 11–42. Mexico: Colegio de México.

Mercado, Roger. 1986. *Periodismo para el pueblo y por el pueblo: Artículos inéditos silenciados por la prensa burguesa del Perú sobre Sendero y otros temas.* Paris: Ediciones Latinoamericanos.

Migdal, Joel S. 1988. *Strong Societies and Weak States: State-Society Relations and State Capabilities in the Third World.* Princeton: Princeton University Press.

Mörner, Magnus. 1977. *Perfil de la sociedad rural del Cuzco a fines de la colonia.* Lima: Pontificia Universidad Católica del Perú.

Moncloa, Francisco. 1980. "Presentación: la realidad del campo y el modelo de desarrollo industrial." In Carlos Amat y León, ed., *Realidad de campo peruano después de la reforma agraria*, 11–16. Lima: CIC y Editora Ital Perú.

Moore, Sally Falk. 1958. *Power and Property in Inca Peru.* Westport, Conn.: Greenwood Press.

———. 1975. "Uncertainties in Situations, Indeterminacies in Culture." In Sally Falk Moore and Barbara G. Meyerhoff, eds., *Symbol and Politics in Communal Ideology: Cases and Questions*, 210–40. Ithaca, N.Y.: Cornell University Press.

———. 1986. *Social Facts and Fabrications: Customary Law on Kilimanjaro, 1880–1990.* Cambridge: Cambridge University Press.

———. 1989. "History and the Redefinition of Custom on Kilimanjaro." In June Starr and Jane F. Collier, eds., *History and Power in the Study of Law*, 277–301. Ithaca, N.Y.: Cornell University Press.

Morote Best, Efraín. 1988. *Aldeas sumergidas.* Cusco: Centro de Estudios Rurales Andinos "Bartolomé de Las Casas."

Moscoso S., Maximiliano. 1965. "Apuntes para la historia de la industria textil en el Cuzco colonial." *Revista universitaria del Cuzco* 22–23: 67–94.

Murra, John V. 1975. *Formaciones económicas y políticas del mundo andino.* Lima: IEP.

North, Liisa. 1983. "Ideological Orientations of Peru's Military Rulers." In Cynthia McClintock and Abraham Lowenthal, eds., *The Peruvian Experiment Reconsidered*, 209–44. Princeton: Princeton University Press.

North, Liisa, and Tanya Korovkin. N.d. *The Peruvian Revolution and the Officers in Power, 1967–1976.* Occcasional Monograph Series, no. 15. Montreal: McGill University.

Oricain, Pablo José. [1790] 1906. "Compendio breve de discursos varios sobre diferentes materias y noticias geográficas comprehensivas a este Obispado del Cuzco que claman remedios espirituales." In Victor Maurtua, ed., *Juicio de limites entre el Perú y Bolivia*, 11:319–77. Barcelona: Heinrich y Comp.

Partido Comunista del Perú. 1988. *Entrevista al Presidente Gonzalo.* Lima: Ediciones Bandera Roja.

———. N.d. *Desarrollar la guerra popular sirviendo a la revolución mundial.* Lima: Partido Comunista del Perú.

Pásara, Luis. 1978. *Reforma agraria: derecho y conflicto.* Lima: IEP.

———. 1982. *Jueces, justicia y poder en el Perú.* Lima: CEDYS.

Paz Soldán, Mariano Felipe. 1877. *Diccionario geográfico estadístico del Perú.* Lima.

Pearce, R. 1983. "Sharecropping: Towards a Marxist View." *Journal of Peasant Studies* 10 (2–3): 41–70.

Pease, Henry, and Olga Verme Insúa. 1974. *Perú, 1968–1973: Cronología política.* 2 vols. Lima: DESCO.

Poole, Deborah. 1984. "Ritual-Economic Calendars in Paruro: The Structure of Representation in Andean Ethnography." Ph.D. diss., University of Illinois, Urbana.

Poole, Deborah, and Gerardo Rénique. 1991. "The New Chroniclers of Peru: U.S. Scholars and Their 'Shining Path' of Peasant Rebellion." *Bulletin of Latin American Research* 10 (2): 133–91.

———. 1992. *Peru: Time of Fear.* London: Latin American Bureau.

Portelli, Alessandro. 1991. *The Death of Luigi Trastulli and Other Stories: Form and Meaning in Oral History.* Albany: SUNY Press.

Quijano, Anibal. 1979. *Problema agrario y movimientos campesinos.* Lima: Mosca Azul.

Rappaport, Joanne. 1990. *The Politics of Memory: Native Historical Interpretation in the Colombian Andes.* Cambridge: Cambridge University Press.

Rasnake, Roger. 1988. *Domination and Cultural Resistance: Authority and Power Among an Andean People.* Durham, N.C.: Duke University Press.

Rénique, José Luis. 1991. *Los sueños de la sierra: Cusco en el siglo XX.* Lima: Centro Peruano de Estudios Sociales.

Rivera Cusicanqui, Silvia. 1990. "Indigenous Women and Community Resistance: History and Memory." In Elizabeth Jelin, ed., *Women and Social Change in Latin America*, 151–83. Atlantic Highlands, N.J.: Zed Books.

Robles Recavarrén, Alejandro. 1975. *Diccionario de la reforma agraria peruana (texto único concordado del decreto ley 17716) concordado con las normas reglamentarias y decretos leyes affinos.* Lima: Agustín Chinga Falcon.

Rosaldo, Renato. 1989. *Culture and Truth: The Remaking of Social Analysis.* Boston: Beacon Press.

Roseberry, William. 1991. *Anthropologies and Histories: Essays in Culture, History and Political Economy.* New Brunswick, N.J.: Rutgers University Press.

Rosen, Lawrence. 1989. *The Anthropology of Justice: Law as Culture in Islamic Society.* Cambridge: Cambridge University Press.

Rostworowski de Diez Canseco, María. 1964. "Nuevos aportes para el estudio de la medición de tierras en el Virreynato e Incario." *Revista del Archivo Nacional del Perú* 28: 1–31.

Salomon, Frank. 1985. "The Dynamic Potential of the Complementarity Concept." In Shozo Masuda, Izumi Shimada, and Craig Morris, eds., *Andean Ecology and Civilization: An Interdisciplinary Perspective on Andean Ecological Complementarity,* 511–31. Tokyo: University of Tokyo Press.

Sánchez, Rodrigo. 1979. *Toma de tierras y conciencia política campesina.* Lima: IEP.

Sandburg, Carl. [1936] 1950. *The People, Yes.* In *Complete Poems,* 439–617. New York: Harcourt, Brace.

Sarmiento de Gamboa, Pedro. [1570] 1960. *Historia indica.* Madrid: Biblioteca de Autores Españoles.

Sarti, Roland. 1985. *Long Live the Strong: A History of Rural Society in the Apennine Mountains.* Amherst: University of Massachusetts Press.

Scott, James C. 1990. *Domination and the Arts of Resistance: Hidden Transcripts.* New Haven: Yale University Press.

Scott, Joan. 1988. *Gender and the Politics of History.* New York: Columbia University Press.

Seligmann, Linda J. 1987. "Land, Labor, and Power: Local Initiative and Land Reform in Huanoquite, Peru." Ph.D. diss., University of Illinois, Urbana.

——. 1989. "To Be In Between: The *Cholas* as Market Women." *Comparative Studies in Society and History* 31 (4): 694–721.

——. 1993a. "The Burden of Vision Amidst Reform: Peasant Relations to Law in the Peruvian Andes." *American Ethnologist* 20 (1): 25–51.

——. 1993b. "Between Worlds of Exchange: Ethnicity Among Peruvian Market Women." *Cultural Anthropology* 8 (2): 187–213.

Shue, Vivienne. 1988. *The Reach of the State: Sketches of the Chinese Body Politic.* Stanford: Stanford University Press.

Sider, Gerald M. 1986. *Culture and Class in Anthropology and History: A Newfoundland Illustration.* Cambridge: Cambridge University Press; Paris: Editions de la Maison des sciences de l'homme.

Silverblatt, Irene. 1987. *Moon, Sun and Witches: Gender Ideologies and Class in Inca and Colonial Peru.* Princeton: Princeton University Press.

SINAMOS [Sistema Nacional de Apoyo a la Movilización Social (National System in Support of Social Mobilization)]. 1977. *Información censal: Población y vivienda, 1972: Dpto. del Cuzco,* ser. 1, vol. 3. Lima: SINAMOS.

Siu, Helen F. 1989. *Agents and Victims in South China: Accomplices in Rural Revolution.* New Haven: Yale University Press.

Smith, Carol A. 1976. "Causes and Consequences of Central-Place Types in Western Guatemala." In Carol Smith, ed., *Regional Analysis*, 1:255–300. New York: Academic Press.

——, ed. 1990a. *Guatemalan Indians and the State, 1540–1988*. Austin: University of Texas Press.

——. 1990b. "Class Position and Class Consciousness in an Indian Community: Totonicapán in the 1970s." In Carol A. Smith, ed., *Guatemalan Indians and the State, 1540–1988*, 205–29. Austin: University of Texas Press.

——. 1990c. "Conclusion: History and Revolution in Guatemala." In Carol A. Smith, ed., *Guatemalan Indians and the State, 1540–1988*, 258–85. Austin: University of Texas Press.

Smith, Gavin. 1989. *Livelihood and Resistance: Peasants and the Politics of Land in Peru*. Berkeley and Los Angeles: University of California Press.

Smith, Michael G. 1960. *Government in Zazzau, 1800–1950*. London: Oxford University Press.

Spalding, Karen. 1984. *Huarochirí: An Andean Society Under Inca and Spanish Rule*. Stanford: Stanford University Press.

Spittler, Gerd. 1983. "Administration in a Peasant State." *Sociologia Ruralis* 23: 130–44.

Starn, Orin. 1991. *"Con los llanques todo barro": Reflexiones sobre rondas campesinas, protesta rural y nuevos movimientos sociales*. Lima: IEP.

Stein, William W. 1961. *Hualcán: Life in the Highlands of Peru*. Ithaca, N.Y.: Cornell University Press.

Stepan, Alfred. 1978. *The State and Society: Peru in Comparative Perspective*. Princeton: Princeton University Press.

Stern, Steve J., ed. 1987. *Resistance, Rebellion, and Consciousness in the Andean Peasant World: Eighteenth to Twentieth Centuries*. Madison: University of Wisconsin Press.

——. 1982a. *Peru's Indian Peoples and the Challenge of Spanish Conquest: Huamanga to 1640*. Madison: University of Wisconsin Press.

——. 1982b. "The Social Significance of Judicial Institutions in an Exploitative Society: Huamanga, Peru, 1570–1640." In George Collier, Renato Rosaldo, and J. D. Wirth, eds., *The Inca and Aztec States, 1400–1800: Anthropology and History*, 289–320. New York: Academic Press.

——. 1993. "Feudalism, Capitalism, and the World System in the Perspective of Latin America and the Caribbean." In Frederick Cooper, Allen F. Isaacman, Florencia E. Mallon, William Roseberry, and Steve J. Stern, eds., *Confronting Historical Paradigms: Peasants, Labor, and the Capitalist World System in Africa and Latin America*, 23–83. Madison: University of Wisconsin Press.

Stoler, Ann L. 1989. "Making Empire Respectable: The Politics of Race and Sexual Morality in Twentieth-Century Colonial Cultures." *American Ethnologist* 16 (4): 634–60.

Stoll, David. 1991. *Is Latin America Turning Protestant? The Politics of Evangelical Growth*. Berkeley and Los Angeles: University of California Press.

Tamayo Herrera, José. 1980. *Historia del indigenísmo cuzqueño, siglos xvi–xx.* Lima: Instituto Nacional de Cultura.

———. 1981. *Historia social del Cuzco republicano.* Lima: Editorial Universo.

Taussig, Michael. 1987. *Shamanism, Colonialism, and the Wild Man: A Study in Terror and Healing.* Chicago: University of Chicago Press.

Tilly, Charles. 1975. *The Formation of National States in Western Europe.* Princeton: Princeton University Press.

Urban, Greg and Joel Sherzer, eds. 1991. *Nation-States and Indians in Latin America.* Austin: University of Texas Press.

Urton, Gary. 1981. *At the Crossroads of the Earth and the Sky: An Andean Cosmology.* Austin: University of Texas Press.

Valcárcel, Luís. 1981. *Memorias.* Lima: IEP.

Valderrama, Mariano. 1976. *Siete años de reforma agraria peruana, 1969–1976.* Lima: Pontificia Universidad Católica del Perú.

Velasco Alvarado, Juan. 1972. *Velasco: La voz de la revolución: Discursos del Presidente de la República General de División Juan Velasco Alvarado, 1970–1972,* vol. 2. Lima: SINAMOS.

Villanueva Urteaga, Horacio. 1982. *Cuzco 1689: Informes de los párrocos al obispo Mollinedo del Cuzco.* Cusco: Centro de Estudios Rurales Andinos "Bartolomé de Las Casas."

Vincent, Joan. 1982. *Teso in Transformation: The Political Economy of Peasant and Class in Eastern Africa.* Berkeley and Los Angeles: University of California Press.

———. 1989. "Contours of Change: Agrarian Law in Colonial Uganda, 1895–1962." In June Starr and Jane F. Collier, eds., *History and Power in the Study of Law,* 153–67. Ithaca, N.Y.: Cornell University Press.

Von Hagen, Victor W. 1976. *The Royal Road of the Inca.* London: Gordon & Cremonesi.

Wallerstein, Immanuel. 1974. *The Modern World System: Capitalist Agriculture and Origins of the European World Economy in the Sixteenth Century.* New York: Academic Press.

Weber, Max. 1947. *The Theory of Social and Economic Organization.* Trans. and ed. Talcott Parsons. New York: Free Press.

Weismantel, M. J. 1988. *Food, Gender, and Poverty in the Ecuadorian Andes.* Philadelphia: University of Pennsylvania Press.

Wolf, Eric. 1955. "Types of Latin American Peasantry." *American Anthropologist* 57 (3): 452–71.

———. 1982. *Europe and the People Without History.* Berkeley and Los Angeles: University of California Press.

———. 1986. "The Vicissitudes of the Closed Corporate Peasant Community." *American Ethnologist* 13 (2): 325–29.

Youngers, Coletta. 1992. *Peru Under Scrutiny: Human Rights and U.S. Drug Policy.* Issue Brief No. 5. Washington, D.C.: Washington Office on Latin America.

Zuidema, R. T. 1964. *The Ceque System of Cuzco: The Social Organization of the Capital of the Incas.* Leiden: E. J. Brill.

——. 1982. "Bureaucracy and Systematic Knowledge in Andean Civilization." In George Collier, Renato Rosaldo, and J. D. Wirth, eds., *The Inca and Aztec States, 1400–1800: Anthropology and History*, 419–58. New York: Academic Press.

Zunz, Oliver. 1985. *Reliving the Past: The Worlds of Social History*. Chapel Hill: University of North Carolina Press.

Index

In this index an "f" after a number indicates a separate reference on the next page, and an "ff" indicates separate references on the next two pages. A continuous discussion over two or more pages is indicated by a span of page numbers, e.g., "57–59." *Passim* is used for a cluster of references in close but not consecutive sequence.

Uprisings, 41–42; peasant, 57f, 79, 99, 107, 241–42n19. *See also* Land invasions; Resistance

Varayuqkuna, 174
Vecinos, 29f
Velasco Alvarado, Juan, 1, 120–21, 182–83, 195; reforms under, 56, 58–72, 79, 175, 184–85, 191, 212–13, 232n3, 233n8
Vilcabamba, 36
Vilcaqunka, 36
Villanueva Urteaga, Horacio, 40
Vincent, Joan, 81–82

Violence, 3–4, 5, 57, 176, 192, 195–96, 205f, 214
Volunteerism, 11f

Waca Chaca Bridge, 33f, 42
Wages, 60, 141–42. *See also* Jornal
Wankas, 37
Wars of Independence, 41, 43, 241n19
Wayna Kapaq, 110
Weber, Max, 108

Yanaconaje, 140
Yaurisque, 46f, 49
Yawar Waqaq, 110
Yerbaje, 41

Library of Congress Cataloging-in-Publication Data

Seligmann, Linda J.
    Between reform and revolution : political struggles in the Peruvian Andes,
    1969–1991 / Linda J. Seligmann
        p. cm.
    Includes bibliographical references and index.
    ISBN 0-8047-2442-3 (alk. paper)—ISBN 0-8047-2443-1 (alk. paper) (pbk.)
    1. Land reform—Peru—Huanoquite. 2. Peasantry—Peru—Huanoquite—Political
activity. 3. Huanoquite (Peru)—Rural conditions. I. Title.
HD1333.P42H837   1995
322.4'4'098537—dc20   94-34937
                                                                CIP

⊛ This book is printed on acid-free, recycled paper.